MEMORY
and
DESIRE

Memory and Desire: Aging-Literature-Psychoanalysis
is Volume 6 in the series
THEORIES OF CONTEMPORARY CULTURE
Center for Twentieth Century Studies
University of Wisconsin-Milwaukee

General Editor, KATHLEEN WOODWARD

MEMORY
and
DESIRE

Aging—Literature—Psychoanalysis

EDITED BY

Kathleen Woodward and Murray M.
Schwartz

INDIANA UNIVERSITY PRESS
BLOOMINGTON

Manufactured in the United States of America

Library of Congress Cataloging in Publication Data
Main entry under title:

Memory and desire.

(Theories of contemporary culture; v. 6)
Bibliography: p.
Includes index.
Contents: Introduction / Murray Schwartz—The
makeup of memory in the winter of our discontent /
Herbert Blau—More images of Eros and old age /
Leslie A. Fiedler—[etc.]
    1. Aging in literature—Addresses, essays, lectures.
2. Psychoanalysis in literature—Addresses, essays,
lectures.   3. English literature—History and criticism—

Addresses, essays, lectures. I. Woodward, Kathleen M.
II. Schwartz, Murray M.   III. Series.
PN56.04M38 1985   809'.93355   84-48851
ISBN 0-253-30300-1

1 2 3 4 5   89 88 87 86 85

CONTENTS

***

ACKNOWLEDGMENTS

This collection of essays, the sixth in our series on *Theories of Contemporary Culture*, had its beginnings in a conference sponsored by the Center for Twentieth Century Studies at the University of Wisconsin-Milwaukee in 1983. That conference was organized with the fine advice and counsel of my co-editor, Murray Schwartz, to whom, along with the contributors to this volume, I owe my first, and affectionate, debt of gratitude.

The work of the Center has flourished under the imaginative and reliable administration of many people at the University of Wisconsin-Milwaukee. I should like especially to thank Dean William F. Halloran, former Associate Dean G. Micheal Riley, and Associate Dean Jessica Wirth of the College of Letters and Science, and Dean George Keulks and Associate Dean Ron Hedlund of the Graduate School for their continuing support. My most profound debt of thanks, however, must go to the superb staff of the Center. To all the people who have guided this book toward completion—Jean Lile, Carol Tennessen, Shirley Reinhold, Rose Both, Jaye Berman, Debra Vest, and John Erickson—I extend my warm thanks for their unparalleled expertise, good humor, and grace under pressure.

Finally, I take pleasure in acknowledging the support of the National Endowment for the Humanities for the April 20–22, 1983, research conference on "Aging and the Imagination: Perspectives from Literature and Psychology," and to Robert Mandel of Indiana University Press for his confidence and interest in the Center's research. I should also note that a goodly portion of my essay in this book was first published under the title of "Instant Repulsion: Decrepitude, The Mirror Stage, and the Literary Imagination in *The Kenyon Review*, 5, No. 4 (Fall 1983), pp. 43–66.

KATHLEEN WOODARD,
Director,
Center for Twentieth Century
Studies

MEMORY
and
DESIRE

INTRODUCTION

***

Murray M. Schwartz

LIKE AGE AFTER YOUTH, introductions look retrospectively at the work that
came before. The essays in this book were written by invitation to explore
aspects of aging and old age as those stages of life are reflected in and reflect
upon the imagination of individual lives. Their authors share literary,
psychoanalytic, and sociological interests, but approach their common
subject in distinctly personal styles. This is not a textbook on aging; it
contains no consolatory or prescriptive schemes. Rather, each essay is
offered to the reader as an invitation to imagine the experience of aging
through some facets of its actuality. Where theory enters, its aim is to
suggest the outline of possible conceptualization despite a desire for sim-
plification. Throughout this book, the reader will find normative statements about life stages, ways of *placing* aging within the evolution of
consciousness, but these statements are counterbalanced by the strong
emphasis on individual idiom that is the unique contribution of the
humanities to the subject of aging. Taken as a whole, these essays approach what Clifford Geertz has called a "thick description"[1] of aging, the
purpose of which is to open our imaginations to a more fully conscious
recognition of the complex and often paradoxical features of maturity.

We do not live in a culture that can depend on traditional ideas about the
relations between generations. How do the aged teach the young when
both are surrounded by promissory images of gratification and lured by
ideologies of self-fulfillment? What claims to wisdom can age authorize in
a culture increasingly democratized by its own technological powers, so
that the young may appear to be more adaptive than the old, and the sense
of history seem more a burden than a source of access to sustaining truths
about a common human condition? How do we distinguish the *experience*
of aging in an age of continuing education and exchangeable parts that
appear sophisticated enough to forestall or even reverse the most palpable
features of biological decline? When the boundaries of generations and
those of life and death itself become ambiguous, as they increasingly seem
to be, large questions such as these play in and through our minds as we
seek to stabilize more local and personal concerns.

Under such general conditions, it seems more than worthwhile to

I

gather and meditate upon explorations of aging that extend and focus our attention simultaneously. Each contributor to this volume has undertaken the task of interpreting the significance of aging through texts that illustrate its primary relations to insistent contemporary issues. Though the texts are not always contemporary or even modern, one purpose of the essays is to introduce the subject of aging more explicitly than before into the study and use of literary, psychoanalytic and, at times, mythic material. By bringing the questions of aging into relations with materials that have been approached more frequently from other perspectives, we hope to achieve a fuller expression of the value of these materials even as we use them to support arguments about phases of life's evolution.

In most of these essays, the metamorphoses of aging are defined against conceptions of the developmental origins of the self. "It could be said that with human beings there can be no separation," wrote D. W. Winnicott, "only a threat of separation; and the threat is maximally or minimally traumatic according to the experience of the first separatings."[2] In its inception, the "I" is a product of concrete, bodily experience mediated by the mother, who reflects an image of psychosomatic integrity in interaction with the child. Both what Erik Erikson has called "basic trust"[3] and what Jacques Lacan has conceptualized as the "mirror stage"[4] of infancy, have their experienced foundation through the responses of an other. The first "separatings" by which we conceive our individuality enact an ironic mastery. That is, we come to imaging our separate selves by assuming a form that mixes elements of the other, the mother and external world, even before the distinction between "me" and "not-me" becomes a reality. We become identified with a reflection of ourselves through the care of the other. When Freud postulated that "the ego is first and foremost a bodily ego," he went on to say that "it is not merely a surface entity but is itself the *projection* of a surface," the construction of images that transform dependency and biological limitation into an expectation of mastery.[5] The sense of personal continuity and trust in the stability of the world of others and objects both depend on the quality of "mirroring" by which we enter a human world, a world of "I's." The ego is rooted in a paradox: separation is attained through the transformational processes of primary identification with the other. The self in its inception is its first object and strives to become identical with its representations in the developmental stages of childhood and youth. In imagination we seek to realize a psychosomatic unity.

Lacan has emphasized the "alienating" effects of the origin of the "I," in so far as it depends on the gestalt of a unifying image. Winnicott explored the use of illusion in a more positive light. The disillusionment of infancy is relative to the experiences through which we recognize and learn to use illusion in the area of playing. Under "good enough" conditions, the incipient "I" is linked to the world in ways that both separate and connect. Winnicott, more cogently than any other theorist, has focused the paradox that inheres in this process. In playing, which begins in the first hours of life, we do not require an answer to the question, "Is this action, are these objects, part of myself or part of the world beyond my creation?"[6]

The transitional objects of early childhood graduate into the field of symbolic action. The play of imagination in maturity and old age can be both a repetition and a transcendence of early experiences of separation, according to the degree to which we achieve consciousness of our symbolic status as individuals. Aging involves repetition of the most fundamental elements of psychic life. In our daily habits we act, fantasize, remember, mourn, and dream according to patterns so ingrained that they structure even the most immediate sensations. But if the passage to and through age were simply the story of repetition and continuity—identity maintenance or the systematic *méconnaissance* that reestablishes our fictions of self-coherence—psychoanalysis and literature could leave its telling to biology and gerontology. Repetition occurs within generational conflict, and continuity of personal style must come to terms with the new and radically irreversible experiences of age, from the concrete reality of bodily change and decline to the more abstract experience of accepting or resisting one's place within the shifting structure of imaginary and linguistic orders that enable us to assign and delimit meaning. What are the distinctive ruptures and cumulative traumas of aging? How are they encountered or abetted by the [re]-formative experiences of the ego? How are we to understand the relation between the experience of self-continuity and the contributions of aging to the recognition and (possible) transformations of the self?

To begin, we could say, anticipating many of the authors in this volume, that aging normally generates a multiplicity of self-images. As post-adolescent habits of repetition seem to cohere or even freeze into sameness and familiarity, a particularity of attachments, or an obsessive style of concern and self-defense, there is also a struggle against the solipsistic attractions of fixation. In old age, the memory of past selves and experiences can simultaneously involve regressive defense and linking motives. The process is by no means simple; few of us simply enjoy or hate the image in the mirror that reminds us of loss or family resemblance to old or dead parents. There is for many an anticipatory element, an "eros of old age," in Leslie Fiedler's phrase, in recognizing that we are becoming as we age what we once desired, though this recognition carries with it an acceptance of loss. In this process, everything depends on our ability to make use of the self as an object of memory and fantasy that simultaneously is and is not equivalent to its present manifestations. The danger of habit is that it forces unity in multiplicity, collapses memory and mourning into mere repetition. But there is no true self-continuity without recognition of

difference in time, only the images of Narcissus and Echo. As John Muller
says, "Discerning these lures of what Lacan calls the imaginary register
may be the chief contribution of aging to personal knowledge."
To use the self generatively as an object of memory and fantasy requires
a space of illusion in age. In Winnicott's model of early development, this
space is not equivalent to Lacan's "imaginary register," though it may
include imaginary relations. For Lacan, the imaginary is the area of
reflected desires, narcissistically bound up in the desire of others who may
respond to our desires. To be caught up in imaginary relations is, for
Lacan, to be ensnared by our images of others' desires. The Lacanian
imaginary register can be understood as a dominant mode of narcissistic
pre-Oedipal relations, and it also seems to govern much of the adolescent's
search for recognition and relation to others. Imaginary relations lack what
W. R. Bion has called "binocular vision,"[7] the capacity to differentiate the
symbolic territory mapped by imagistic and linguistic representations
from the lived relations these fields structure and articulate. "Binocular
vision" distinguishes *and* merges map and territory; it replaces imaginary
relations, the duplicities of desire, and the cult of self-identity, with desire
understood as both open and limited. It is coordinate with entry into the
symbolic order in Lacanian psychoanalysis.

Winnicott's "space of illusion" or play space is the area in which "binocular vision" may come to realization as we work through the crises of
childhood and adolescence. We become aware of ourselves as parents *and*
children, or the "parents" of aged parents. We identify ourselves through
the desires of others *and* we appropriate elements of the symbolic order for
our own use. We confront the psychic murders of adolescence with our
earlier position reversed and survive the attacks we once inflicted. We
repeat *and* reverse oedipal relations. The contribution of aging to personal
knowledge derives from an apparent paradox, like the paradox at the root
of ego development, but now the self as other is both within ourselves and
between ourselves and others. "Binocular vision" entails recognition of this
paradox without final resolution.

In Winnicott's concept of play, illusion refers to the third or transitional
area of experience, between delusory equation of what is created by
projection and perceived as real, on the one side, and a rigid discrimination
of self and objective reality on the other. Illusion is not simply an alternative to the other two areas of experience, but a suspension of their
opposition. "There is a direct development," Winnicott wrote, "from
transitional phenomena to playing, and from playing to shared playing,
and from this to cultural experiences."[8] This process includes both renun-
ciation and recuperation of early relationships. (Wordsworth captured this
precisely in "Intimations of Immortality": "At length the Man perceives it
die away/And fade into the light of common day.")

Varieties of playing, uses of illusion, can thus be seen as the threads of continuity that enable us to differentiate and recapitulate past experiences as we negotiate the crises of middle and old age. Such continuity, as Winnicott emphasized, is always precarious, dependent not only on the quality of the earliest interplay of the child and parenting figures, but also on prevailing social, economic, and cultural conditions. One cannot "play" when the demands of survival are too great, when pain subsumes the capacity to engage the social world, when isolation or ghettoization of age groups enforces too much conformity to behavioral expectations. Winnicott's idea of playing argues for individual idiom within an environment that "holds" but does not contain its possibilities. It includes, among other activities, the sustained concentration of socially validated work.

But, as many of the authors in this book show, the binocular vision of maturity is susceptible to dislocation, and can become a double vision of unreconcilable or uncanny alternatives. The space of illusion can fail to achieve its integrating aims and yield instead to a regressive search for the imaginary unities of youth. Or we may be confronted with a violent return of the repressed, a rupture of all sense of continuity. Old age, the prospect of loss without reparation, absence that cannot become potential presence, throws us back to archaic anxieties at the limit of thought. "The self, in its autonomy, is an atonement structure," wrote Hans Loewald, "a structure of reconciliation, and as such a supreme achievement."[9] In old age the latent ambiguities of this complex statement may preoccupy psychic life. What "autonomy" is there in the face of death? What are the limits of "atonement," given its connotations of guilt overcome and reconciliation achieved? A structure of reconciliation has both passive and active reference. Past reconciliations become structure and also the way to structure; their stability and lack of completion show in later encounters. At the extremities of existence, the entire structuring process may be called into question, as the achievements of selfhood are confronted inevitably by another paradox, the presence of non-being. Can we mourn the loss of *ourselves?* The ultimate paradox may be that the knowable reality of the self is its *symbolic* status, beyond which nothing is thinkable.

Erik Erikson has postulated that the wisdom of old age lies in the achievement of "integrity," which he imagines as "the acceptance of one's one and only life cycle and of the people who have become significant to it as something that had to be and that, by necessity, permitted of no substitutions."[10]In this vision, the "might-have-been" of incomplete reconciliation has become, as in Freud's attitude toward death, acceptance of *Ananke*, necessity, beyond the space of illusion and the process of substitution, even substitution in imagination. It is as if one could stand outside existence looking in at one's life as a final atonement, like Yeats's Chinamen in "Lapis Lazuli," transcending "Every accidental crack or dent." In the space of illusion, which, after all, *is* the space of Yeats's poem, the gaps and fissures of integrity are not necessarily the material of despair, Erikson's polar alternative to integrity, but the source of a different wisdom, which lies in the recognition and communication of the ultimately paradoxical structure of the self, neither fully present to itself nor imaginable as total lack of being, but within unknowable limits of our existence. In this wisdom, symbolic action perpetuates our lives. We have art, the work of the imagination, including the art of self-fashioning, in order not to *perish* of truth, as Nietzsche said.

The foregoing summary, though necessarily abstract, is meant to be a touchstone for the essays that follow. The essays may be thought of as markers on a map whose complete territory remains to be delimited. We begin with Herbert Blau's eloquent meditative scanning of aging as it is embodied in the interplay of his own experience with his enormous repertoire of literary and psychoanalytic knowledge. Every issue in subsequent essays is brought within the compass of his essay, which defies summary and should be read with free-floating attentiveness to its nuances and suggestiveness. The openness of Blau's exploration should warn us against too easy an identification of the significance of aging in our time, yet it offers an image of our condition that helps explain why the imagination of aging has become so important to our cultural moment. Living in "a culture sending mixed signals about age," we need to sort the signals from the noise before we can even decipher their mixture. Many of the signals are ominous in the poetry and drama of aging, but the social exploitation of the concerns and expectations of the aged may be our most mixed blessing, as we deprive ourselves of *their* experience by making it more like everyone else's. Blau's essay retrieves for our contemplation much of what we need to think through and think with as we struggle to clarify a subject that prompts varieties of evasion.

Against evasions and censorship of consciousness in old age, Leslie Fiedler presents the archetypal image of the "dirty old man," that is, the erotically desiring male facing his imagination of impotence in its comic and tragic forms. Through his own tragi-comic encounters with the junk mail promising relief from the bodily anxieties of "senior citizens," he takes us back to the stories, myths, and texts of the *Senex* pursuing the pleasures of erotic gratification generated by and against the onset of the inevitable demise of *virtú*, in both its Latin meaning of potency or strength and its moral implication of right behavior. In the context of the ancient dream of eros recovered, the Faustian myth can be read as a variation that prefigures our culture's obsession with the paraphernalia of rejuvenation, "the quest for a kind of *ersatz* immortality in the flesh, with which we have sought to satisfy ourselves since the death of God and the loss of the hope of Heaven." Fiedler's essay enlarges the "space of illusion" by exposing some delusory pursuits of happiness so prevalently found in traditional and popular myths, but he also raises with inimitable poignancy the possibility of a time in life beyond erotic desire, a rebirth of sublimation in a culture that seems to have renounced it forever. However we read the ambivalence of erotic desire in old age, the dirty joke may be on us.

From Blau and Fiedler, who speak in distinctly personal styles, we move to Norman Holland's essay about personal styles or identity as it informs an entire life cycle. Using Freud's "Little Hans" case history and material from the life of its actual central character, Herbert Graf, the former stage director of the Metropolitan Opera House, Holland tells the story of identity as the thematic continuity he finds in the variations of Graf's self-representations from childhood to age. From Little Herbert's encounters with Freud and his family, Holland abstracts the oedipal expressions consistent with the mature Graf's style of being-in-the-world. Beyond the pleasure principle, and shaping all of its expressions, the identity concept elicits a representation of the most tenacious pattern of personality, the normative counterpart of what Freud called a "destiny neurosis." Holland's essay is thus both a theory of life's thematics and an illustration of thematic theory.

In his identity theory, Holland conceptualizes change as variation on a formal constant, or identity theme, which each individual brings to the epigenetic crises of development theorized by Erikson. Identity is thus always *within* the interplay of theme and variation, and discontinuity is explained as further variation of some kind. Aging and old age return us to childhood in transformations of the same "kernel sentence" in which we began, the difference being that our mental and bodily faculties decline, and this double movement gives rise to a kind of paradoxical development in which we are both more and less than we were before.

Identity theory is answered by John Muller's study of Louise Bogan's life and poetry from a Lacanian perspective. Where Holland sees thematic variation as the defining feature of aging, Muller offers a radically different kind of reading. Emphasizing how the contemporary *Pilgrim's Progress* of identity theory reinforces "a very American, individualistic and optimistic" view of life, Muller interprets Bogan's achievement through her ability to accept and embody in her poetry "what Lacan calls a 'total distinction' between the register of the mask (the captivating visual lure of the scopic register) and the evocative field of speech, poetry, and symbol." This "total distinction" is at the root of the differences between some versions of American and French psychoanalysis. Thematic continuity assumes but does not seek to explain the special importance of the symbolic order in human development, but for Muller, following Lacan, "the journey of desire from primal other, to others, to the Other . . . , the symbolic order, constitutes the *only distinctive psychoanalytic characteristic of aging.*"

Here, then, we have a crux of theoretical difference by which the reader can measure the truth of several essays. For Muller, affirmation of ourselves as "ego-identities" is our "perduring illusion," which comes to face the limit of its efficacy in maturity and old age, as we "realize the fundamentally unrealizable nature of the wish for the completing object," the other who will fulfill our desires. For Holland, no such limit or lack is articulated in normal development. Instead, he emphasizes the unifying process that continues to transcend the vicissitudes of change, not as an illusion but as a sustaining self-representation through which we relate to others.

Muller's "perduring illusion," is not, of course, the same as Winnicott's "space of illusion," which names a different continuity, not the continuity of the "I" but the continuous possibilities in development for the use of objects and others to reconcile continuity and discontinuity. The distinction is, perhaps, difficult and elusive, but none the less crucial for that. In Kathleen Woodward's essay, for example, the "mirror phase of old age" involves experiences of discontinuity between the "I" and its reflection in mirroring relationships. Both literally and metaphorically, we may look in the mirror and not see ourselves reflected, and such experiences are more or less traumatic according to the degree of our narcissistic dependence on mirroring responses and the provisions for true self-recognition in the social arena. If old age brings with it a perception of one's image as alien, can we say that a thematic continuity of personal style adequately explains the fate of the ego?

Woodward elegantly follows the character of Marcel in Proust's *The Past Recaptured* through his conflicting attitudes toward aging in order to prepare the reader for her general speculations on the significance of mirroring in old age. Her thesis, that there is a "mirror stage of old age," draws primarily on three sources: Freud's theory of the uncanny, which explains the experience of the double in literature and life as a revival of an image once familiar but repressed, returning to consciousness as a sign of immortality for "primitive" peoples and later in history as a harbinger of death; Lacan's theory of the mirror stage of infancy through which the "I" is constructed; and Simone de Beauvoir's *The Coming of Age.* She postulates a distinct phase of old age, the obverse of Lacan's mirror stage, in which the self confronts its biological and social representations with an attitude of repudiation or denial. The sense of wholeness may be threatened by the image of bodily decline in a reversal of the developmental process. The self may no longer include the image of a realizable psychosomatic integrity, and aggression may be directed against the signs of death "outside." We struggle, then, to resolve a finally unresolvable contradiction that has critical social as well as personal implications, for the extent to which we collectively repudiate the aging body to preserve the image of narcissistic integrity is the extent to which we tolerate or engage in hostility toward the aged among us.

Woodward's essay is especially important in its implications for contemporary society, given its fascination with the olympic body of youth and media-induced images of aging as a curable affliction, but the failure to achieve symbolic continuity is most intensely scrutinized by Ellie Ragland-Sullivan in her interpretation of Oscar Wilde's *Picture of Dorian Gray.* Against the background of a Lacanian depiction of the life cycle (her essay may be the first Lacanian literary analysis to attempt a full-scale drawing of the stages of life as they are implicated in the production of a work of art), she pictures Wilde's projection of his superego conflict into a text which tells the story of his own severe limitation. Wilde was trapped between Desire and the Law, doomed to witness a portrait of his guilt in a caricature of old age because he could not find entry into what Lacan called "the Name-of-the-Father," the sexually differentiated cultural universe beyond imaginary gratifications. In Ragland-Sullivan's elaborately developed theory, Wilde was fixated between the stage of sexual identity and the earlier narcissistic position. He could only encircle the question of his place in society without ever answering it. In the *Picture of Dorian Gray,* he represents a gray area between psychic reality and social expectation. Never having accepted the law of time, he presents a monstrous picture of old age, a metaphor of psychic sterility.

We turn from the failure of generative aging in Oscar Wilde to two quite different feminist perspectives. Diana Hume George approaches women poets from fifty to seventy with the questions of a daughter: What can they teach me? What is the nature of their psychic journeys as they age? She finds in their courageous self-confrontations a double movement—toward explorations of the images of parents at the origin of self-awareness, and simultaneously, through this commemoration of oedipal and pre-oedipal struggles, a reconstitution of self. Her essay moves from description of the poets' themes of dependency and loss to a theoretical position drawing on the work of Woodward, Jane Gallop, and Julia Kristeva and then to an interpretation of Muriel Rukeyser's "Double Ode," a poem which embodies the feminist/psychoanalytic issues that have been transposed to theory. In the "eternal double music" of exile from the parents, especially the mother of infancy, and return in imagination to that first home, Rukeyser exemplifies the "psychoanalytic" heroism of the woman poet discovering her own potential space in age. It is a space without fixed boundaries, a space of confluence and recurrence, mediating past and present to appropriate parental powers without assuming their image.

Mary Lydon continues this theme in her study of Marguerite Duras's cinematic transformation of the Mother/Daughter relation. In age, Duras presents the double image of an old woman who has "joyfully assumed regression" to master in word and image the powerful freedom of child's play. Duras's mother, driven by rage to literally battle the sea that inundated her rice fields, comes to exemplify a courageous madness. The mother *(la mère)* and the sea *(la mer)* merge in Duras's legend to become *le merle*, the mother who is at once absent and present, everywhere in the consciousness of Duras's cinematic narrations yet also silent and inaccessible to others. This representation of the mother, "as ambivalent as it is fierce," informs Duras's challenges to convention and her own fierce determination to embody and transform that originary legend in the letter, in language played against the power of the image. Duras thus assumes in her old age the power of a daughter liberated by her submission to and control of psychic fluidity and an associative freedom "that embraces the past and future at once."

Lydon's essay gives the reader access to an intricate and subtle process of self-transformation. Lydon's interpretation brings into clear focus the way in which a woman without power assumes her own identity, and therefore becomes a power in her own right. The psychological struggle between mother and daughter becomes an instrument of social change because Duras is able to give it symbolic expression as an old woman who is continuing to fashion herself in public consciousness. The power of Lydon's essay derives from her recognition of the resonance betewen the psychological and social dimensions of Duras's example.

William Kerrigan's essay takes us from contemporary revelations of the mother/daughter relation back to Ancient, Medieval, and Renaissance texts. Though his texts seem a great distance from twentieth-century issues, Kerrigan actually deals with masculine counterparts to the subjects of the feminist essays. With a broad sweep of reference, he explores the thesis that wrath serves a creative function when directed against the self and others. By dignifying anger, Kerrigan positions the reader to regard the rage of Shakespeare's Prospero as an essential element in his gradual control of oedipal repetition. The angry father uses his rage, enacted in the storm that opens the play, to bring his enemies into the space of his imagination, and this appropriation of their freedom then permits him to enact scenes of reversal of both their crimes and his vengeful desires. He can then renounce the incestuous elements of his exiled state and admit the thought of death into consciousness.

In John Milton, wrath is directed against his own unspent, stainless youth, and Kerrigan suggests that the astonishing creative energy of his old age derives from this self-rebuke against unlived potential. In his final section, Kerrigan forcefully develops this idea in connection with Renaissance polemics against the orthodoxy of the Augustinian life model, and concludes the broad scope of his essay by questioning Erikson's depiction of the life cycle in so far as it overlooks the creative power of wrathfulness. Like George's and Lydon's, Kerrigan's essay can be seen as a celebration of the mastery achieved through lifelong oedipal struggles.

Rage, however, can obliterate as well as generate a creative resolution of self-conflict in age. Old age *guarantees* nothing, certainly not a space of illusion, and *King Lear* remains our most powerful dramatic embodiment of this fact. As Carolyn Asp reads the play, the terrible reality of Lear's regressive claims on his daughters challenges the family and the cultural order itself in their holding functions. By his demand for a reflection of his global narcissism in words of love, Lear fractures the mediating capacities of every civilizing structure in a patriarchal universe. *King Lear* enacts the double-binding ramifications of an absolute refusal in old age to accept difference from childhood. The failure of the aging patriarch to negate his mortality gives rise to the most painful mortality, which Lear resists even to the moment of his death. He wants to be the child of his daughters; he becomes the support of Cordelia's dead body. He wants to feed on the signs of love; he is deprived of nurturance in its most concrete forms. He wants to see literal substitutes for the provisions of infancy; he becomes an hysterical actor on a barren stage, outside the sight of others, except for those whose language and bodily form return in riddles or disguised or mutilated expressions of repressed or negated desires. In Western literature there is no more complete representation of the pain provoked by a foreclosure of play space in old age. Lear's drama is an inversion and perversion of Winnicott's conception.

"The terror of the play," Asp writes, "lies in the spectacle of so little wisdom garnered at the price of such immense suffering." As witnesses to the tragedy, we see paternal expectations of solace in old age before a shattered mirror. Asp reads a moral: who can escape the imagination of exposure to the possibilities of Lear's suffering? Which of us can say that the repressed will not return? As Yeats wrote in "Vacillation," "No man has ever lived that had enough / Of children's gratitude or women's love."

But Yeats could also write that "Man is in love and love's what vanishes. / What more is there to say?" At the end of life, whether quickly or in prolonged Lear-like agony, the space of illusion narrows to solitude and we become, at best, a presence in the memories of others or in the collective memory of the Other through the works that remain. It is fitting, then, that this book should conclude with an essay on Samuel Beckett's *The Unnamable*, a work that Gabriele Schwab shows to embody a final use of transitional experience in the imagination of extreme age. Suspended between life and death, Beckett's narrator voices his paradoxical condition: "Where I am there is no one but me who am not." Yet he copes with the disintegration of his body by giving voice to his fragmented state, sym-

bolizing the limits of the symbolic. Language becomes the site of mourning and his refuge in dying. A text like *The Unnamable*, Schwab concludes,
shows that the modes of being in the intermediate area are not exclusive
but compatible with a hyperreflexivity and a lucid use of the function of
judgment. How much speech of the dying, unheard or confused with
infantile babble, gropes toward this use of language? It may be that
Beckett bespeaks an integrity for our time in the space of narration
between life and death.

Notes

1. Clifford Geertz, "Thick Description: Toward an Interpretive Theory of
Culture," in his *The Interpretation of Cultures* (New York: Basic Books, 1973), pp. 3–
30.

2. D. W. Winnicott, "The Place Where We Live," in his *Playing and Reality*,
(New York: Basic Books, 1971), p. 108.

3. See, for example, Erik Erikson, *Insight and Responsibility* (New York: W. W.
Norton, 1964), p. 115.

4. Jacques Lacan, "The Mirror Stage as Formative of the Function of the I"
(1949), in *Ecrits*, trans. Alan Sheridan (New York: W. W. Norton, 1979), pp. 1–7.

5. Sigmund Freud, *The Ego and the Id* (1923), trans. Joan Riviere, rev. and ed.
James Strachey (New York: W. W. Norton, 1962), p. 16.

6. See, for example, Winnicott's "The Use of an Object and Relating Through
Identification," in *Playing and Reality*, p. 89.

7. W. R. Bion, *Learning from Experience* (London: Heinemann, 1962), p. 86.

8. D. W. Winnicott, "Playing: A Theoretical Statement," in *Playing and Reality*,
p. 51.

9. Hans W. Loewald, "The Waning of the Oedipus Complex" (1978), in his
Papers on Psychoanalysis (New Haven and London: Yale Univ. Press, 1980), p. 394.

THE MAKEUP OF MEMORY IN THE WINTER OF OUR DISCONTENT

***

Herbert Blau

Fifteen apparitions have I seen;
The worst a coat upon a coat-hanger.
W. B. Yeats, "The Apparitions"[1]

. . . no doubt the discovery that they have grown old causes less sadness to many people than it did to me. But in the first place old age, in this respect, is like death. Some men confront them both with indifference, not because they have more courage than others but because they have less imagination.
Marcel Proust, Time Regained[2]

Enough my old breasts feel his old hand.
Samuel Beckett, Enough[3]

MY MOTHER WORE LIPSTICK until the day she died. She also wore it into the grave. That last fetish of an appearance was not quite her own, but she would certainly have approved the cosmetic ministrations of the undertaker, which corresponded to her vanity and a taste for excess. There was always too much lipstick, and nothing any of us could say about it would dissuade her. She was simply unembarrassed. By decorum, by our taste, by time. The lipstick was the insignia of a self-enamored presence which everybody adored. It had nothing to do, I think, with refusing to age. My mother, though born in Brooklyn, was not sufficiently American to be fixated on youth. If that were so, the makeup might have been applied more subtly, with more restraint. Instead, there was a bright penumbra of crimson on her lips and a lurid swath of rouge upon her cheeks. There was nothing surreptitious about it, as with the aging Gilberte in *Time Regained*, who even blew her nose with caution lest her makeup show its colors, as Marcel observed one day amidst his disenchantments, the "sumptuous palette" in her handkerchief.[4] So far as aging was on my mother's mind— as she brushed incessantly her thinning black hair before the mirror like a triptych in her bedroom—it was as if she adorned it with a sort of bedizened satisfaction on her face.

The triple image in the mirror did not signify, moreover, any division in the self, no splitting of identity. It would never have occurred to my mother that anybody could be more than one. The overlaid and successive selves which constitute a life in the solipsistic mirrors of the postmodern would have seemed too burdensome a luxury for a woman whose abundance and major pleasure were in admiring what she was. Or if, to my surprise, she were thinking in those sessions of self-reflection through multiple facets of a past, the variousness of cast-off roles, what was being repeated in the mirror was the role she really preferred. She seemed to treasure the image and gazed at it through the long afternoon, humming or murmuring, until she almost seemed asleep.

She also liked to have her picture taken. She was not at all like the mother of Roland Barthes, who would place herself in front of the camera's lens *"with discretion,"* for there was always a touch of theatricalism in the painted propriety of my mother, a primping into a posture before the click. Writing of his mother in those delicately confessional passages of *Camera Lucida* which seem retrospectively like a premonition of his death, Barthes says: "She did not struggle with her image, as I do mine: she did not *suppose* herself."[5] Nor, I suppose, *ex*pose her self either, the desire for which—*full* exposure, the inexhaustible *manifestation* of the singularity of our being—we struggle for and against all our lives. The struggle continues even when, resigned to age, we think we're merely giving up the ghost. Whatever it is that we may be withholding, now or then, it is naturally a losing cause. "He that has eyes to see and ears to hear," wrote Freud in an early study of hysteria, "may convince himself that no mortal can keep a secret. If his lips are silent, he chatters with his fingertips; betrayal oozes out of him at every pore."[6]

So, who are you fooling? my mother might say, no hysteric. There was nothing like a supposition in her face. No *struggle* with an image either. The makeup was never applied evenly or ever the same, just a blur and not a line around the mouth. Proust speaks of "the inaccurate language of our own vanity,"[7] but I wonder, for there was something impeccable in the overdoing. If Proust is right, maybe not vanity at all. So, what are you hiding? she'd say as if, even painted an inch thick, concealment were in vain, as it is without makeup in the pretense of unconcealment. Despite the makeup and because of it—like the undisguised specificity of the illusoriness of theater—the import of the image was always there, legible, laughable, emblematic, mortifyingly bare. She seemed, through the inexpungeable red gaudiness of the coverup that made me blush, totally and infectiously exposed. Whatever my mother may have been when younger—and some early pictures show her as lovely and unguarded with no makeup at all—she seemed perfectly masked by what she had become, and all the more beguiling for that.

Barthes speaks of "the figure of sovereign *innocence*" which he perceived in a faded sepia print of his mother as a little girl. What she seemed to have inherited from no one, not the parents who loved her badly, sustained itself as an "assertion of gentleness"[8] which distinguished her with age. When she gave herself to a photograph like an elemental goodness it seemed to him to "replace a moral value with a higher one—a civil value."[9] My mother was too narcissistic for that. Freud wrote of neurotics who fetishize the body as a sexual object, "limiting their susceptibility to influence." As I've already indicated, my mother was similarly unsusceptible. But when she caressed and fondled her body—even as she grew heavier and the skin slackened with age—it was, as Freud suggested, a systemic persistence of that primary narcissism—not at all abnormal, and not easily surrendered with age—which is "the libidinal complement of the egoism of the instinct of self-preservation,"[10] of which the lipstick seemed a literal inscription. It is this narcissism which, as Lacan restates Freud, stands between the subject and the desire for death, although there was something in the ablutions that seemed like a preparation for death. My mother was surely exploitative, but with no loss of an alluring motherliness in her auto-affection, maybe all the more motherly, or nurturing, as a result. I am seeing her now, obviously, through the leniency of the years, still struggling with an aversion in my ever-lasting delight over the memory of this patently self-indulgent and imperturbably funny woman. If there was no civil value in what she offered to a lens, there was something older there, sovereign but far from innocent, maybe a mythic value—though I, like Barthes, also have an aversion to myth.

It has been said—and Barthes reminds us—that Jews have renounced the Image in order to protect themselves in the diaspora of illusion from worshipping the primacy of the Mother. But my mother was not *that* Mother, nor a mere Jewish mother either. Like the kindness of Barthes's mother which, he says, belonged to no system and, at the limit of morality, was "specifically *out-of-play*,"[11] my mother's self-engendering was a thing unto itself, immodest, inimitable, heterodox and—as I grew older, the image of her image, its *remembrance*, becoming mine—retrospectively unique. She could cook an entire meal without rising from her chair because everybody, seduced, quite willingly did the work. "Would you mind taking the milk out of the ice box. Could you get me a little salt. Sit, peel the potatoes." Neighbors would do her shopping for her. Or my father would drive her around. Why were we glad to do her bidding, though it often seemed absurd? In Freudian terms, she seemed to occupy as she aged "an unassailable libido-position which we ourselves [had] abandoned."[12] Perhaps it was because she spared us the good example, had no mere opinions, made no claims—even when she was overtaken by sickness—about gracefully growing old.

I realize as I say this that my mother was at most a year or two older when she died than I am now, but she would never have supposed—as I prolong the expectancy of a youthful middle-age—that she was anything other than old and, even before her hair whitened (how white, when she lay dead, its thinning blackness was!), she merely took for granted that death was near at hand. Whatever the motives in her makeup, she was not surprised by time. "I had not a single grey hair, my moustache was black," says the narrator of Proust's novel, as he questions the revelation of "the terrible fact"—that he had grown old, everybody having laughed when he referred to himself as young:

> And now I began to understand what old age was—old age, which perhaps of all the realities is the one which we preserve for longest in our life as a purely abstract conception, looking at calendars, dating our letters, seeing our friends marry and then in their turn the children of our friends, and yet, either from fear or from sloth, not understanding what all this means, until the day when we behold an unknown silhouette, like that of M. d'Argencourt, which teaches us that we are living in a new world. . . .[13]

Within her narrow compass, my mother knew her world. She was decidedly afraid of death and, as with the makeup, uninhibited in pain. Through her rimless red lips would come a boundless cry, not quite archetypal because so distinctly hers. "Gas, gas," she'd say, as if squeezing it from her breast, and then the cry ascending, *"it's kill-ing meee!"* But as the gas subsided, if it was ever really gas, her shameless humor revived. "What'd you want I should do, dance?" she'd say to my father when he said she almost scared us all to death. It made no difference how painful the gas, the makeup was indelibly there.

My mother did not so much, as she grew older, want to be approved or wanted, like others her age. She never reproached anybody, as the elderly sometimes do, with not giving her enough love. As for giving love herself, none of us felt denied, but she was one of those whose aging endowed her—if it wasn't there before—with the gift of being loved. But if that was insufficient she could always love herself. That was not at all true of my father who, when he suffered a double stroke which left him in a wheelchair and blind in one eye, took it as a sign of weakness, almost a personal fault and, in the excess of pride with which he had lived, refused any solace or therapy and virtually inflicted upon himself the lonely humiliation of death. When I flew across the country to visit him, the television would be on. He'd stare intently at the screen no matter what was there, never looking at me with his single eye, as if cancelling the oedipal contract and asking, among all the hopeless desires, that we forget his crippled being, as if he'd never been at all. Not so my mother, in sickness or in health. She was not an accomplished woman, far from that, but she wanted to be remembered, remembered there and then, and remembered for what *she* remembered in the festivity on her face.

Proust speaks of those for whom our love "has been so nearly continuous that the image we retain of them is no more than a sort of vague average between an infinity of imperceptibly different images. . . ."[14] By some aboriginal inspiration my mother had averted that, or almost, as she also thwarted time, arranging in the mirror to her personal satisfaction the englistered gaze she'd present to death. Her hair thinned and grayed for all the brushing, but as I look at her image now it's only the photographs that age.

Amidst the *clichés* of old photographs, the redoubled quick of memory—which to Proust seemed less reliable than its involuntary return—this view of my mother may be no more than a trick of imagination, which doesn't necessarily improve with age. If I were, to be truthful, and I am trying to be, making up this portrait of my mother, adorning it here and there, overdoing it a little bit, that would itself be a prospectus of age, the correlative of her makeup, the autobiography of the auto-affection, a semblance of a self-assumption, which is what autobiography is, the conversion of all otherness into the bodily legend of a self, the necessary fiction of age. "In the people whom we love," Proust observes, "there is, immanent, a certain dream which we cannot always discern but which we pursue." If we stumble in the pursuit it's because, as he adds, there cannot help but be something like error and aberration in all our loves.[15] As the loves accumulate and fail, the dream recedes. Which may be why we mostly think the imagination is more active in youth which is, besides, thought to be closer to the other Mother who is, as mistress of illusion, sovereign in the aging dream.

"Hear him," writes Wallace Stevens of the child whose "Questions Are Remarks," before whom objects arise without history or rhetoric and whose question, even about the mother, seems complete. "He does not say," not yet, as the aged Stevens says in the poem, " 'Mother, my mother, who are you,' / The way the drowsy, infant, old men do."[16] I have not been saying that either, not yet, the remark as question, "Mother, my mother, who are you?", which awaits a further time, though I am edging toward it now. But as I recall the memorial makeup on my mother's face, that testamentary lifemask in the funeral home, it occurs to me that it is only by virtue of the imagination that, coming of age, all the remembered promises narrowed down, the prospects may seem more limitless than they were before. That's because the bottomless source of the future is the

inexhaustible past, as it is in Proust when Marcel discovers, through an
irruption of repercussive memory on the uneven paving stones, that the
only real paradise is the paradise that is lost.

In the famous passage on involuntary memory, Proust speaks of how
"the simplest act or gesture [of the past] remains immured as within a
thousand sealed vessels,"[17] the breaking open of which releases anxiety
about the future into an appetite for life that is immense. In Proust, as in
Stevens, this anamnesis comes through a kind of seasoned amnesia, or
parapraxis, the grace of drowsiness, like my mother's before the mirror, an
unsubsiding attentiveness to the dimming rhetoric of age. Memory, for
Proust, is not only a mental category. There is, as well, an "involuntary
memory of the limbs" to accompany that other memory set off by the
madeleine dipped in tea. This corporeal memory, torpid as it is, a sterile
imitation of the other, nevertheless outlasts it and may be awakened by the
will of chance through a kind of nurtured desperation. As Stevens says in a
last poem, "Need names on its breath / Categories of bleak necessity"
which, "just to name," attains by "right of knowing, another plane."[18] He
writes of that categorical imperative elsewhere as a poverty in the space of
life, familiar to age, where we come upon a feminine figure, "the sibyl of
the self, / The self as sibyl, whose diamond" *is* poverty, a sort of bejeweled
exhaustion whose earthly ground is need. The sibyl's shape seems, in
"The Sail of Ulysses," an avatar of the imagination whose object, as in
Proust, is absence and whose energy is depletion:

> . . . a blind thing fumbling for its form,
> A form that is lame, a hand, a back,
> A dream too poor, too destitute
> To be remembered, the old, shape
> Worn and leaning to nothingness,
> A woman looking down the road,
> A child asleep in its own life.[19]

Which is the unnamed old man, in the poem entitled "A Child Asleep in
Its Own Life," whose mother is not complete, the unnamed old man who
broods on all the rest of the old men, those we shall become, "Distant, yet
close enough to wake / The chords above your bed to-night."[20]

Speaking of distance, it is certainly a long way from the uneducated
egocentricity or the nurtured narcissism of my mother to the elegant
solipsism of Stevens and Proust. But I want to move from the remembrance of her image to some further thoughts about memory and the
imagination and—what is more typical of the rest of us—aging and its
discontents, or the uneasiness of aging as the span of life increases and the
time for it recedes.

I said of my mother that she seemed to reflect a mythic value, but that I have an aversion to myth. That's because "we never lived in a time / When mythology was possible," as Stevens says in a last poem, like Freud in his final work. What we recover from time, then, if we recover it at all, is an image which "must be of the nature of its creator," as this remembrance of my mother is consubstantial with my self, *fictive* because remembered, its substance out of mind. "That," says Stevens, "raises the question of the image's truth."[21] I don't deny it: what is mirrored in memory is the mirror. Imagination is a function of memory whose expanse is a great divide. It is a division which seems to widen with age, like the aggravation of a grievous fault. That fault is mirrored, as Lacan suggests, in the motor incapacity of the child fumbling for its form, as if born through something forgotten, "an original organic disarray" in the *"specific prematurity of birth. . . ."*[22] It is as if our failures of memory are archaic but propitious, arising "in the dimension of a vital dehiscence [or . . .] negative libido" which is constitutive of what we are,[23] and which seems to return in the specific maturity of age, when we are really old, like the old man asleep in the child's life. Or was it the other way around?

That question is a remark. As we fear a loss of being with age, there is also, with so much more to remember, an anxiety about forgetting. It's like the compounding of the amnesia in our normal psychic life, which may be the trace of that original fault. When I say amnesia now, I mean our tendency to forget, just that, the *necessity* of it. For the truth is we're always forgetting. We think we're putting things aside—out of caution, fear, tact, dismay—only to discover they're no longer there. There is in the selective inattention, screening, slips, oversight, and censorship through which we mature inevitably a point of diminishing returns—or the unexpected virulence of the return of the repressed.

Henry James advised the novelist to be one upon whom nothing is lost. He was speaking of a kind of absolute pitch of remembrance that you're unlikely to be born with and must attain, not only with the experience of age but, by right of knowing, with the rigor of art. "Rigor of beauty is the quest," said William Carlos Williams in *Paterson*, that palimpsest of up-welling age which seems a renewal of life. "But how will you know beauty when it is locked in the mind past all remonstrance?" Locked as the mind is, things escape us, even when memory is as active as it is in Williams, who is forced to roll up the sum "by defective means."[24] Even when the means, though defective, are subtle beyond thought, as they are in Proust and James, there is something in the mind which, as James says of the American scene, puts out interrogative feelers, the questions which aren't remarks but only endless questions. Like: where is our life in memory when it is not being remembered—or remembered *as being?* It is a response to that question which led in Freud to the concept of the unconscious in psychoanalysis, where we have grown familiar with the child asleep in the old man's life, awakened as he is by the vicissitudes of the instincts in the rolling up of age.

Freud restates the problem of what escapes us at the opening of a note on what the unconscious has come to mean about a dozen years after *The Interpretation of Dreams:*

> A conception—or any other mental element—which is now *present* to my consciousness may become *absent* the next moment, and may become *present again*, after an interval, unchanged, and, as we say, from memory, not as a result of a fresh perception by our senses. It is this fact which we are accustomed to account for by the supposition that during the interval the conception has been present in our mind, although *latent* in consciousness. In what shape it may have existed while present in the mind and latent in consciousness we have no means of guessing.[25]

It is, however, the imagination which presumes, guessing at the shape of an absence—a sibyl's shape?—and bringing it back alive, through some affinity with the unconscious in which the latency abides.

The unconscious doesn't seem, at first, like the most natural setting for the aged, so far as we expect them to be wise, restrained, and stabilizing agencies in our lives without the license of the still-unruly libidinal desires. "O sir, you are old," they say to King Lear; "Nature in you stands on the very verge / Of his confine" (II.iv.1414-43). There are multiple connotations of nature in *King Lear*, but here it suggests the life which has not only reached its limit but needs to be controlled. "You should be ruled," says Regan (II.iv.143), as if addressing the unconscious itself, which we normally think of as the domain of the irrational. But it is not quite that. In the unconscious system, as Freud describes it, there is "no negation, no dubiety, no varying degree of certainty"—all of which, as anxiety, are liabilities of age, when the natural functions weaken and the somatic vitality declines. The processes of the unconscious are, moreover, timeless, neither ordered temporally nor altered by the passage of time, all of what we have known and done and still to be imagined enabled there, bearing "in fact . . . no relation to time at all."[26]

Unconsciousness is a regular, vital, and inevitable phase in the activity of our thought. As Freud taught us in perhaps his greatest teaching, the unconscious—what we think of as irrational—is our oldest *mental* faculty, as dreams are the deepest registers of thought. It is, however, a deprivation in the processes of the unconscious that we are liable to suffer with age, injury to its civilizing virtue by encroachment on its civil rights. For the social ordinances continue, through all the relaxing of taboos, to see that the unaging libido is ruled so that the elderly act their age, letting the troublesome child sleep. Of course, it is those still shaken by the specific prematurity of birth, the unreconciled children who—as the aged breed past all expectations, not always with an aging grace—grow impatient with their almost obscene ubiquity. So we consign them with mixed feelings to a sort of exiled behaviour which, as the children themselves join the multitudes of age, they may later come to regret. It is this pressure upon the old, often unspoken and solicitous, to *be* old, to act their age and at the same time contain the incontinence endemic to age—not only the loose bowels of the insufferable body but the unseemly persistence of regressive desire—which causes the elderly to be wounded in their narcissism,[27] egregiously injured where the ego was and, unfortunately, unsufferably, where the id still is.

It was that—being wounded in her narcissism—which Proust's Aunt Leonie, hypochondriac as she was, never let happen to her, and which my mother, admiring her image, seemed to refuse through all the appeals, jokes, and even insults about her makeup. For all their self-indulgences, they were fortunate that their obsessions seemed to have a natural charm, witty in its way and invulnerable, which kept them from being resented and left them independent in their dependencies and undeterred by age. While they were both quite conscious of approaching death, they wanted—as Stevens says of the aging Penelope waiting for her lover-husband in "The World as Meditation"—"nothing [it] could not bring her by coming alone."[28] "If I live to be a hundred . . . ," my mother would often say, only to indicate that there was nothing she wanted from life that had to rely on that. Nor would the promise of such longevity cause either of those women to abandon her idiosyncrasies, which were a mark of self-possession, in order to accommodate pleasures neglected before and made possible by age. They would both have been indifferent to the overcompensations of some of our Senior Citizens who, in a culture sending mixed signals about age, find themselves dancing to the media-sponsored tune of recovered youth which is inevitably the delusive diminuendo not of the sibyl's shape but of the siren's song.

Much has been said and done, true, with the most benevolent of intentions, to guide those who are aging in making the best of the years that are left, instead of relinquishing them to a feeling of uselessness and another period of self-denial. But as with everything else in American life which emerges from neglect in persuasive numbers, the elderly have become sellable prospects in the marketplace of amelioration. There is that other poverty in the space of life which, pensioned off, also makes the aged better consumers and tourists, as well as a voting bloc. For every Gray Panther there are thousands at Disney World. There's surely no reason whatever why the aged shouldn't enjoy their belated measure of material blessings, and I'm uncomfortable deriding the pleasures that others have been waiting for. Yet some of the aged themselves are looking askance at

the newly abounding solicitations to the diversions from the more un-
speakable needs, like my seventy-five-year-old aunt who returned from
Florida because she was tired of pretending she still liked to dance, flirt
with octogenarians, and play shuffleboard.

When the opposing pressure is off, *not* to act their age, my guess is that
the elderly, more likely than not, want to acknowledge age as it is, meeting
it as equals, as the man meets the Echo in Yeats's poem, shouting, "a secret
to the stone," which consists of a question made, now that he is old and ill,
of all he has said and done: "I lie awake night after night," he says, "And
never get the answers right." The poem suggests that our narcissism can
also be wounded by being diverted from the question, which is asked in
various ways until it culminates in this:

> O Rocky Voice,
> Shall we in that great night rejoice?
> What do we know but that we face
> One another in this place?[29]

But when, confronted with the question, the others look away, what we
can see in the community of the aged are the newer signs of rejuvenation
masking the older disguises and avoidance. What is powerful in the later
poems of Yeats is not only the spectacle of the intrepid old man, still horny,
letting himself be shameless and mad, but that he never forgives the
ignominy of age, its bodily decrepitude, which threatens the sexual drive.
Remembering, however, that love has pitched its mansion in the place of
excrement, he turns over like a bagman the smelly detritus of life, the
"mound of refuse" which constitutes a past, and from which—if there is
any life and poetry left—they will have to be made: "Old kettles, old
bottles, and a broken can, / Old iron, old bones, old rags, that raving slut /
Who keeps the till"[30] and who, even through my mother's mask, inevitably
disfigures life.

There are some newer literary theorists for whom age is no excuse and
who might raise more than an eyebrow over the hysterical feminine figure
at the till picking up the libidinal cost. It is perhaps worth remarking,
however, that Yeats anticipates in this passage not only the plays of
Beckett, with their exhaustive enumeration of the grotesque comedy of
age, with its amputated paternity and ashbins of being, but the
postmodern strategy of *bricolage*, starting from the littered ground up. If he
borrows, as Derrida says of the *bricoleur*, from the scattered text of a
heritage that is more or less coherent and more or less in ruins,[31] he does
so not with the callow parapraxis of postoedipal desire but with an older
passion from the depths of age. Yeats's own critique of the solutions of
humanism can be devastating, but what is clear beyond cavil is that there is
for him no adequate response to the problem of aging in the ceaseless play

of signifiers through an infinitely deferrable end. "Those images that yet / Fresh images beget" come from the "fury and the mire of human veins" and not from language alone, though the language is charged with the complexities of blood and age, as it tries to imagine a place where "blood-begotten spirits come," beyond language, beyond life.[32]

"I am old, I belong to mythology," says the Old Man who introduces Yeats's last play, *The Death of Cuchulain*. But we recognize it as a desperate wish-fulfillment as he goes on to assault "that old maid history"[33] which makes the assertion a tenuous proposition—what caused Stevens to say that we live in a time when mythology is impossible. "I spit! I spit! I spit!" the Old Man repeats as the stage darkens on his rage and the curtain falls. "Myths are anonymous," says Lévi-Strauss,[34] but the voice behind the Old Man is surely not; and even Cuchulain, who fought the waves, receives six mortal wounds in his perfect narcissism. The "flesh my flesh has gripped / I both adore and loathe," says the Singer at the end of the play, as he sees the image of Cuchulain in the bloodbath of the Post Office, as the muscular body of myth gives way to the illusions of history and the insoluble questions of age.[35] While Yeats is able to imagine the Chinamen of "Lapis Lazuli" whose ancient, glittering eyes are gay, the attritions of history are such, its depredations upon love's body, that—while soul may clap its hands and sing, like the severed head of Cuchulain, for every tatter in its mortal dress—there's nothing like a starry *jouissance* making any the less onerous the awful debilities of age.

"I do not myself find it agreeable to be 90," wrote Rebecca West just before she died, "and I cannot imagine why it would seem so to other people. It is not that you have fears [though you do] about your own death, it is that your upholstery is already dead around you."[36] As Proust remarks, however, speaking of fragments of existence and fugitive things, there are those capable of living with the delusion that they *can* talk to the furniture because, while uncertain of themselves, they believe it is really alive.[37] And sometimes, too, the memories arise, furtive, out of focus, alien, like fantasies of a past, and those who are talking to the furniture can talk to no one else. ". . .[E]very fixation at a so-called instinctual stage," writes Lacan, "is above all a historical scar: a page of shame that is forgotten or undone, or a page of glory that compels."[38] Speaking of certain almost incommunicable "prodigies" of experience, Henry James despairs of dealing with them directly or objectively. "We want it clear, goodness knows," he writes in "The Altar of the Dead," "but we also want it thick, and *we get the thickness in the human consciousness that entertains and records, that amplifies and interprets it.*" The more elusive the memory or blurred with age, the more necessary it is, as James says of these prodigies, for the fragility of the memory to preserve itself, imperiled as it is, by *"looming through some other history*—the indispensable history of somebody's *normal* relation to something."[39] It is, then, through the loomings and laminations of the remembered—the thickness of a doubled consciousness—that, facing one another in this place, we may restore ourselves to the future, which is history unfolding in the indispensable other. "*You speak. You say:*" says Stevens in "As You Leave the Room," as he recapitulates, sparely, his poetic career. Has it been merely what skeletons think about? Is he no more than "A countryman of all the bones of the world?"[40]

There is something in the disposition of the major modernists—Stevens, James, Proust, Mann, Woolf, Joyce, Eliot, Marx, and Freud—that has an affinity with age and aging, as we do not encounter it among the offspring of the dead fathers of the postmodern, which, to the extent that it disclaims history in favor of an uninterrupted present without the impediment of remembrance, lacks the thickness. It is a disadvantaged history, of course, the history of the modern, because it is a history dominated and written by men. But we are, at the moment, thinking of aging in that history which, even when made and written by women, is the only history I can imagine in which we come to age. You'll have to forgive me—it may be a fault of age—that I am not good at imagining, even as we move through outer space and science fiction or marginal cultures with no conception of history, the outside or the end of history. Such as it is, the deepest experience of the modern seems to occur not *as* it occurs but through an aura of time as reversal and repetition, the reaching back through a kind of belatedness to the memory reconceived. "Now, here, the snow I had forgotten," says Stevens, or the other, the one who speaks, who *says*, certifying in the evanescence of remembered snow the reality disbelieved. "And yet nothing has been changed except what is / Unreal, as if nothing had been changed at all."[41]

The reaching back is, according to Proust, the distinctive work of the artist whose struggle is "to discern beneath matter, beneath experience, beneath words, something that is different from them," although it is possible, like Stevens, to speak of poetry as words about things which wouldn't exist without the words. A literature which thinks, however, of history as coded by words and words by history will distrust such talk as further mystification, there being—according to recent literary thought—nothing beneath words but more words, the only or major difference. Yet Proust is concerned with another difference brought on, perhaps, by the failing names for things which *do* exist in a world made out of words: "exactly the reverse of that which, in those everyday lives which we live with our gaze averted from ourself, is at every moment being accomplished" by all that "which we falsely call life." What one hopes for, then, is not only the capacity to live a life, but to *have* lived it, to have the experience *of* our experience, the secondariness, so that we can make "visible to ourselves that life of ours which cannot effectually observe itself and of which the observable manifestations need to be translated and, often, to be read backwards and laboriously deciphered."⁴² In this reading backwards, in the *literariness* of the idea of translation itself, there is—as in the talking cure of psychoanalysis—the suggestive power of repetition, bringing into consciousness the life which without being *said*, that is, *repeated*, would not in a sense have been lived at all—as if the origin of the experience we think the cause of it, *the one beneath*, is the capacity to think it the cause. In this respect, it is well to remember, as Lacan points out, that the amnesia of repression is one of the most lively forms of memory, which may be invoked by psychoanalytic process to the extent that it *is* a literary process. There is a sense, too, in which the voids of memory with age are an opening into imagination, so long as the aged are not made to feel that a failing memory is a felony of sorts. "Incomplete and dim memories of the past," writes Freud, are the substance of tradition and "a great incentive to the artist," as they might be to the person grown old, "for he is free to fill in the gaps according to the behests of his imagination. . . ."⁴³

But what about the forgotten aged without, perhaps, this poetic instinct for repossession, so damaged by history, the scars so thick, not the consciousness, that the memories, receding, are not only fragile but so deeply lodged and distorted in the unconscious that—even in the presence of the other with a "normal relation to something"—they are almost inaccessible?

I suspect that is the more general condition of aging in our time when history, accumulating in the self-consciousness of history, still looms as Marx described it, as the nightmare from which we are trying to awaken. There is, moreover, the liability with age that, along with the recurrencies and coming attractions of memory, we accumulate the reruns of repression, the social masks, the powers of imagination weakened by the character armor, a myriad of defenses, baffles, screenings, evasions—those supersaturated symptoms of the civil order displaced into the psyche from whence, recycled, they show up in the performance of everyday life as nothing but a repertoire of stage fright. Our vanity and our passions, says Proust, "our spirit of imitation," intensify the anxiety of the performance, along with abstract intelligence and habit, especially habit, the great deadener, according to Beckett. For Proust and Beckett, as for Freud, undoing the work of repression means travelling "back in the direction from which we have come to the depths where what has really existed lies unknown within us."⁴⁴ If art is a discipline of *de*conditioning, erasing habit, it may occur in age by accident, as senescence strips us of vanity. But there is just as likely to be in the process of growing old a compounding of those same habits and passions through long-formed reflexes of self-imitation, encouraged by the weakness of others, which is a pass of safe conduct through the perils of change.

What we see in Proust as in Beckett, who studied Proust and Freud, is a powerful drive to bring into consciousness all of what belongs to it. So long as it remains in a primary or inaccessible state it constitutes part of our life which, in its essence, remains unlived. Unfortunately, the censorship is resourceful not only in the civil order but at every level of the psychic systems, and "what belongs to consciousness," as Freud remarks, "is not always in consciousness. . . . The truth is that it is not only what is repressed that remains alien to consciousness, but also some of the impulses which dominate our ego and which therefore form the strongest functional antithesis to what is repressed."[45] As we age in this condition we are doubly impaired, self-deprived, twice distanced. There's no reason at all to believe that age will necessarily release inhibition by reducing the temporal claims of life, as we might expect. We are more likely as we age to go on preferring what Proust, and Eliot, considers that death-in-life which we elaborate for ourselves with gaze averted from the interior of being that is being-denied. "When we have arrived at reality," said Proust, "we must, to express and preserve it, prevent the intrusion of all those extraneous elements which at every moment the gathered speed of habit lays at our feet."[46]

But for those who, even when they've grown old, have not arrived at such reality—unless age itself, the raw fact of age, felt, is unequivocally that—the gathered speed of habit is itself an habituated momentum. There is also the possibility that, as Freud points out, the materials of primary repression are likely to have developed over the years in "unchecked and luxuriant fashion," ramifying "like a fungus, so to speak, in the dark" and taking on those extreme forms of expression which, when translated by analysis and revealed to the neurotic, seem alien and frightening.[47] As for the aged, such expression may look like habit when, to alleviate the terror, the damming of the eventually damaged and illusory strength of instinct is diverted into something akin to obsessional neurosis. Once again, it is the undoing of habit, so far as habit is not a comfort but a deterrent to desire, which is, I would think, the deepest wish of age.

The inability to reduce the symptoms below a certain level without destroying the civil value, which Barthes saw in his mother, caused Freud to speak forlornly, at the end of a long clinical career, of civilization and its discontents. It's as though he were in mourning for the irreversible aging of a world which doesn't know what to make of its history, like so many of the elderly who feel that time has invalidated all they have seen and known, and much of what they've believed—never more so than in our own time, when the abrasive momentum of history, swifter than ever before, has left still-remembered values almost geologically behind. So it is that in the graying of time they involuntarily assume another role, which seems somehow like a congestion of history, a cardiac arrest, which maybe needs a triple bypass. Unlike my mother, who seemed to design the role on her face in the image of a desire with an unembarrassed past, like a refusal to forget its promise, we find ourselves playing roles that seem intolerably miscast, and like most obedient actors—in the economy of a theater which reflects the economy of death—we don't say anything about it because we're thankful to have a part, however diminished, particularly as we age. And as we speak then the lines that have been written for us or, like aging actors doing walk-ons watching dolefully from the wings, what might be better remembered has been substantially lost. It's as though something in our history has deprived us of age in the winter of our discontent.

Thus we may become old, as it were, unseasoned, bereft, caught up in a process in which biological destiny, played out in the *mise-en-scène* of the unconscious, is either over before we know it or happening to someone else, while we wonder where it began. Where, indeed, does it begin, although we think we know where it ends? "If I am no longer young," writes Jules Renard, "I should like to know at what hour of what day my youth left me," as we feel it leave the dashing Vronsky in Tolstoy's *Anna Karenina* at the moment when, in a catastrophe of self-perception, he discovers the fatal bald spot on his head. In *The Death of Ivan Ilych*, a worse calamity befalls when Ilych, hanging the drapes in his affluent new home, bruises his side against the knob of the window frame. It's as if there's an acceleration of age through the illusions of normality and the residues of benighted youth. The terrible pain subsides, but what returns, with a sense of pressure in the side and queer taste in the mouth, is a general irritability that mars an enviable life, as if something pernicious and ungraspable had been there all along, "and nothing he could do would deliver him from *It*. And what was worst of all was that *It* drew his attention to itself not in order to make him take some action but only that he should look at *It*, look it straight in the face: look at it and without doing anything, suffer inexpressibly."[48]

Ilych wants to attribute his illness to the bruise in the side which is, however, but the memory-trace of an unlocalized horror which causes him to scream for three days before it falls away "from two sides, from ten sides, and from all sides."[49] It has a long tradition of impossible representation. In the medieval play *Everyman*, the coming of death is impressively proclaimed to the last unbelieving vanities of life. Today, one of the troubling vanities is longevity itself, and the prospect of an indefinite extension of life in whatever indeterminable forms, through the mutations of genetic engineering and the marvels of intensive care. Here the problems of aging run into the ethics of an intolerable dying, as well as the ghostlier demarcations of the origins of growing old. As Ronald Blythe puts it in *The View in Winter*, "In hospitals up and down the land lie finished lives that have been cut dead by death." Instead of death announcing itself to us—whether as the antic in the hollow crown or the insidious bruise in the side—"we may have to announce ourselves to death."[50] As we anticipate meanwhile, with exercise and better diets, an older age for us all, I am inclined to feel, as they apparently did in other shorter-living generations, that no matter where we are in life—whether nubile, lucent, lucky, or senescent—we live our lives in death which, like the unconscious, has no beginning or end, but is rather the medium of the illusion which is the eventuality of life.

Aging, I think, has no established period in our lives. But I am now making the necessary distinction between aging and merely being old. Proust gives us in *Time Regained*, like a natural historian, a scrupulous and often ruthlessly stunning taxonomy of old age. With the question of aging, however, there is the question of perception: who is doing the perceiving? and from what bias or coign of vantage? Some of the specimens in Proust's museum, or rather *Kunst* or *Wunderkammer*—those late Renaissance collections of the marvellous and the strange—seemed older or younger, repulsive or attractive, depending on perceptual distance: "it was dependent upon the spectator, who to see them as young had to place himself correctly and to view them only with that distant inspection which diminishes its object like the lens selected by an oculist for a long-sighted elderly person; old age here, like the presence of infusoria in a drop of water, was made apparent not so much by the advance of years as by a greater degree of accuracy in the scale of the observer's vision."[51] Beckett, in his essay on Proust, speaks about the infection of the object by the subjectivity of perception, the disease of perception itself where, when the object is human, we are dealing with differing systems of synchronization that are, as in the perception of age from within or without, more than likely to be hopelessly out of phase.

There are those, besides, who are hopelessly out of phase within themselves. I have known some, officially young or looking unaged, colleagues, even students, re-encountered friends, who seem to me unfathomably old, as if born with an overdose of entropy. Or you can see the curded promise in the complexions of verdigris. It is often the outward projection of depressing self-contempt. Marcel remarks too, amidst the geriatric figures of the Guermantes party where the past came rushing back, some who were "not old men, they were very young men in an advanced stage of withering."[52] They hadn't ripened with age because, with specific prematurity—"the marks of life . . . not deeply scored"[53]—they were absolute for death which, as Proust conjectured, seemed indifferent to them, as if there were not enough life to be bothered with in the end. "Ripeness is all," says the dispossessed Edgar in *King Lear* (V.ii.11), after he meets *his* blinded father and learns more of what it is to be desperate and old. In a world where the gods seem to be killing us for their sport, one may *want* to die, as Gloucester does, though in a kind of talking cure Edgar constructs the necessary suicide and recovers his father miraculously to life. He helps him to see with younger eyes sharpened by betrayal, madness, and degradation, which still have to look on death. In the last scene, when age seems stretched so far "upon the rack of this tough world" (V.iii.315) that it seems to suffuse the living with the dead, it is Edgar who says before the dead march to the promised end: "The oldest hath borne most; we that are young / Shall never see so much, nor live so long" (V.ii.326–27). It is strange how moving and accurate these strange lines feel, even now, when we're likely to live longer.

There is, however, a deference to the endurance of age which seems to belong to a forgotten world. Yet the atrocities inflicted upon age in *King Lear* should be chastening in still another way: aging and dying are universal, true, but aside from the fact that some, like Cordelia, die wantonly before their time, there is a scandal of aging, too, in which age is hastened unnaturally by the viciousness of history and the pollution of politics, so that while life expectancy stretches here, in the same old tough world there multitudes are wracked, old, terribly old, even the children are old, with the age that comes of misery in an uncommiserable time. Here, as we try to adjust our attitudes about aging as the aged wax and increase, we can be sentimental about the respect for the elders of other cultures where the price of such respect—as with the astonishing magnitudes of their mortuary art—is that people are being starved if not tortured to death. "World, world, O world!" exclaimed Edgar when, as if at the beginning of historical time, he first saw the bleeding eyeballs of his mutilated father. "But that thy strange mutations make us hate thee, / Life would not yield to age" (IV.i.10–12).

Death defeats all, they used to say, including wealth and power. But there is an acrid disease of age, an odor of age, that is an excretion of power, not only the seepage of the body's organic failing but of caste and class, something sullen in the economic disposition of things, an expense of spirit in the historical waste of shame. "The train smelled like the inside of an old man's hat—smelled of darkness, hair, tobacco," writes John Hawkes in *The Lime Twig:* "there were smells coming off the woman too, smells that lived in her despite the odor of coke and burning rails. Smells of shoe black and rotting lace, smells that were never killed by cleaning nor destroyed by the rain. The woman's strong body, her clothing, her hairpins and hair—all were greased with the smells of age."[54] So far as some come to age, it is not, as we see in Hawkes, by living for life but *against*

life, or as if there were no more to living than oblivion on the brain,
yielding not so much to age but to a sort of breathing extinction in the
disgrace of history. At the same time there are those, like certain characters
in Dostoyevsky, who even when young seem to be untellably old, as if
they've lived several lives over and would continue to live, however hide-
ously, through the last fell inch of life, and who—in the wild fringe
benefits of that inch exultant!—seem to live more life than our social
security of scientists ever dreamed. That fervor to live comes from a
resistance to death almost deranged which is not quite the poetic rage,
rage, so moving in Dylan Thomas, against the dying of the light.

We die, we know it, what is there to know? except that it can't *be* known,
and if you have a certain kind of temperament this will drive you crazy, as
our greatest literature knows. I must admit, though we have been looking
elsewhere for better attitudes toward dying, that my imagination has been
enduringly stirred by such literature, almost to the point of joy, all the
more so because it's unbearable, like the final suffering of the heroic Freud.
The irony of such suffering, like his labors, is that it seems outside the
scope of any conceivable model of aging. For most of us the tragic burden
is too great, as it always is with tragedy. We don't have the gift, we're not
prepared to pay the cost. And besides, we weren't chosen. Which is why,
today, in the absence of tragedy, we're rather relieved with other forms. As
for the illusions of other cultures which serve to reappropriate the suffering
of age and the brute fact of dying into the ceaseless continuum of something unnamable and maybe other than being, I don't pretend to understand them. When, however, I think of aging and the imagination, there is
an elegance of cold certitude which seems to me enviable if not emulable,
utterly moving and irreducibly right. Few minds will come to this because
it is a condition of mind which understands that the imagination's deity, if
one must have a myth, is an unswerving and implacable goddess, "Maiden
of icy stone / With no anatomy," whose service is unsparing of the ego that
refuses to be dissolved, as it is of the language which falsifies itself in the
vicinity of death, to which you can only bring a life—if you have enough of
it to offer:

> What brings me here? Old age.
> Here is the written page.
> What is your pleasure now?[55]

I am quoting from a beloved teacher, a poet, a critic, an implacably
stubborn and controversial man whose wisdom exceeded the faults of his
age, which he knew only too well.

When the marks of life *are* scored, you can only hope you know the
score. "I became my own obituary," said Sartre in his autobiography,

sometime before he died.[56] Which is not to say his life *is* his death, but rather an accounting of it, a reckoning, which can only occur at the inception of age by living it retrospectively. Which inevitably means the assumption of a solitude that can only be realized in the being-for-death. Freud speaks of it as the death instinct in *Beyond the Pleasure Principle*, the urge to restore some earlier state of things where the organism was at rest. Thus, the amazing proposition of Freud that, whatever course it takes, the aim of life is death. Or, as Lacan approaches it through the poetics of the Freudian discourse, the death instinct is associated with the repetition compulsion as the essential expression of "the limit of the historical function of the subject,"[57] the subject being the one who, splitting off from the ego and passing into language, "brings back into the present time the origins of his own person,"[58] becoming the one who *has been*. Lacan borrows from Heidegger the possibility in death of something which is "ownmost, unconditional, unsupersedable, certain and as such indeterminable. . . ." The possibility as a limit "is at every instant present" in what the subject-as-history "possesses as achieved. The limit represents the past in its real form, that is to say, . . . the past which reveals itself reversed in repetition."[59]

One of the sources of anxiety about the new omnipresence of the aged, particularly in America, is still our delinquent sense of history, the correlative of which is the sequestering of the aged in historyless communities, the time-warped parcelling out of memory in condominiums and nursing homes. "Today people live in rooms that have never been touched by death," wrote Walter Benjamin in his essay on the storyteller Leskov, "dry dwellers of eternity. . . ." If he anticipated almost half a century ago the current critique of the ghettoizing of the aged, Benjamin also sees in death the source of narrativity, the tale that must be told. It is in the imminence of death that the "unforgettable emerges" and "man's knowledge or wisdom, but above all his real life—and this is the stuff that stories are made of—first assumes transmissible form. . . ."[60] (As we shall see, however, there is something of a problem in the enunciation of the subject in the system of transmission.) We may deduce from Freud and Lacan that the life which comes rushing back in death—say, in the stereotype of drowning—arises from the desire for death through which we affirm ourselves in life. The onrush of a return is long prefigured in the circling back of instinctual life. In the memory-trace of desire, there is a movement toward otherness which, more than the instincts of self-preservation or self-assertion, moves the subject to its own proper death.

If Freud qualifies the disturbing notion of the death instinct by speaking of the sexual instincts, conservative as they are, as the true life instincts— "Eros, the preserver of all things"—that's because he also sees the life of the organism moving in a "vacillating rhythm" through "ever more compli-

cated *detours* before reaching its aim of death." Freud's thought, and the
retrogressive path he is describing, is not unlike the circuitousness of
storytelling itself, from Borges back to the *Arabian Nights*. Much has been
made of this in new literary theory, and I'm not going to labor it now.
"What we are left with," says Freud, for all the detours, is what has been
posited early in the work, "that the organism wishes to die in its own
fashion."[61]

But there's the problem, since dying in one's own fashion may no longer
be, for that subject, self-fashioning. "We obey," said Stevens, "the coaxings
of our end."[62] Without misprizing, or minimizing, the less abstractly
teasing simple pains and fears, the chills and fevers of the elderly abreast of
death, I also sometimes think there is no such thing as aging even when
people *are* old, because they miss the coaxings, through too long obedience, perhaps, to something other than the end. So, while everybody
has a story to tell as the unforgettable emerges, it appears to be forgotten
and the story isn't being told because it *hasn't* achieved transmissible form.
While it may be moving at times to see old people suspended in themselves
like Yeats's long-legged fly upon the stream, their minds moving upon
silence, the silence may not be much sustenance, or substance. And for
such—as for any of us for whom the bleak necessity remains silent when it
would be categorically better spoken—there is only further pain. "What I
seek in speech," says Lacan, "is the response of the other. What constitutes
me as subject is my question." Remarks are insufficient. What is the
question of the person growing old? I suspect the question is: *Why me?* "In
order to be recognized by the other," says Lacan, "I utter what was only in
view of what will be." So, too, with the memories of age, which are not
merely part of one's personal history but a rhetoric, a petition as well,
seeking the one who *can* respond: "In order to find him, I call him by a
name that he must assume or refuse in order to reply to me."[63] But the
deepest pathos of age may be when nobody responds because, for whatever reasons, the name has been forgotten.

If there were such a thing as the poetics of aging, we might say it is a
failure of the imagination to have imagined, as one nears the exhaustion of
life, "the absence of imagination" which is "[it]self to be imagined," as
Stevens observes as if thinking of Proust, Swann's Way, the Other Way, the
depleted circling of the essential solitude: "the great pond and its waste of
lilies, all this / Had to be imagined as inevitable knowledge, / Required, as
necessity requires,"[64] after the leaves have fallen in "The Plain Sense of
Things." Plain as it is (for Stevens), a poem of winter and its discontents, it
has something of the bereft beatitude of the "yellow leaves, or none, or
few" of Shakespeare's sonnet where, in a kind of double take on the falling
leaves—the few were none, *there*, then fallen—we come with age to the

"Bare ruined choirs where late the sweet birds sang" (Sonnet 73, ll. 1–4). But whether they sing or not depends, I suppose, on the presence of the imagination in the imagining of its absence, "imagination dead imagine," as Beckett said, beyond his seventieth year, in the ironically elegiac voice which brings to age the nothingness which is a little less, *lessness*, words doing their best in the metonymic incapacity of words and age, their Negative Capability, what Stevens calls elsewhere figures of capable imagination, reflecting the nothing that is not there and the nothing that is.

The life so short, the craft so long to learn, we learn from poetry which learns from age, as in *Lear*, how nothing will come of nothing with more than nothing seems. "Now that I'm entering night," writes Beckett in *Enough*, who is intimate with nothing, "I have kinds of gleams in my skull."[65] "The sedge has withered from the lake / And no birds sing," wrote Keats, who never lived to be old, about another sibyl's shape, in "La Belle Dame Sans Merci," and I hear instead of the absence of the song the negative of the absence, the no-birds *sing*, as in "the palm at the end of the mind" the birds also sing, in the sumptuous bleakness at the end of Stevens's poems, as they do on the golden bough of Yeats's Byzantium, another creation of age which arises, out of the consciousness of being old, from the foul rag and bone shop of the heart. It is a richness in the categories of need, like "the cry of the leaves [in Stevens] which do not transcend themselves" but, like Shakespeare's leaves not quivering but shaking *against* the cold, give one the feeling, through "an exertion that declines" of "the life of that which gives life as it is."[66]

Without that feeling—and its achievement is a lifetime's exertion which accident may impair—what can there be in old age but even in the garrulousness of the old an unspoken confusion, not "the chatter that is then true legend,"[67] as the early momentum subsides, and then the loss of anticipation, sclerotic time, the same agitations of uncertain desire, lamed eros, panic, the dying fall, not to mention the specific and unfigured incapacities, the accretions of disease, dry mouth, sore knuckles, brittle skin, weak knees, dim eyes, running sores, varicose veins, longer healing, palsy, arthritis, short and repellent breath, odors, gas, gas, unsubsiding, angina, cancer, senility itself, unsphinctered helplessness and shamed dependence, the litany of unaccountable somatic disasters and unnameable agonies that testify in the lamentations to something that was, when it was here, never entirely known, and only the emptiness tangible now, that absence, babbling, dread, now, when the last failed apprehension of it is gone, in "the stale grandeur of annihilation."[68]

For the real impediment to an aging which is other than mere attrition is, for all we've appeared to live, the mere appearance of living, which is not quite the same as what I've tried to recall in the hyperbolic figure of my madeup mother, the commemorative living of an appearance. Nor have I been, in remembering her, recommending that inheritance as anything like a paradigm of age, for I have no illusion through all its remembered charm about the boundaries of her triple mirror nor, after having spent so much of my life aging in the theater, the mirrored limits of any appearance.

"How swift life runs from January to December!" writes Virginia Woolf in *The Waves*. "We are all swept on by the torrent of things grown so familiar that they cast no shade."[69] It is never enough to have made the most of our time or to live out an impalpable future, for we always desire, in the virility of the present moment, the thing which went before, and our fear about the future is, even before it comes, that it was never meant to last. Among the torrent of things grown so familiar that they cast no shadow are the things we meant to do that we've never done for want of time, opportunity, or courage, and few of us will be able to avoid that. Most of those who say they do, lie, which is perhaps another form of commemoration. Among the things that are disappointing in age is the inability to be any wiser or more courageous, or to meet principle any more squarely than you did when you were young, though you are older and you know the time is running out when, with some last scruple of integrity, you can keep the promise to yourself. I would like to say a good deal more about the best of our desires and the embarrassment of knowing that they will never be fulfilled, not because desire is endless and always desiring desire, but because for one good reason or another we've grown comfortable failing ourselves. I suppose, however, that to know these things of oneself is part of the meaning of aging and of having been, at the limit of the historical function of the subject, one who has been as much as he can be after all, and more because one knows it.

But there is also a perturbation of aging that comes, just over the threshold of consciousness from want of consciousness, a last sad intimation of the life we've never lived because essentially unremembered, so that there is a sense of having suffered somehow an irreparable loss that, because not known, we cannot even mourn. "It is poverty's speech which seeks us out the most," writes Stevens in old age about the older philosopher dying in Rome. "And you—it is you that speak it without speech. . . ." There is a sensory plenitude in the grace of this remembrance, "Your dozing in the depths of wakefulness, / In the warmth of your bed, at the edge of your chair, alive / Yet living in two worlds. . . ."[70] But when, in the declensions of an ending, there is a solitude without sense, the mere poverty of the unremembered, it adds to the last depreciations of age another discontent, and what was once, if memory serves, a rite of passage out of time is only, now, without then, more time to be endured.

Notes

1. "The Apparitions," in *The Collected Poems of W. B. Yeats* (New York: Macmillan, 1960), p. 332.

2. *Time Regained*, in Vol. III of Marcel Proust, *Remembrance of Things Past*, trans. C. K. Scott Moncrieff, Terence Kilmartin, Andreas Mayor (New York: Random House, 1981), p. 970.

3. *Enough*, in Samuel Beckett, *First Love and Other Shorts* (New York: Grove, 1974), p. 60.

4. Proust, *Time Regained*, p. 721.

5. Roland Barthes, *Camera Lucida: Reflections on Photography*, trans. Richard Howard (New York: Hill and Wang, 1981), p. 67.

6. Sigmund Freud, *Dora: An Analysis of a Case of Hysteria*, intro. Philip Rieff (New York: Collier, 1963), p. 96.

7. Proust, *Time Regained*, p. 976.

8. Barthes, *Camera Lucida*, p. 69.

9. Barthes, *Camera Lucida*, p. 67.

10. Sigmund Freud, "On Narcissism: An Introduction," in *General Psychological Theory*, intro. Philip Rieff (New York: Collier, 1963), p. 56.

11. Barthes, *Camera Lucida*, p. 69.

12. Freud, "On Narcissism," p. 70.

13. Proust, *Time Regained*, pp. 973–74.

14. Proust, *Time Regained*, p. 878.

15. Proust, *Time Regained*, pp. 869–70.

16. Wallace Stevens, "Questions Are Remarks," in his *The Palm at the End of the Mind*, ed. Holly Stevens (New York: Vintage, 1972), p. 353.

17. Proust, *Time Regained*, p. 903.

18. Stevens, "The Sail of Ulysses," p. 393.

19. Stevens, "The Sail of Ulysses," p. 393.

20. Stevens, "The Sail of Ulysses," p. 393.

21. Stevens, "A Mythology Reflects Its Region," p. 398.

22. Jacques Lacan, *Ecrits: A Selection*, trans. Alan Sheridan (New York: Norton, 1977), p. 4.

23. Lacan, *Ecrits*, p. 21.

24. William Carlos Williams, *Paterson* (New York: New Directions, 1963), p. 11.

25. Sigmund Freud, "A Note on the Unconscious in Psychoanalysis," in *General Psychological Theory*, p. 49.

26. Sigmund Freud, "The Unconscious," in *General Psychological Theory*, pp. 134–35.

27. See Ronald Blythe, *The View in Winter* (New York: Harcourt Brace Jovanovich, 1979), p. 9.

28. Stevens, "The World as Meditation," p. 381.

29. Yeats, "The Man and the Echo," in *The Collected Poems*, p. 338.

30. Yeats, "The Circus Animals' Desertion," in *The Collected Poems*, p. 336.

31. Jacques Derrida, "Structure, Sign, and Play in the Discourse of the Human Sciences," in *Writing and Difference*, trans. Alan Bass (Chicago: Univ. of Chicago Press, 1978), p. 283.

32. Yeats, "Byzantium," in *The Collected Poems*, pp. 243–44.

33. William Butler Yeats, "The Death of Cuchulain," in *The Collected Plays of W. B. Yeats* (New York: Macmillan, 1953), p. 439.

34. Claude Lévi-Strauss, *The Raw and the Cooked*, trans. John and Doreen Weightman (New York: Harper & Row, 1969), p. 18.

35. Yeats, "The Death of Cuchulain," in *The Collected Plays*, p. 445.
36. Rebecca West, quoted in *The New York Times*, 16 March 1983.
37. Proust, *Time Regained*, p. 909.
38. Lacan, *Ecrits*, p. 52.
39. Henry James, preface to "The Altar of the Dead," in *The Art of the Novel: Critical Prefaces*, ed. R. P. Blackmur (New York: Scribner's, 1962), p. 256.
40. Stevens, "As You Leave the Room," p. 396.
41. Stevens, "As You Leave the Room," p. 396.
42. Proust, *Time Regained*, p. 932.
43. Freud, *Moses and Monotheism*, trans. Katherine Jones (New York: Vintage, 1955), p. 89.
44. Proust, *Time Regained*, p. 932.
45. Freud, "The Unconscious," in *General Psychological Theory*, p. 139.
46. Proust, *Time Regained*, p. 934.
47. Freud, "Repression," in *General Psychological Theory*, p. 107.
48. Leo Tolstoy, *The Death of Ivan Ilych and Other Stories* (New York: Signet, 1960), p. 133.
49. Tolstoy, p. 155.
50. Blythe, *The View in Winter*, p. 4.
51. Proust, *Time Regained*, p. 989.
52. Proust, *Time Regained*, p. 979.
53. Proust, *Time Regained*, p. 929.
54. John Hawkes, *The Lime Twig* (New York: New Directions, 1961), p. 72.
55. Yvor Winters, "To the Moon," *The Collected Poems of Yvor Winters*, intro. Donald Davie (Chicago: Swallow Press, 1978), p. 185.
56. Jean-Paul Sartre, *Les Mots* (Paris: Gallimard, 1968), p. 171.
57. Lacan, *Ecrits*, p. 103.
58. Lacan, *Ecrits*, p. 47.
59. Lacan, *Ecrits*, p. 103.
60. Walter Benjamin, *Illuminations*, ed. Hannah Arendt, trans. Harry Zohn (New York: Schocken, 1968), p. 94.
61. Sigmund Freud, *Beyond the Pleasure Principle*, p. 33.
62. Stevens, "Sail of Ulysses," p. 392.
63. Lacan, *Ecrits*, p. 86.
64. Stevens, "Sail of Ulysses," p. 383.
65. Beckett, *First Love*, p. 54.
66. Stevens, "The Course of a Particular," p. 367.
67. Stevens, "Sail of Ulysses," p. 391.
68. Stevens, "Lebensweisheitspielerei," p. 384.
69. Virginia Woolf, *The Waves* (New York: Harcourt, Brace, 1931), p. 216.
70. Stevens, "To an Old Philosopher in Rome," pp. 272–73.

MORE IMAGES OF EROS AND OLD AGE:

The Damnation of Faust and the Fountain of Youth

✳✳✳

Leslie A. Fiedler

SEVEN YEARS AGO (at a point when I had just turned fifty-nine, which is to say, was entering the seventh, the mythological *last* decade of life), I began a series of ongoing meditations, the first stage of which I provisionally fixed in an essay called "Eros and Thanatos: Old Age in Love."[1] In it, I speculated on what it meant to have become, insofar as love still moved my failing flesh (and it did, it *did!*), a "Dirty Old Man," not just in the eyes of those around me, but in my own deep imagination as well. I had introjected, I discovered, a primordial and persistent image of the pathetic yearning of the aged for the barely nubile young, a myth to be found almost everywhere in the culture which had bred me: in the dirty jokes we told each other on the streets of my childhood, in the fairy tales my parents read me before I could read them for myself, in classic texts by Shakespeare and Chaucer and Charles Dickens which I had "studied" in college and graduate school, and finally in certain works of High Modernism, which in the bad old days of my adolescence we still had to enjoy behind our teacher's backs—Thomas Mann's *Death in Venice*, for instance, and Ronald Firbank's *The Eccentricities of Cardinal Pirelli*.

To understand better the roots of the fascination and horror with which our society has traditionally regarded the kind of love whose most honorable name is "pederasty" and whose most pejorative is "child molestation," as well as my own ambivalence toward it, I tried to isolate, analyze, decode the archetypal image of the *Senex*, the *Geros*, pursuing an elusive and ultimately taboo beloved: the *Puer* or *Puella*, *Kouros* or *Kore*, who flees from him faster than he can run. I say "him" and "he" because the sex of the pursuer is in the most ancient stories mythically male. That of the pursued, however, is optional, either, or sometimes ambiguously both, since, archetypally, the impossible beloved is an ephebe on the androgynous

37

verge of genital maturity. Especially in earlier versions of the tale, the myth is often rendered comically—ending in the ridiculous discomfiture of Crabbed Age, most often by betrayal and cuckoldry. But there are pathetic undertones from the very start; and later versions become fully tragic (without, however, ceasing to be in some sense absurd), ending in the death of the old man.

Indeed, it seemed to me then—and seems to me even more clearly now—that the thanatic ending was implicit in the myth from the start. The archetypal pursuit of the *Puer/Puella*, that is to say, represents not merely the incestuous desire of the father for his own offspring, the inverse of the infamous Oedipus Complex, whose frustration can be played for the laughs. On a deeper and darker level, it stands for a kind of narcissism once removed, since what the *Senex* yearns to embrace is the image of his own youth reincarnated as flesh of his flesh and bone of his bone. Like all narcissism, therefore, it implies finally a desire to embrace death: the desperate dream of forever delivering oneself (even at the cost of life) from the lifelong fear of extinction for which ordinary orgasms provide a temporary relief.

The Myth of the Dirty Old Man portrays the quest for that final solution as not merely impossible, but as somehow unseemly because (in the words of my earlier essay), "In a culture like ours . . . the flight to the anodyne of sex has long been considered . . . for the old totally inappropriate . . . we do not merely quite properly ask that the old be treated with dignity, we (more dangerously) demand of the old that they behave with dignity, impose decorum on them as a burden and a chore" (p. 236). Though this is still to a degree true even in our age of, theoretically, "sexual liberation," it has become by the end of the twentieth century only half of a double truth: a double bind, in fact, imposed on the aging by a culture which though it has never really stopped requiring of them decorous restraint, also urges on them unflagging sexual performance. Surely, I must have been dimly aware of this even back when I was not quite sixty; but I did not manage to bring it to full consciousness.

Now, however, that I have passed my sixty-fifth year and have become officially one of the Golden Aged by registering for Social Security and Medicaid, I am reminded almost daily of our society's conflicting demands on the old. My name has apparently been fed into the computers of companies who in an attempt to make a fast buck evoke images of *eros* and *thanatos* drawn from both sides of that double bond. If their advertising brochures have not moved me to purchase the products they tout, they have at least impelled me to meditate further on sex and aging. Much of the unsolicited Golden Age junk mail I receive—offers of special deals on life insurance without physical examination or on bargain cemetery plots and caskets, for example—exploit the prescience of impending death implicit in the Myth of the Dirty Old Man: that awareness of our mortality which simultaneously exacerbates and cools the desire of the old to couple with those so young they do not yet know they will ever die. Moreover, like that archetypal tale, they urge us "to go down dignified," to "Provide! Provide!" against the loveless eternity which lies beyond the brief span of loving and begetting which is our life in time. "Find out all the advantages of mausoleum crypt ownership NOW" one such leaflet reads; "If you plan ahead the decision can be made without the pressure of emotion."

How debased and trivial and essentially false are such assurances that we can confront the threat of death without troubling emotion—shorn, as they are, of the traditional promises of immortality or the hope of Heaven. Only the guarantee of "perpetual care" for the gravesite to which our ashes will be consigned is provided. Yet somehow these secular travesties of consolation have for me the same kind of baleful fascination as the obituaries in the daily newspapers and the alumni magazines of schools I have attended, which I consult to see what old friends have predeceased me, and how many total strangers of my own age or younger have already died. Contrary to what they seem to promise, however, such ads begin by aggravating rather than allaying the primal *timor mortis* we are heir to. But, perhaps precisely because of their banality, their final effect is to exorcise the bad dreams stirred in me by the myth of *Eros* as *Thanatos/Thanatos* as *Eros*—in which I am unsure whether the lovely ephebe I pursue in rapid eye motion sleep is the image of my irrecoverable youth or that of my inevitable demise.

In any case, I arise on the morning after oddly refreshed, delivered from my oldest incubus. "Let the dead bury their dead," I declare to whomever will listen, and "We must endure our going hence even as our coming hither." Then I go to my mail box prepared to heave the latest installment of commercial *memento mori* into the wastebasket unread. But looking down, I see that the new day's batch of mail "For elderly eyes only" is disconcertingly different from what I had been expecting. The letterheads this time read not "Forest Lawn Cemetery and Mausoleum" but "S/40," meaning, I discover, sex after the age of forty. And the large print on the cover of the enclosed brochure raises the ante even higher, assuring me that " 'The One a Night' pill ensures maximum erotic satisfaction for men in their 40s . . . 50s . . . 60s . . . 70s . . . 80s. And even older." "Age is no longer an excuse for sexual senility," it goes on, the tone now halfway between reassurance and mild rebuke, "you can have the power to love no matter how old you may be." And lest any still remain doubtful, there are signed testimonials from satisfied users of Corazine-DL or NSP-270, written in language simple and gross enough for the least literate. "I am 69 years old. Since I started your pills . . . I want sex every day. . . ." "I can get a hard and long lasting erection—so long that my wife was going to hide my pills . . . but I don't let her know where I keep them." "I am 76. After the first 30 capsules, my penis became firm. I am proud of it and when I urinate I think I am holding someone else's."

It is tempting to dismiss such crass appeals as irrelevant to anyone but the pathologically insecure, and yet I must confess that from the start I sensed behind them the presence of a myth of eros and old age, especially appealing perhaps to our time and place, but surely ancient in its origins. Superficially, they seem based on a naive faith, very twentieth-century, very American, that science can cure all the ills of our flesh, plus an equally unquestioned modern belief that one of those ills—the supreme indignity, in fact, that befalls us as youth departs—is the loss of potency. Such advertisements though they make a show of being addressed to women as well as men, clearly speak primarily to males, who, in a time which considers sexual inadequacy more unseemly than indecorous lust, are in a particularly difficult spot, because wearing as they do the physical sign of erotic readiness in full sight, they can deceive neither themselves nor their partners when "sexual senility" overtakes them.

But in any time since we separated ourselves from other mammals by divorcing sex from periodic estrus, the fear of being eventually unable to get it up, of failing finally to cut the mustard, must surely have haunted the males of our species, leading them to seek—in eternally deluded hope— some nostrum or charm or spell which might guarantee perpetual potency. True enough, in the heyday of orthodox Christianity, when the devout were taught to pray for deliverance from desire rather than to regard its inevitable waning as a disaster, that primordial fear and the delusive hope it begot were seldom publicly confessed. It is hard to believe, however, that they did not live on subliminally at least, finding expression, like other repressed human responses, in the encrypted form of myth.

Indeed, though I somehow failed to notice it in my earlier essay (for reasons which I trust will become clear before I am through), there *is* in our tradition a myth which in its tripartite structure reveals the dialectical interplay of ambivalences created by the tension between our natural dread of sexual failure and the teachings of the Church. Beginning with a nightmare evocation of impotency in old age, that archetypal story turns in its second stage into a wish-dream of restoring youth and genital vigor with a magic potion, then lapses into a night-terror again as the miraculous recovery turns out to have been a hoax or a diabolical trap. In its classic form, it was, after the invention of printing, reembodied over and over by dramatists and poets and musicians including Christopher Marlowe, Goethe, Paul Valéry, Gounod, and Berlioz. Nor has it ceased to haunt us in post-Gutenberg times, being reimagined in such movies as Brian De Palma's *Phantom of the Paradise*.

Like everyone else in the dying twentieth century, therefore, I have long been haunted by that archetypal tale. In fact, I once acted the part of its protagonist in a production of Valéry's *Mon Faust*, which is in truth quite explicitly erotic. For a long time, however, I thought of it not as a fable of *eros* and old age but solely as a myth of the *hybris* and consequent damnation of the scientist: the prototype of certain pop classics of the nineteenth century like *Frankenstein* or *Dr. Jekyll and Mr. Hyde*, as well as the pulp fiction and comic books of the twentieth century, in which the image of the Modern Prometheus becomes the caricature of the "Mad Scientist" plotting the destruction of the world, but achieving only his own.

Very early on, however, the myth of Faust—the "studious artisan" who is archetypally old—was conflated with that of Don Juan, the indefatigable sexual athlete who is archetypally young. That process had already begun with Marlowe, whose Dr. Faustus, though not really old, is nonetheless seeking in his forbidden studies a sexual New Life. Despite all his grandiloquent talk about wanting to "make the Moone drop from her Sphere" and "the Ocean to overwhelme the world," what he actually asks for once he has sealed his infernal bond, is "a wife, the fairest maid in *Germany*." Moreover, his final request of Mephistopheles is to "have unto my paramour / That heavenly *Hellen*,"[2] who represents the erotic ideal of pre-Christian paganism. Domestic bliss is apparently not in the power of Marlowe's Devil to bestow; what he can grant the amorous doctor—and even this perhaps only in illusion—is a kiss from Hellen which sucks away his soul. Though this seems to me an anticlimax to his vaulting ambition, verging indeed on absurdity, no reader, I think, has ever managed to laugh at it, since most of us have continued to dream to our own day the Faustian dream, believing on some level, whatever our conscious morality, that sexual consummation is more devoutly to be wished than the power to re-order the Cosmos or confuse the Elements.

That dream was, at any rate, still being dreamed by Goethe, when at the end of the eighteenth century (at the very moment America and Romanticism were being invented), he wrote the first version of a poetic drama he spent the rest of his life emending and revising. On a conscious level, he sought at first only to turn the story of Faust into a bittersweet tale of seduction, sentimental and domestic enough to please the bourgeois taste of his own times. But before he was through, he had, without quite knowing it, turned it into a myth of Endless Love in a form that would still remain viable when damnation had become a metaphor, sex was no longer regarded as sinful, and earthly science had begun to inspire the faith formerly reserved for God.

This transformation of the archetype Goethe accomplished first by making his Faust unequivocally old—and then grafting on to his legend that of the Elixir of Life or the Fountain of Youth, which had long flourished independently, particularly in the lore of the Alchemists. Goethe's Faust, that is to say, is rejuvenated only after he has quaffed at a Witches' Sabbat a "filthy brew" that takes twenty years off of his life. There has been no doubt from the start about why he seeks thus to reverse the process of aging; since Mephisto has assured him that if he takes his medicine he will learn once more "with intensest pleasure / How Cupid stirs within and bounds about. . . ." And this time the Spirit which Denies keeps his promise, providing the rejuvenated Doctor with a real, live, flesh-and-blood girl: a village *Fräulein* "decorous . . . virtuous . . . a little pert as well" and, best of all, eminently seducible.[3]

Though the actual seduction of an all-too-human Gretchen seems at first an even more comic anticlimax to the Faustian quest than the illusory possession of a ghostly Helen, it, too, debouches in terror. First the child she bears to Faust dies at her hand, then Gretchen herself perishes, leaving him still young to be sure, but lonelier than ever and burdened with guilt. It would appear then that the horror with which Christianity had taught the pagan world to regard unbridled passion ("the wages of sin is death") persisted still in the unconscious of Renaissance atheists like Marlowe and apostles of the Age of Reason like Goethe. Not even in America, which had declared its Independence from the traditional belief systems of Europe, were writers delivered from the Faustian nightmare of damnation. Not for quite a long time anyway.

And how could they have been, since two hundred years before the appearance of the Deists who framed the Declaration, New England had been settled by a generation of True Believers, who read side by side with the Bible, *Pilgrim's Progress*, and *Paradise Lost*, chapbooks containing the legend of Faust. Small wonder then that as late as the mid-nineteenth century, the image of the Satanic Pact is still to be found at the center of the novels we have come to consider the masterworks of the period. The secret motto of *Moby Dick*, Melville confessed, was "I baptize you not in the Name of the Father, the Son and the Holy Ghost, but in the Name of the Devil"[4]; and Hawthorne spoke of his *Scarlet Letter* as a "hell-fired book." Nor did these descendants of the Puritans ever suggest—like Goethe in the final version of his *Faust*—that their Fausts would be some-how ultimately saved. Captain Ahab goes down to destruction with blasphemy on his lips, and Chillingsworth becomes the Dark Spirit he serves, "a serpent manifest."

To be sure, a counter myth of rejuvenation without guilt, a dream of finding without diabolical aid the innocent Fountain of Youth, has also possessed the American imagination from the start. Even before the WASP founders of New England had sought to persuade the Indians of the icy North that sex without marriage was sin, explorers from Southern Europe had sought to discover from the aboriginal inhabitants of Florida the exact location of those miraculous waters. It was, indeed, the hope of finding that Fount which persuaded them in the first place to dare the dangers of an Atlantic crossing. Moreover, though their mythic quest failed literally, it succeeded symbolically, creating an enduring image in the deep psyche of the world of Americans as New Adams and Eves, eternally young in the Garden of the New World. That we ourselves have introjected that image is attested by the fact that on the very beaches where Ponce de León once sought the fabled waters, we can find at this moment withered refugees from winter and their own senility acting out in unsuspected caricature the myth of eternal youth. Meanwhile, all up and down America, other aging Americans pursue rejuvenation by sipping Geritol, popping Vitamin E, dieting, jogging, or submitting their sagging flesh to the cosmetic surgeon's knife.

The whole foredoomed effort represents, in one sense, the quest for a kind of *ersatz* immortality in the flesh, with which we have sought to satisfy ourselves since the death of God and the loss of the hope of Heaven. But specifically for the aging, it represents also and chiefly the dream of turning back the clock permanently: which is to say, not only of becoming young and potent once more, but of staying that way. In our time, moreover, especially in these United States, we have persuaded ourselves that such a reversal of entropy does not require, as the Faustian Legend suggests, striking a bargain with Evil and eventually paying the price, since presumably lily-white Science can now provide without the risk of damnation (in which, anyhow, we no longer believe) what Black Magic so delusively and dangerously promised. Science or quasi-science or, at the very least, pseudo-science—including the nostrums of the pillpushers on which I began by reflecting, the behavior modification techniques of sexologists like Masters and Johnson, the psychotherapy of Freud and Jung and Wilhelm Reich—has, in short, become for us the true Fountain of Youth, the new Alchemy.

Indeed, in the popular mind, Dr. Freud has long since achieved a mythological status almost equivalent to that of Dr. Faustus: feared by some as one more subverter of the moral order in league with the Powers of Darkness, but seeming to many more a secular saviour, capable of "scientifically" delivering us all from repression and impotence. Freud, however, though he did teach that "full genitality," erotic maturity, was a blessing rather than a primal curse, was essentially a believer in sublimation and restraint, a champion of monogamy and the nuclear family. Nonetheless, however misguidedly, advocates of sex without responsibility or guilt evoked his holy name in the decades just before and after World War I. When, however, following the next World War, a new generation of Sexual Revolutionaries appeared to whom "sublimation" and "maturity" were dirty words—when in short the Sexual Revolution and the Youth Revolution were fused into one—they turned away from the Founding Father of psychoanalysis to his most heretical ex-disciple, Wilhelm Reich.

Half Shaman, half scientist—and in the end quite mad—that apostate from Freudian orthodoxy became a major influence on certain Jewish-American novelists of the fifties: most notably, perhaps, Isaac Rosenfeld, Saul Bellow, Paul Goodman, and Norman Mailer, whom he persuaded that sexual repression is the cause of all the ills which beset us—not only neurosis and impotence, but cancer and capitalism and war. Reich preached, moreover, and such writers believed, that the way to salvation, both personal and social, was to seek with the aid of Orgone Therapy (and to celebrate in fiction) the Perfect Orgasm. Inevitably, the Reichian re-definition of love "as the search [not] for a mate, but . . . an orgasm more apocalyptic than the one which preceded it"[7] led to a detachment of *eros* from the myths with which it had been traditionally associated, like that of Romeo and Juliet or Tristan and Isolde or even Cinderella. Instead, it was associated in the work of such writers, on the one hand, with the Quest for the mythical Holy Grail, and on the other, with the legend of an actual Fountain of Youth.

In Mailer's essay, "The White Negro, Superficial Reflections on the Hipster" (the closest thing to a manifesto produced by the generation of Reichian apologists), the latter identification is spelled out in full. "It is not granted to the hipster to grow old gracefully—he has been captured too early by the oldest dream of power, the gold fountain of Ponce de Léon, the fountain of youth where the gold is in the orgasm." But, of course, both Grail and Fountain are ultimately unattainable, which is to say, the dream of youth and potency eternally restored never dies because it is never fulfilled. This, indeed, Mailer himself goes on to confess ("the apocalyptic orgasm . . . remains as remote as the Holy Grail"),[6] but he is wrong about the cause—suggesting that such failure is due to remaining knots of neurotic violence in the "hipster," which inhibit full genital release. No, if the myth itself begins with hope and ends in frustration, this must be because we have all of us always, on some level or other, *wished* it so, since the wish is father to the dream.

Only in the mythic imagination of the self-hating WASP is even the "Negro" immune to the desire to be delivered from the endless round of tumescence and detumescence by growing old. And Mailer, far from being a "Negro," is a "Jew," which is to say, his archetypal opposite not just in the deep psyche of the gentile world but in that of all Jews exiled in that world. Who of us educated in the United States, Gentile or Jew, is not possessed by the archetypal image of Shylock—the castrating Old Man, the Patriarchal Enemy of Young Love, threatening the innocent eroticism of pre-Christian Europe with the knife he is eternally whetting on his boot, and the Law in whose name he claims to speak: "Thou shalt not commit . . . ," "Thou shalt not covet. . . ."

Nor does it help much that Mailer has ostensibly rejected his Judaic heritage, embodying his erotic fantasies in prepotent goyish protagonists and declaring himself heir apparent to antisemitic Ernest Hemingway. The literary tradition out of which Hemingway comes is, whatever Mailer may believe, a Puritan one, which from the start sought to subvert the myth of the Fountain of Youth. The earliest story I know, for instance, in which a major American author deals with that myth is Hawthorne's "Dr. Heidegger's Experiment," which opens with the good doctor offering to four aged friends, three men and a woman, a potion he claims to have been drawn from the fabulous Fount. Typically, Hawthorne leaves some doubt about whether this claim is literally true, but it scarcely matters, since the waters *work*, psychologically at least. In a very little while, the author tells us, "they were young: their burning passions proved them so," which is to say, lust and jealousy soon has the males, inflamed by the restored "witching beauty" of the withered hag with whom they had entered, at one another's throats. But even as they struggle, what is left of the potion spills and they find themselves old again. "The Water of Youth possessed merely a virtue more transient than wine," Hawthorne comments editorially; and Dr. Heidegger concurs, declaring, "I bemoan it not, for if the fountain gushed at my very doorstep, I would not stoop to bathe my lips in it. Such is the lesson you have taught me."[7]

Long before Hawthorne ever made it into print, however, American writers had already learned that lesson, which few of them in fact have ever forgotten. Indeed, the first mythological character created by an American author who succeeded in capturing the imagination of the world was Washington Irving's Rip Van Winkle; and he—fleeing rather than seeking a wife—adds rather than sheds the Faustian twenty years, leaving him safe on the further side of passion. Besides, the only figure in our literature of equal archetypal resonance is Huckleberry Finn, whom Mark Twain imagined—dreaming himself back twice twenty years to when he himself was a boy—fixed forever in "innocent" boyhood, or in other words, safe on the *hither* side of sexual maturity. Small wonder then that at the heart of many native works we especially cherish, similar anti-Faustian protagonists appear: old before their time, or younger than they have any right to be, but in any case, impotent. Think, for instance, of Cooper's eternally virginal backwoodsman, Natty Bumppo, evading marriage like Civilization itself; of Poe's sexless, almost bodiless Roderick Usher, dying without issue; of Hawthorne's eunuchoid *voyeurs* from Clifford Pyncheon to Miles Coverdale; of Melville's castrated hero-villain Ahab and his saintly impotents, Bartleby and Billy Budd; of Henry James's libido-less romantics from Christopher Newman to Lambert Strether, whose Happy Ending is *not* to get the girl; of T. S. Eliot's Gerontion and J. Alfred Prufrock, etc., etc.

To be sure, as early as Henry Miller, there were efforts to create a counter image of the American hero as tireless cocksman. Moreover, not merely did Mailer and Bellow attempt, in their quite different ways, to follow his example, but so also in theirs did Philip Roth and Jack Kerouac and countless others now forgotten. From the vantage point of the eighties, however, and in the entire context of our literature, all their efforts seem, in mythic terms, if not quite un-American, at least eccentric or irrelevant. Certainly, none of their prepotent protagonists has come to possess our imaginations like the genital cripples and refugees from sex of our central tradition. Not Mailer's Sergius O'Shaughnessy or Stephen Rojack, surely, or even Roth's insatiable Portnoy, who is almost redeemed by his last-minute impotence in the land of his ancestors. Roth, as a matter of fact, despite his commitment to the Sexual Revolution is drawn over and over into confessing the fear of phallic failure which lies just below his superficial bravado. Indeed, one of his most moving stories is the comic-pathetic "Epstein," whose aging anti-hero finds in the bed of a complaisant neighbor not the "apocalyptic orgasm" he is seeking but a heart attack.

Indeed, many practicing novelists in the last decades of the twentieth century—especially as they grow older—find it easier to identify with eunuchs than with studs. As I began to write this essay, for instance, there lay open on my desk Kurt Vonnegut's most recent novel *Dead Eye Dick*, whose protagonist turns out to be—not unexpectedly—a "neutered pharmacist" called Rudy Waltz, a symbol (the author tells us in a defensive preface intended for critics like me) of his own "declining sexuality."[8] Yet Vonnegut remains a favorite writer of young readers, as well as of the no-longer young generation which first discovered him in the time of the Counter Culture, identifying even then with his earlier eunuchoid characters like Mr. Rosewater.

How could they not since, though to one degree or another they actually lived the "sexual revolution" which Mailer preached, at a less conscious level they were possessed by the mythology of the Comic Books which they had grown up reading behind their parents' backs. And at the heart of that mythology is Siegel and Shuster's "Man of Steel": an impotent savior of mankind, who, nonetheless, could not—either as Clark Kent or Superman—ever make it with Lois Lane. It is only that Super-Eunuch, perhaps, who has in this century achieved for the American mass audience the archetypal status of Rip or Huck; though for a smaller audience which still prefers words on the page to images on the screen, two characters created by Nobel laureates who have died rather recently, have similarly escaped the texts in which they first appeared and come to live the free lives of myths.

I am referring, of course, to Hemingway's stoic *castrato*, Jake Barnes, and his dark shadow, Faulkner's emasculated *voyeur* and (with the aid of a corn cob) rapist, Popeye, whose name, of course, evokes once more the pop mythology of the Comics. But this seems fair enough in light of the fact that *Sanctuary*, in which he appears, borders on being shameless sensationalist schlock. It has consequently not only been regarded with suspicion by the guardians of High Culture, but the author himself felt obliged to apologize for it publicly, claiming that from the start he had intended it to be a pornographic potboiler: a way of making a quick buck by giving the mass audience a cheap masochistic thrill.

Whatever we think of it (and I esteem it very highly indeed), it would be foolish to deny that *Sanctuary* is basically an extended dirty joke in rather poor taste. Yet it is something more and less, since the laughter stirred by its grotesque situations and caricatured *dramatis personae* is being constantly undercut by horror and revulsion. We tend to laugh anyhow, as we do at *any* story about someone who can't get it up and is obliged therefore to get his kicks by peeping at someone else who can. Only thus can we exorcise the horror evoked in us by the suggestion implicit in such stories that a similar fate may await *us*—if we live so long. The darker and deeper wish/ fear embodied in the image of impotent rape, however, along with its implied message that rape is a confession of impotence, is no laughing matter. And it is precisely its ability to take us thus beyond laughter which makes *Sanctuary* peculiarly American—different, at any rate, from the classic "dirty books" of Europe, whether they be grimly ironic like the Marquis de Sade's *Justine* or blithely good-humored like John Cleland's *Fanny Hill*.

To be sure, as we have already noticed, certain twentieth-century American writers have tried to naturalize such European "pornotopias," dreams of eternal youth and unflagging potency. But there is something deep in the American psyche (certainly, in my own) which finds profoundly alien all such fantasies of sex and sadism without responsibility or guilt. What appeals to us more is the model provided by Mark Twain's *1601, or a Fireside Conversation*, the sole piece of hard porn produced by a major writer of our own nineteenth century. Written in 1876, when Twain had just passed his fortieth birthday and was already beginning to create the myth of pregenital innocence which has haunted us ever since, it remained for a long time a secret even to many of his most ardent admirers. At first, indeed, he seems to have wanted it that way, distributing it only in letter form to a small group of close male friends—including a Protestant minister from Hartford, a poet from Buffalo, and a rabbi from Albany. And though he eventually had it printed (at West Point, of all places!), it was in a limited edition of fifty. Nonetheless, he is on record as having said it was one of the few pieces of his own at which he had ever laughed aloud; he seems to have believed its early readers who tried to convince him that it was a minor masterpiece which should not be allowed to disappear.

Subsequent critics, however, have not concurred. Indeed, *1601* is scarcely mentioned in any "scholarly" studies to this very day, and it is not even listed in the compendious bibliography of his work which appears in the third volume of Robert Spiller's *The Literary History of the United States.*[9] Yet it repays hard reading, being essential not only to an understanding of Twain's own troubled attitudes toward sex but of the culture which produced him. Despite the fact that it is set in the court of Queen Elizabeth I and written in what he intended to be the colloquial British English of the seventeenth century, this presumable extract from the diary of "an old man who feels his nobility to be defiled by what he has to report" is prototypically American.[10] and perhaps the most American thing about it is that though it is pornography, gross and explicit, there is in it *no* fucking and sucking.

For the first ten of its fifteen pages in fact (except for a fascinating aside attributed to Sir Walter Raleigh, about how "in ye uttermost parts of America they copulate not until they be five and thirty years of age . . . / and do it then but once in seven years" [p. vi], it is almost purely scatalogical: a long discourse on farting. Then in its closing paragraph, without transition or motivation, it switches, becoming, in fact, a classic version of the myth of impotence and old age which I had set out to discover: "Now was Sr. Walter minded of a tale . . . about a mayde, which being likely to suffer rape by an olde archbishoppe, did smartly contrive a device to save her maydenhedde, and said to him: 'First, my lord, I prithee, take out thy holy toole and piss before mee,' which doing, lo! his member felle, and wolde not rise again," (p. xi).

Superficially, the disastrous ending of *1601* (with its refrain, "and wolde not rise again") resembles that of the Myth of the Dirty Old Man. But this time around the Senex is cheated of the inappropriate consummation he so shamelessly desires, not by death but by detumescence and we are moved therefore through pathos to laughter and beyond. And this is indeed something new: something peculiarly American, perhaps, as I have already suggested, as well as peculiarly modern. The archetypal story which I examined in my earlier meditation assumes that sexual desire and phallic potency (however unseemly they may be in the aged) never cease as long as life lasts. Consequently, what is presented as problematical is the propriety rather than the possibility of sex in the shadow of death. Twain's dirty little story, on the other hand, represents a transitional stage on the way to the myth which informs the brochures of the sexpill hucksters who invade my privacy with each day's mail, in which the propriety of con-cupiscence at an advanced age is taken for granted, while its possibility is assumed to be (without medical intervention) doubtful in the extreme.

Truly, the fear of impotency seems to have grown rather than dimin-ished in direct proportion to our loss of any sense of sex as sinful or shameful or indecorous. I am, however, by no means convinced that in the depths of our troubled psyches, even the most enlightened and liberated among us, the Immoral Minority to which most of us would like to think we belong, are not moved still by the guilts reflected in and reinforced by the Myth of the Dirty Old Man. How hard we find it, for instance, not to snigger at public displays of affection between crabbed age and youth, though we have presumably learned to be ashamed of such titters and the archaic guilts which prompt them. After all, we live in an era when the Sexual Revolution has succeeded to a point where compulsory one-night stands in youth and required mateswapping in middle age have come to seem the norms of bourgeois life. To be sure, like all revolutions, it has failed as well since neurosis and cancer, war and the profit motive have not disappeared as promised with the release of old repressions.

Nonetheless, psychologically we *have* changed, have we not, even those of us who have reached an age where it might well seem advisable to make a virtue of what is if not yet quite a necessity, will be soon enough—by abandoning the ultimately doomed pursuit of yet one more sexual climax, and one more beyond that. A wedge has been driven between us and what was long considered wisdom. No longer can we really understand, much less sympathize with, for instance, the cry of relief of Sophocles, when at age eighty sexual desire finally ceased to trouble him; "At last I have been delivered from the harsh taskmaster." Similarly, the New Testament verse which reminds us that some have become eunuchs for the sake of the Kingdom of Heaven—and suggests that more of us should—dismays and repels us. And we are even more dismayed to learn what was long kept secret from the vulgar by his privileged acolytes, that Sigmund Freud himself (which is to say, the putative father of sexual liberation) gave up sex completely after reaching the age of forty. He did it, to be sure, in the name of secular sublimation rather than Christian chastity but for a long time now sublimation has become as dirty a word as its non-psychoanalyt-ical equivalents: dignity and decorum and self-restraint. Under whatever name, we are through with the denial of the flesh forever, which is to say, for as long as life lasts.

Or so at least I used to think when I was young. At this point, however, I must confess that though the harsh taskmaster drives me still, I find it difficult, having come some fifteen thousand times in my life, to look forward to my fifteen thousand and first orgasm with the utopian hope-fulness of youth, or for that matter, to contemplate the possibility of its being my last with the dismay of middle age. Thus also, having—coward that I am—already died a thousand deaths, I find I can entertain the notion of my own inevitable extinction with similar equanimity. And I am therefore able to believe that in some ultimate sense the two concomitants of aging, impotence and death, like the two myths which embody them, are inextricably bound together.

In any case, it has become possible for me at long last to imagine myself uttering—with whatever vestigial ambivalence—the Sophoclean sign of post-erotic relief. I know now, I am trying to say, that from the start I must have *wished* for ultimate impotence quite as deeply as I feared it; even as I must have yearned for the final obliteration of consciousness as fervently as I dreaded it. Nor do I wish to be delivered of the dark side of my ambivalence in regard to either. Indeed, I suspect that if ever I became immune to the longing to be done living and loving, I could, to be sure, cast a colder eye on the ads for Corazine-DL and NSP-270, but I would also (and it is a price I will not pay) no longer be able to remember what had once seemed to me so heartbreakingly funny about Mark Twain's dirty little joke.

Notes

1. Leslie Fiedler, "Eros and Thanatos: Old Age in Love," in *Aging, Death, and the Completion of Being*, ed. David D. Van Tassel (Philadelphia: Univ. of Pennsylvania Press, 1979), pp. 235–54.

2. Christopher Marlowe, *Dr. Faustus*, Vol. II of *The Complete Works of Christopher Marlowe*, ed. Fredson Bowers (Cambridge: Cambridge Univ. Press, 1973), pp. 169–70, p. 178, p. 219.

3. Johann Wolfgang von Goethe, *Faust*, trans. Louis MacNeice, abr. ver. (New York: Oxford Univ. Press, 1960), pp. 72–73.

4. Herman Melville, *Moby Dick* (New York: W.W. Norton, 1976), p. 479. In *Moby Dick*, Ahab's remarks are given in Latin. I have rendered them in my own words.

5. Norman Mailer, "The White Negro: Superficial Reflections on the Hipster," in *Advertisements for Myself* (New York: G.P. Putnam's Sons, 1959), p. 347.

6. Mailer, p. 347.

7. Nathaniel Hawthorne, *The Complete Novels and Selected Tales of Nathaniel Hawthorne*, ed. Norman Holmes Pearson (New York: Random House, 1937), pp. 950–51.

8. Kurt Vonnegut, *Deadeye Dick* (New York: Delacorte Press/Seymour Lawrence, 1982), p. xiii.

9. Mark Twain, *Date 1601. Conversation as it was by the social fireside, in the time of th Tudors*. (West Point: Carles Erskin Scott Wood /United States Military Academy Press, 1882), prefatory matter.

NOT SO LITTLE HANS:
Identity and Aging
***
Norman N. Holland

"Aging"—we use the word two ways. In one, we are talking about growing old. We "become" elderly. We "reach" old age like a destination. When we age in this first sense, we begin to experience the paradoxes and losses of old age that poets and sufferers have eloquently and painfully phrased over the centuries.

To understand that sense of "aging," however, I think we need to understand another, more general, sense of the word. In this deeper sense, we use "aging" to mean just that we are passing through time as all things do. We simply participate in the evolving that every object in the universe shares. We age, in this meaning of the term, from the moment of birth, as a wine ages from the moment it is casked.

In the first, specific sense, we grow old; in the second, general meaning, we grow older. Growing old (in modern American youth culture) is purely and simply a bad thing, while growing old*er* may be a good thing. To understand aging in the specific sense, however, we need to understand the more general process, the aging that is simply "we grow older."

To address both that general sense and the specific "growing old," I want to consider one special person, the first child ever to be psycho-analyzed, the Little Hans of Freud's famous case history. I know Hans only at isolated points in his life, two in particular: when he was brought to Freud to be cured of a phobia at the age of four and three-quarters and then, as a mature artist, when at the age of sixty-eight he looked back upon his own distinguished musical career.

By considering Little Hans at two points in his aging (his growing old*er*) separated by decades of that process, we can see what has changed and what has remained the same. We can, in short, see an . . .

IDENTITY AGING

We age—we grow—in two ways as children. One way, we learn all kinds of cognitive and other skills. We learn that we can be separate beings and that we can tolerate the poignant mixing of love and hate implicit in our separateness—that is, we learn to trust in Erik Erikson's sense. We learn to obey others' rules and formulate rules of our own. We learn to walk and to talk and to read. We learn to understand and imagine the ideas and feelings of others. We learn to plan and to plan our place in a world of gender and generations, of male and female, and of parents and children, in short, an oedipal world.

This kind of growth we share with the vast majority of our fellow humans. Most of humankind learns to crawl, to stand up, to walk, to talk, to find places, to understand stories, to engender and be gendered. As we age in cognitive matters, we share that growth with other children. We become like the other humans in our culture.

At the same time, we grow in individuality. We acquire a character, although perhaps that is too strong a word. It comes from Greek *kharax*, a pointed stake for scribing a line or a brand on a surface, a metaphorical surface that was perhaps the original version of John Locke's *tabula rasa*. *Kharax* is cognate with *gash*, human character as a gash cut in a featureless infancy, and that is too strong for what I intend.

I don't think "character" has that etched, immutable quality, and therefore I prefer "identity." That word has acquired more and more complicated meanings for me, but here let me simply say it is (among other things) a *representation* of character. Identity is to character as the history book is to history.

We see identity in this sense very early in life. Margaret Mahler, who set up perhaps the most intense and astute laboratory team for watching children, reports that, by the children's twenty-first month, her team found it no longer possible to group the toddlers simply by general criteria. The processes of their individuation were changing so fast they were no longer characterized by one or another of the classical psychoanalytic phases (oral, anal, phallic, oedipal). Each child had become an individual, very distinct and different from any other child.[1] Mahler is telling us that the growth of individuality had, by the twenty-first month, become as visible as the other kind of growth, the growth in body and mind that many children in the culture share.

What, then, is the relationship between these two kinds of growth? Proust speaks of "our permanent self, which continues throughout the whole duration of our life" and "our successive selves which, after all, to a certain extent compose it."[2] His metaphor, a series of selves composing a more permanent self, suggests one way of thinking about the changing and unchanging aspects of ourselves. We could simply think of the separate selves as adding up into a larger self.

Another model suggests that the two kinds of selves just exist side by side. A paradigm suggested by two psychologists, Michael Lewis and Jeanne Brooks, distinguishes an "existential self" which differentiates this individual from all others and a "categorical self," consisting of the categories through which we consider ourselves. The first is the subject of verbs like "I see," "I close my eyes," or "I feel pain." The second is the self that undergoes physical and social changes, and it is the one—the only one—psychologists can test.[3] In their thinking, there simply *are* these two kinds of selves.

I prefer to think of that relation between unchanging and changing selves as, in philosophical language, a dialectic or, in the language of psychology and physiology, an information-processing feedback. That is, the relation between the two kinds of growth is one of control. The child *uses* the ability to walk or talk to become more itself. The more itself the child becomes, the more distinctive becomes its way of walking or talking. It is the ability to walk and talk and run and ride and read that *lets* us become more of a person. Conversely, it is the kind of person we are becoming that determines how we walk and talk and run and ride and read. Each of these kinds of growth feeds into the other. The more skills we have the more we can mature as a person. The more we have matured as a person the more skills we can acquire.

In other words, the child is like a craftsman discovering a new tool or like an artist with a new medium. At the end of his life, Picasso began to make small blue glass figurines. They turned out, as it happens, pleasantly bawdy, less angrily sexual than some of Picasso's earlier ribaldries. The blue glass allowed Picasso to express new aspects of Picasso. Conversely, the new aspects of Picasso brought into being blue glass that looked like no other blue glass before. In doing so, he was, like any child, engaging in two kinds of aging and growth, one which is shared (or at least sharable—anybody can work with blue glass) and one which is highly individual; one in which he acquired a new skill, a skill that his culture rewarded, and one in which we see that *this* child (or artist) is different from all other children.

In other words, this artist-child has an identity that sets certain standards and values for performance in the world. The artist-child acts out into the world, and the world reacts to those actions. Then the child feels either satisfied or dissatisfied, pleased or anxious, guilty or free, at the world's reaction according to its own standards. The cumulating history of these experiences becomes, then, the artist-child's identity. (By identity, of course, I still intend somebody's *representation* of character, not some set of traits carved on the tabula rasa of infancy.)

More precisely, a model of child development that posits an identity governing a feedback loop involves three elements. First, the child has motor and other systems for acting on the world, for trying out hypotheses. Second, the child has a sensory system for comparing the response of the world to his hypotheses with what he wanted, his standards. Third then, and this is the role of identity, there must be standards (values, beliefs, wishes, demands, needs—ultimately a style) from which the child builds actions and hypotheses and against which he compares their consequences.[4]

If we adopt such an information-processing feedback model, development through the familiar psychoanalytic stages (like the oral or phallic), ceases to be something passively "done to" the child by drives, parents, environment or society. Rather, an active child with a developing identity marches through an "epigenetic landscape" of questions posed by his own biology, his parents, and the social and environmental structures they embody. The questions they pose the developing child elicit answers that he tries out. He puts forth actions and hypotheses which in turn produce consequences, closing a feedback loop. The child compares those consequences against the standards his identity seeks and is reinforced or not as the case may be.[5]

In effect, we can read the development of any given individual as the particular answers he chooses (because they re-create his identity) to questions that his body and family pose or that he shares with other children who have his biology and culture. And, of course, the answers he arrives at become part of the identity he brings to the questions he gets thereafter. Development—the aging of the young—thus becomes a dialogue (or, as in perceptual theory, an information-processing feedback) between identity on the one hand and on the other, biology and culture.[6]

By using the word "identity," I am calling on developments in the psychoanalytic theory of human character made possible by the concept of identity formulated by Heinz Lichtenstein and further developed by Murray Schwartz, myself, and others at the Buffalo Center for the Psychological Study of the Arts.[7] Lichtenstein suggests that one think of a human's identity as a mixture of continuity and change, and he proposes the most telling way I know to put that dialectic of sameness and difference into words: his concept of identity as a theme and variations.

Think of the sameness in a person as a theme, an "identity theme." Think of the differences as variations on that identity theme, like musical variations or, since the theme is verbal, like transformations of a linguist's "kernel sentence." I can derive an identity theme from the recurring patterns in a person's life just as I would state the theme of a piece of music or the theme of a Shakespearean play. I would express it, not in theoretical language (diagnostic terms like "paranoid," trait-words like "competitive," or structural terms like "id"), but in ordinary language, as close as possible to the words that a person might use to describe his own behavior. My aim, as interpreter of identity, is to symbolize the potential space between myself and the person whose identity I am formulating in terms we can both own.

It is this representation of another that I propose as the governor of the feedback which is aging. Thus identity has a paradoxical existence. It is an agency, as it were, acting from the self out into the world. It is a consequence, the cumulating return from those actions. But it is also a representation, my representation of someone's identity, even my own. In this sense, identity is a hypothesis someone puts forward like any other, with which to test experience, in this instance, one's experience of another person (or oneself). The perception of another person, his or her identity, is like any other perception. Agency, representation, consequence—identity is an ARC. One must keep in mind all three elements. Dropping any one will lead to all kinds of absurdities.

Identity, then, is not a conclusion, but a relationship—in two senses. It is the relationship I maintain between myself and the world and in which I develop, showing both change and continuity. It is also the relationship within which I read identities in my particular way as a function of my own identity, like the identity of . . .

LITTLE HANS

In January 1908, when he was four and three-quarters years old, Hans developed a phobia. He became terrified of going out into the street. His father, one of Freud's first disciples, consulted the master. Freud suggested that the father carry on analysis by questioning his son and interpreting the answers the boy gave. Only once did the father take Hans to see "the Professor" for some especially powerful interpreting.[8]

At the time Freud treated him, Hans had achieved training for both bowels and bladder. Indeed, he took pleasure in showing off these accomplishments, for example, by a mastery-game in which he would go into a cupboard ("my W.C.") and take out his "widdler" and pretend, "I'm widdling."

Consider then these bits of Hans's dialogue with his father (here, "I") as variations from which to infer a theme or themes, as (to use jargon) "chosen behaviors":

> *I:* "You'd like to have a little girl."
> *Hans:* "*Yes, next year I'm going to have one*, and she'll be called Hanna too."
> [p. 87]

> [*Father:*] So on April 26th I asked him why he was always thinking of his children.
> *Hans:* "Why? *Because I should so like to have children; but I don't ever want it; I shouldn't like to have them.*"[p. 93]

I: "Have you always imagined that Berta and Olga and the rest were your children?"
Hans: "Yes, Franzl, and Fritzl, and Paul too" (his playmates at Lainz), "and Lodi." This is an invented girl's name. . . . [p. 93]

Hans: And really I *was* their Mummy."
I: "What did you do with your children?"
Hans: "I had them to sleep with me, the girls and the boys. . . . [p. 94]

I: "When you sat on the chamber and a lumf came, did you think to yourself you were having a baby?"
Hans (laughing): "Yes. Even at _____ Street, and here as well. . . ." [p. 95]

Hans: "This morning I was in the W.C. with all my children. First I did lumf and widdled, and they looked on. Then I put them on the seat and they widdled and did lumf, and I wiped their behinds with paper. D'you know why? Because I'd so much like to have children; then I'd do everything for them—take them to the W.C., clean their behinds, and do everything one does with children." [p. 97]

For the theme that runs through all these (and other such) claims by Hans, one could say simply that he is showing a wish to identify with a parent typical for a child his age. One can, however, say a bit more. Hans defines that identification in relation to children. He does not say, as I might perhaps have said at his age, I want to be like my father because he does important work that controls this family. He says, I want to do what a parent does for children.

My word "like" points to another aspect of Hans's identification, as it appears in his last (as Freud says) "triumphant" fantasy:

April 30th. Seeing Hans playing with his imaginary children again, "Hullo," I said to him, "are your children still alive? You know quite well a boy can't have any children."
Hans: I know. I was their Mummy before, *now I'm their Daddy.*"
I: "And who's the children's Mummy?"
Hans: "Why, Mummy, and you're their *Grandaddy.*"
I: "So then you'd like to be as big as me, and be married to Mummy, and then you'd like her to have children,"
Hans: "Yes, that's what I'd like, and then my Lainz Grandmummy" (my [the father's] mother) "will be their Grannie'." [pp. 96–97]

As Freud sums it up, "Instead of putting his father out of the way, he had granted him the same happiness that he desired himself: he made him a grandfather and married *him* to his own mother too" (p. 97). Hans thus shows both the wish to be and the wish to be like his father, and he grants the more realistic of the two to his father: his father can be *like* Hans.

There is still a further special quality to Hans's identification: he identifies with a parent through *actions*. He marries his mother, but even as he says that, his father tells us, he is playing with his imaginary children. He is "doing for" them, as when he takes them to the toilet or puts them in his bed, and he is "doing for" his father when he marries him off to Grannie.

In short, in tracing the themes of someone's identity, psychological words like "identification" compare the individual to other individuals. "Identification" helps me write about a process Hans shared with many other children. If, however, I want to get at the individuality of Hans, "identification" smoothes off the uniqueness. By using words more like the individual's own, we can keep data about that unique quality of the individual identity. Here, from what Hans says, I can propose a theme: *to be (like) a parent by doing for children (or parents)*.

A theme of "doing for" leads me to much else in little Hans's life. I am thinking of such episodes as his tapping on the sidewalk and wondering if someone were buried underneath, his wish to crawl under the rope blocking off a space in the public gardens, his wish to smash through a window, or his butting his head into his father's stomach, all efforts to break into or through. I remember his prancing about, saying "I'm a young horse" or his making a row with his feet when he sat on the potty to make a *lumf*. I am thinking, too, of his dream of the two giraffes (parents) in which sitting down on top of the crumpled giraffe (mother) meant taking possession of it. All these episodes involve action, but more particularly all involve crossing the boundaries, especially those between the inside and outside of Hans's or someone else's belly or behind.

These enactments and re-enactments, it seems to me, also served Hans as adaptations. They enabled him to control or master things, as his game of pretending to widdle in the cupboard or play at loading and unloading packing cases demonstrated his mastery of urination and defecation. What Hans seemed to need to master was the general problem of things coming from the inside to the outside. He was particularly troubled by the birth of Hanna, but also widdling, *lumf*, and his own dire imaginings coming physically into the world.

At the same time, however, Hans emphasizes the literalness of these things, their actual look and sound. I am thinking of the way he enjoyed watching and being watched while urinating or defecating, or his looking at his parents' and playmates' widdlers, or the way he observed the activities on the loading platform across the street. He carefully distinguished the kinds of flushing the W.C. made, perhaps also the different sounds of male and female urinating, and certainly his mother's "coughing" during childbirth.

Much of Hans's looking and watching took the form of penetrating into forbidden places. He wheeled his way into the bathroom to watch his mother going to the toilet. He coaxed his way into the parental bed. He blundered into the room containing the bloody evidences of Hanna's birth. He used his sensing and his "doing" to "get in" or to see how others got in. Most important, he got out on the dangerous balcony of the apartment to watch the loading dock across the street, the site (no pun intended) of his phobia.

Similarly, in the fantasies with which he resolved his neurosis, he imagined actions. He let a penknife drop out from between a doll's legs to simulate the birth of his sister. He imagined that the plumber (who, in an earlier fantasy, had taken his "widdler" away) now gave him a bigger widdler and a bigger behind. Here, he is not "doing for" so much as "being done for."

I find it helpful to bring these various themes together into one central identity theme by means of a kernel sentence like those used in the earlier versions of transformational (Chomskyan) grammar.[9] I could state Little Hans's identity theme this way: he either got his body into situations or got something into or out of his body by either being done for or by doing for others in parent-child ways. We could put these possibilities into a schematic form:

getting my body into a situation   being done for   a child
getting something into my body   by   as
getting something out of my body   doing for   a parent

One can transform such a form and content, such a syntactic and lexical kernel, into an infinite number of sentences, yet never lose the essence represented by the kernel—just like an identity theme.

For example, you can substitute into a term like "parent" not only Hans's literal father and mother but parental persons, such as "the Professor" or the still more powerful plumber. Similarly, "a situation" can be transformed into any of the forbidden rooms or places Hans got into or it might refer to Hans's much larger effort to get into the family matrix of male-female and parent-child. "Getting something out of my body" could refer to doing *lumf* or getting rid of his "nonsense." "Getting something into my body" could be sitting on a dreamed giraffe or imagining a plumber attaching a new widdler or in a much larger sense taking in the affection and admiration Hans wanted from his parents.

I can read Hans's method of identification as a subtle combination of the basic terms of his identity theme: getting something into his body (a baby when he identifies with his mother; a bigger widdler when he identifies with his father); getting his body into the oedipal dialectic of parent and child, male and female, by acquiring a bigger widdler from the plumber or the Professor-doctor (being done for) or by getting his fantasies out of his body in his characteristically energetic way (doing for).

Similarly, I can understand his "choice of symptom" as a function of his identity. Action being his way of forcing himself into the world, when that possibility becomes dangerous, he meets the danger by inhibiting action. He fears lest something be done to him by the biting horse (father) or the loaded horse (mother). Conversely, he fears lest he do to father or mother something that would get him into a dangerous situation—and he stays home.

In one sense, of course, Hans is doing nothing more than meet the normal oedipal question: how shall I fit myself into a world divided into male and female, adult and child? And he is trying to answer it in the only language he has, the familiar excremental, intrusive, inside-and-outside symbols of the anal and phallic stages of childhood.

Nevertheless, he turns those shared symbols into highly individual actions. Perhaps, therefore, we can speak of Hans's unique identity even at this early stage. Finally, however, the only way to tell if I have over-read the boy's words is by looking back on his fourth year from some later time. Now, at last, we can look back at Little Hans by virtue of the generous candor of . . .

NOT SO LITTLE HANS

On February 5, 1972, *Opera News* published a memoir in which the former stage director of the Metropolitan Opera House, Herbert Graf, identified himself as Freud's Little Hans.[10] Herbert Graf was the son of Max Graf, the writer and musicologist who was one of Freud's first adherents. Originally, the career of opera director being unknown as such, young Graf had tried to become a singer, but he soon established himself as a director, traveling here and there as he was invited to stage various productions. After directing a number of operas in Europe, he came to the United States in 1934 to escape Nazi persecution. He first made his mark here with a series of strikingly novel and controversial productions in the Philadelphia Orchestra Series of 1934–35. From 1936 to 1965, he worked with the Metropolitan Opera in New York, retiring from that position to become general manager of the Grand Théâtre, the opera house of Geneva. He was twice married, and by his second wife he had a daughter. He died on April 5, 1973, five days before his seventieth birthday.

As an adult Herbert Graf left behind a record of many choices from which one could infer an identity theme and variations. Not so much the ever more eminent series of positions he held in the world of opera, nor the individual productions he staged—it would be hard to infer Graf's particular contribution in so collective an enterprise as opera.[11] Graf, however, left the long personal memoir in *Opera News* and three books on the production of opera: *The Opera and Its Future in America* (1941), *Opera for the People* (1951), and *Producing Opera for America* (1961).[12] For a psychoanalytic

literary critic like me, such writings record thousands of words he chose
and from those choices I can frame an identity theme for the adult Little
Hans.

The most important choice he made, of course, was opera. In his
memoir, he describes himself as a student standing in line for half a day to
get tickets for standing room. "Even the most makeshift productions were
enough to fire my imagination, and before long I began to try my hand at
duplicating the wonders I'd seen in the opera house—first with a toy
theater I built with my sister's help at home, and later in school productions." Graf spent one summer in Berlin where Max Reinhardt was
directing three theaters: "That Reinhardt summer was the turning point in
my life. I felt it was my mission to do for opera what Reinhardt had done
in the spoken theater."[13]

Once Graf had chosen his career, subsequent choosings took place
within the framework established by that first, basic choice. Opera became the medium and the limits for the development of his identity, both
giving him freedom and restricting that freedom. For example, Graf made
his name in America by his innovative productions in Philadelphia, but he
felt stifled under the conservative Metropolitan administration. "New
productions, in the sense of new costumes and scenery, were very rare
indeed," and he felt most productions had "a dusty, museum-like appearance."[14]

As in his ambition to be the Reinhardt of opera, Graf always longed for
the new, and this trait lends his writings a sort of gee-gosh, juvenile
enthusiasm. "I had been in New York for a short visit during the summer
of 1930 and had marveled at the wonders of America," he wrote in 1951.
"What could be more desirable for a young stage director who had
experimented on new opera productions in pre-Hitler Europe for nine
years, than this highly interesting opportunity to put his experience to
work in a big city of the fabulous New World?"[15]

He saw America very much as the New World, claiming that "opera in
Europe is solidly entrenched in historic tradition." By contrast, he held a
view of American opera so romantic as to border on fantasy:

> Here, in the first decades, were simple vigorous people, struggling to conquer
> the physical wilderness around them and achieve a measure of security and
> wealth. They were building their new world without the chains of old
> concepts and with pride in their personal freedom. In their minds, in their
> busy days, there was no place for the elaborate, glamorous entertainment of
> European kings and dukes, grand opera, which still bore traces of its aristo-
> cratic origin. They were content with their simple folk songs, in church and
> home. Later, when their material existence had been made secure and they
> could enjoy music in concert hall and theater, they listened to simple operas
> in English, stemming from the English ballad operas of the eighteenth
> century.[16]

"The new folk opera," he wrote of the late eighteenth century, "was ultimately an enormously creative force in the development of later opera. It had new blood in its veins; it stemmed from the people. It replaced the stagnant artificiality of aristocratic Baroque opera, which was decaying. The pompousness of antique gods and heroes gave way to realistic portrayals straight from the hearts of a simple people."[17]

This romantic belief in a *Volk* and its music had come with his first enthusiasm for Max Reinhardt's productions. "What impressed me most was the realistically detailed handling of the crowd scenes in such epic plays as *Julius Caesar* and Rolland's *Danton*." "As soon as I got back to Vienna I begged permission to stage the forum scene from *Julius Caesar* in the school gym, but since I paid a good deal less attention to the nuances of the big speeches than to the howling and whistling of the Roman mob, the dean soon called a halt to the whole venture."[18]

In the contrast Graf draws between wealthy, older artistocrats, associated with pomposity and chains and deans, and a more vital, primitive, poorer *Volk*, associated with simplicity and freedom and a New World, I hear an artistic version of the struggle of the generations. As part of that struggle, Graf set out in his New World career to make young American equal to older European opera in the eyes of the world:

In the end American opera will not be an unimaginative imitation of opera in Europe, but rather, as an integral part of American community life, it will become a new and even more exciting art form. The American opera of tomorrow will embody the dynamic, creative spirit of the American people in a cultural achievement recognized and honored not only in the United States but throughout the world.[19]

Under the signs, "European," "American," "old," "new," "aristocratic," and "folk," I sense more universal meanings: child and parent. Hence I feel two themes working here: a deep commitment to the new; then a strong wish for equality between the new and the old, but based on a firm recognition of the differences, even aggression, between them.

In his work Graf continually emphasized cooperation and sharing, which I read as a continuation of this rivalrous reconciliation of young and old. He translated the theme of cooperation into a style of production for the "young" opera: "The more true-to-life approach of folk opera called for natural acting, scenery, and costumes. This opera centered around a dramatic idea, of which every element now became the servant—not, as formerly, the master."[20] Graf idealized this cooperative approach to production and proposed it for all opera:

In its original form, the music drama comprised words, song, orchestral music, action, scenery, costumes, lighting, and a theater plan. It was a unique alliance of *all* arts—poetry, music, the dance, painting, sculpture, and architecture. Although each of these was a brilliant prima donna in her own right, none tried to overshadow another. Instead, they worked together as a perfect ensemble in the service of a common purpose.[21]

But, he noted, "If the dramatic concept is abandoned, these several elements split apart as independent, self-centered star effects created by singers, dancers, conductors, stage directors, designers, and architects. Opera then becomes 'grand opera'"[22]—a genre of which he thoroughly disapproved, which he had described a few paragraphs before as a "dream world." I see an analogy in all this equalizing of the older, European generation and the newer, American one or Graf's smoothing down of "star effects" to the sixteen-year-old's concern with the crowd scenes of Rolland or Shakespeare, "the howling and whistling of the Roman mob," to the exclusion of "the nuances of the big speeches." Europe and America, parent and child, mob scene and star's soliloquoy, all are to be equal.

In Graf's efforts to diminish the star effects of prima donnas, he also minimized his own role: "I've always felt that the stage director is opera's 'invisible man,' or should be. It's the very nature of his job to stay behind the scenes and leave the spotlight to the work itself." Not only was he himself no genius; neither was the director he most admired:

> Look, I'm not a "brilliant" stage director in the style of a Reinhardt or a Zeffirelli, and even though I can appreciate that sort of virtuosity, it's neither part of my nature nor my aim. I'm a professor's son, an earnest worker, a know-how man who believes that certain aspects of operatic know-how can be passed along to others. People say Toscanini was a genius, but for me his ideas, his artistic insights, weren't the stuff of "genius," *that* came out in his amazing power to put his ideas across—simple, straightforward common sense, conveyed with the thrust and impact of revelation. In that sense he trained everyone who ever worked with him.[23]

Yet elsewhere in his memoir, he reminds us that his own "professional life runs parallel to the emergence of the director as prime mover of the production," and his own democratic encouragement of young singers enabled him to create the very "stars" he warned against. Thus Graf's concern with cooperation embodies ambivalence toward those cooperated with and those cooperated against—to the degree they either became or began "above" the crowd. In effect, he would like to deal with the rivalry of parents and children by having us all be children playing—creating—together.

This leveling of the exalted to the ordinary provides Graf with his ambivalent solution to conflict, as in his remarks about his father. (Interestingly, he does not refer at all in the memoir to his mother.) His father was "an extraordinary man, the most extraordinary I've ever known" (and Graf's acquaintances included Toscanini, Fürtwangler, and other musical greats). Graf describes his father as a failed composer but a "formidable scholar" of literature and aesthetics, "equally at home in philosophy and science and quite capable of talking mathematics with Einstein, which he did." But he was also part of the crowd: "One of my most vivid boyhood memories is seeing him on the crowded footboard of a trolley headed for the Sunday soccer match at the Hohe Warte, one hand on the railing, the other clutching his most cherished book, a well-worn, annotated copy of Kant's *Critique of Pure Reason*." He was also a sexual being, "a true Viennese, in every sense: he knew how to enjoy a glass (or more) of wine and the company of pretty women."[24]

I can only guess how these themes came out in Graf's family life or his particular productions.[25] I can see fairly clearly, however, how this operatic ideology expresses personal themes. Graf quite explicitly symbolizes the competing traditions of opera in family images:

> Opera was a child born with a silver spoon in its mouth. Taken about to the parties of the nobility, it soon became spoiled and precocious. Its patrons used it to show off their wealth and social position. Like any spoiled child, it soon lost control of its qualities. The elements of opera became ungoverned prima donnas, each working for its own aggrandizement rather than for the sake of the whole—and the music drama.[26]

I detect in another of Graf's analogies a certain malicious pleasure in seeing this spoiled child or ungoverned woman humiliated in the New World: after 1929 in America, "Opera, scion of the European aristocracy, has had to take off its top hat and go around among the great public seeking support." More positively, "Opera has become the adopted child of the rank and file of music-lovers."[27]

In order for ordinary Americans to enjoy opera, Graf insisted on performances in English (over a great deal of rather snobbish opposition). "If opera is to reach the people, it will have to speak the language of the people." "My greatest professional satisfaction in the United States is associated . . . with productions to bring opera to the people." For the same reason, Graf devoted himself to producing opera for radio, movies, and television, even going so far as to copyright a design for a television opera theater. He was greatly interested in the practical details of putting opera on television, because he saw in television "the opportunity of bringing opera to bigger audiences than ever before," another form of sharing. Moreover, "Television can be the most decisive medium for forcing opera to take off its top hat and enter the American home."[28]

Graf was much concerned with "financial practicabilities and technical possibilities." Pages of his first, 1941 book are devoted to the dollar sums achieved (or not) by this or that fund-raising scheme. I have already mentioned his concern with the practical details of theater and set design or television production. His figures of speech could run to the practical, too:

> I looked again at my blueprint of the people's opera. No, it was no impossible dream; it was the inevitable result of existing forces. There can be no further doubt about its eventual realization. The site and the tools for building the people's opera are ready; the time is ripe. Let us start production.

He used this building metaphor to conclude *Opera for the People*. He used a similar figure to end *Producing Opera for America:*

> We have come to the end of our survey of operatic production in Europe and the United States. Our proposed program for opera in America lies before you. I hear some voices saying, "Dreams!" I can only reply that the real fantasy is in thinking that opera can establish itself successfully in America in any other way. It must build solidly on the foundations already in existence, and take advantage of the forces presently at work in America. These foundations and these forces are not dreams—they are the only real facts. From these foundations opera in the United States will rise and find its proper place in American cultural life.

Both the metaphors and the book titles attest Graf's concern with practicality.[29]

Graf, however, was not an unambivalent doer. Victoria Hattam, my onetime associate at the Buffalo Center for the Psychological Study of the Arts, has written for me her own theming of Graf. She too calls him a "man of action" and points out how energetic he was throughout his career, even during periods of unemployment. At the same time, despite Graf's energy, Hattam remarks the many times in the memoir that he uses words like "luck" and "good fortune." He describes all the major events in his career this way, she points out: his first directing job, his first associations with Toscanini and Bruno Walter, and his first engagement at the Met. For example, at the beginning of the interview, Graf says, "As luck would have it, my professional life runs parallel to the emergence of the director as prime mover. . . ." After the Philadelphia experiment of 1935–36, "That left me without a regular engagement for the coming year—a gap luckily filled by Walter's invitation to stage *Fidelio* in Paris." His engagement at the Met: "As luck would have it [Edward] Johnson's spring trip to Europe coincided with my own directorial wanderings. Wherever he went . . . there it was on the theater posters: 'Stage Director: Herbert Graf.' Poor Johnson, he must have thought it was a conspiracy! Finally he offered me a Met contract for the 1936–37 season." "Others," suggests Hattam, "might have spoken of their efforts being finally recognized and rewarded, but these are not characteristic expressions for Graf."[30]

In the same way, Graf externalizes his helplessness and frustration when confronted with the conservative "system" of the Metropolitan. "New productions, in the sense of new costumes and scenery, were very rare indeed." Although there were marvelous singers, "the dismal look of their surroundings, plus lack of onstage rehearsal, . . . gave most of our performances a dusty, museum-like appearance." Yet he stayed with the Met for twenty-nine years! "Yes, I was back every season—mostly frustrated, but doing what I could within the system."[31] In the interview, he describes himself as not much of a "fighter," and I have heard stories of his being tyrannized and shamed by Rudolph Bing, the artistic director. Truly, he was "opera's 'invisible man.'" Evidently his tendency to "do" was balanced by a tendency not to do—by passivity. Hattam sums this trait up more precisely: "He sets a discontinuity between the action and the externalizing."

Hattam is not the only student of Little Hans to state the discrepancy between Graf's drive toward action and the passivity he showed toward the leading figures of the operatic world. Melvin Kalfus in a long, as yet unpublished monograph, has studied not only the case and Graf's writings but accounts of his stagings as well. Kalfus concludes that the boy Hans developed in two directions as a result of Freud's therapy; he developed a True Self and False Self as described by D.W. Winnicott.[32] The True Self was a "rather feminine desire for creative individuality," and the False Self was his need to identify with and comply with the idealized, fantasy father. Thus Graf could submit to Bing and other ogres, he could minimize his own talents in relation to Zefirelli and other more glamorous directors, and he could make himself into the "invisible man of opera"—all aspects of this False Self. At the same time, his True Self could listen to the creative promptings of his unconscious fantasies and design impressive stagings. But the True Self always ran up against the limits imposed by the False Self.

Perhaps because of these conflicts, Graf prized a quality that would undo that gap between inner and external circumstances: not fighting, not anything "brilliant" or devious, but what Hattam calls "straightforward action." For example, Graf applauded the new generation of "'well-rounded' performers" who can act, "but the more we stress surfaces and rely on technique to make a point the more we risk losing the real expressive power opera has to offer." The older singers may not have been good actors, but they had "clear, meaningful delivery."[33]

The key value for Graf was "the ability to sing meaningfully," "personal expressiveness," the same thing he prized in Toscanini, "his amazing power to put his ideas across."[34] I hear Graf valuing the ability to take something from inside, a feeling, an idea, and concretize it, first through the physical voice, then through the responses of ordinary people who love opera. I hear in the mature Graf's artistic values something like the boy

Hans's need to act out his inner fantasies, giving them reality and testing them against reality: blueprints and foundations, what will work, "clear, meaningful delivery," "crystallized." At the same time, however, as Kalfus suggests, he limits these fantasies lest they rival or conflict with powerful, fatherly men. In effect, Graf put a cap on his own career.

But what of . . .

IDENTITY AND AGING

which we seem to have lost track of in a welter of arias and singers? It seems to me that identity theory has given us a powerful means for relating the growth of infancy—Hans's learning to make his way into a world of gender and generations—and the growth of the adult: Herbert Graf's making *his* way as a director of opera.

I can think of three strategies for reading back from Herbert Graf to Little Hans. In the first, I could draw analogies between specific events in the adult's life and specific events in the child's. For example, I might see Herbert Graf's statement that he is or should be "opera's 'invisible man'" outside the playing space as an adult version of the boy perched on the balcony of his parents' apartment watching the carts going into and out of the loading dock across the street. Such readings, however, are necessarily both speculative and reductive.

I can do somewhat better if I consider units larger than events—traits: the adult's traits in relation to the child's. I might regard the adult Graf's preoccupation with the practical details of production, indeed his whole career as a director, as an extension of Little Hans's tendency to deal with his fears and fantasies by acting them out. Graf wanted to appeal to people in general, to the various "stars" in an opera to cooperate toward a shared musical idea, and to create an American opera separate from European—I could read all those as continuations of Little Hans's generous impulses to "do for" the other children or for his father. By dealing with traits, I enclose more of Hans's life.

Identity theory asks for and allows me a third, still larger way of tracing the development from Little Hans to Herbert Graf, opera director. It lets me see both individual incidents and larger traits as parts of a whole life that can be understood as a theme and variations. We have considered a great many particulars of Graf's life, his ideals for opera, his view of his own career, his choice of occupation, and his activities as a theater designer. One can describe these particulars as variations on certain basic themes. Five occur to me.

i. Graf commits himself to the new against the old, contrasting the "dusty, museum-like," the "antique" or "stagnant artificiality," "pompousness," aristocrats, chains, deans, and bad parents (or a spoiled child) with the young, "free," "new blood" of a "folk." He is committing himself, I think, to child against parent.

2. At the same time, he wants to reconcile the two in an "alliance," "combining" them to become "rich and complete." His father is a "universal man" who nevertheless has the common touch. Toscanini is a genius because he has a peasant intelligence.

3. He stresses cooperation toward a "common purpose." In a production, every element is to be the servant, none the master, so as to form a "perfect ensemble." There are to be no "stars."

4. He concerns himself with practical details: roots, blueprints, foundations, buildings, to be contrasted with "surfaces," "exhibitions," dreams, or a "dream world."

5. He values in singers, conductors, directors, or himself the transformation of inner, inarticulate feelings into outer realities: personal expressiveness, voicing.

To read Graf's identity more fully, I would want to bring these five themes together into a closer unity by means of a centering "theme of themes" or an identity theme. I can bring themes 1, 2, and 3 together under the general idea of uniting competitive groups of old and new into a common whole. Themes 4 and 5 seem to me to come together as the transformation of inner feeling to outer work. I would phrase a total identity theme for Herbert Graf, then, as: *to unite competitive age-groups into a common whole by transforming inner feelings to outer work.*

If the theme is to be truly helpful, I should be able to unfold each of the key terms ("competitive," "age-group," "common," "whole," and so on) into the details of Graf's behavior from which I abstracted the several themes, and I think the passages I have quoted show that I can.

Conversely, I can test such a theme by seeing how well it fits some episode that did not enter into its formulation. Graf provides one striking instance, his adult recall of a (perhaps the) key episode in his early childhood:

> When I was still very young, I developed a neurotic fear of horses. Freud gave me a preliminary examination and then directed treatment with my father acting as go-between, using a kind of question-and-answer game which later became standard practice in child psychiatry. Freud documented my cure in his 1909 paper, "Analysis of the Phobia of a Five-year-old Boy," and as the first application of psychoanalytic technique to childhood neurosis the "Little Hans" case, as it's popularly known, is still a classic study in the field.
>
> I remembered nothing of all this until years later, when I came upon the article in my father's study and recognized some of the names and places Freud had left unchanged. In a state of high excitement I called on the great doctor in his Berggasse office and presented myself as "Little Hans." Behind his desk, Freud looked like those busts of the bearded Greek philosophers I'd

seen at school. He rose and embraced me warmly, saying that he could wish for no better vindication of his theories than to see the happy, healthy nineteen-year-old I had become.[35]

It is tempting to see in Graf's statement that Freud "directed treatment" (specifically, the questions and answers between the father and the son) the prototype of Graf's later choice of a career as a similarly behind-the-scenes, "invisible" director of actors in dialogue. I would be making a speculative analogy from one incident to another, however. We do better to keep in mind the whole man, theme as well as variations.

Graf's thematic concern with outer work shows in his attention to "names and places," to Freud's "Berggasse office," and his immediate resort to action to express his inner feelings: "In a state of high excitement I called. . . ." Graf makes two other characteristic progressions in the first paragraph. He moves from "neurotic fear" to "standard practice," from inner feeling to outer work. He also moves from "very young," "preliminary examination," and "first application," to a "classic study," "popularly known," including all the age groups, Hans his father, and "the great doctor."

The second paragraph develops an age-group contrast between the "high excitement" of "myself as 'Little Hans,'" and Freud, "like those busts of the bearded Greek philosophers I'd seen at school." (Unconsciously, I think, Graf is attacking Freud the way he condemned older, operatic styles as "dusty, museum-like" or "antique.") As in the first paragraph, the language shifts from inner thought ("his theories") to external affirmation ("the happy, healthy nineteen-year-old"), from Freud as bearded philosopher to Freud warmly embracing.*

Once we have read Hans's behavior and Graf's as themes and variations, the continuities between the two become almost anticlimactically obvious. Each identity theme has two components that match the components of

---

*Comparing Freud's recollection of the interview with Graf shows a different identity differently perceiving the same events.

> One piece of information given me by Little Hans struck me as particularly remarkable [wrote Freud in his Postscript to the case]; nor do I venture to give any explanation to it. When he read his case history, he told me, the whole of it came to him as something unknown; he did not recognize himself; he could remember nothing; and it was only when he came upon the journey to Gmunden that there dawned on him a kind of glimmering recollection that it might have been he himself that it happened to.

Freud characteristically treats Hans's reappearance in terms of facts and information (Freud's need for reality) which are to be explained scientifically. In the same way, answering criticisms of analysis being applied to a child, Freud wrote, "But none of these apprehensions had come true. Little Hans was now a strapping youth of nineteen" (shifting from fancies to facts, from the fears of others to the evidence, different from Graf's expressive move, from Freud's ideas to Freud's work). Freud speaks of Hans's "glimmering recollection" that "dawned on him" resorting characteristically to an explanation by means of a decisive moment (as in his theories of traumatic repressions, the boy's crucial sight of female genitals, the primal murder of the father, and the like).

the other theme. Hans's doing for others or being done for by others becomes the adult Graf's need for sharing and cooperation. The adult, with a career, however, has a sense of external purpose the child lacks. Similarly, the boy's excremental and exploratory efforts to get his body into situations or something into or out of his body become the adult's concern with personal expressiveness, transforming inner feelings into outer work, to be sure, a work that much involved Graf in getting into and out of special spaces. Discrete events such as Hans watching the cars loading and horses working from his parents' balcony and Graf's being the "invisible" director outside the acting space connect, not in some simple one-to-one way, but within the context of a total individual represented by such themes as the transformation of inner feelings into outer work.

Thus it becomes possible to rethink elements of Hans's childhood in the light of Graf's adult life. For example, after the trauma of his sister's birth, Hans was suddenly taken ill with a sore throat. He had interpreted the birth (partly) by his mother's coughing. One can understand his sore throat, then, through the identity themes as his "uniting" competitive age groups (adult theme) or "getting his body into a situation" in which he does as a parent does (child theme). In this vein, his subsequent tonsillectomy gives the enactment (or variation on the theme) yet more meaning: he will have major treatment for his cough just as his mother did. Reading through identity thus leads to a theme not touched in the original interpretations, Hans's identification with his mother through his own actions (as by making a row with his feet or having a *lumf* baby).

The purpose of reading a life by means of a theme and variations identity is to see the continuity from youth, even infancy, to maturity. I am not assuming, however, that such a theme is intrinsic to Little Hans or Herbert Graf, "in" them in some sense. It is my interpretation of them or Hattam's or Kalfus's. Nor do I mean to imply that this is the only reading of Graf-Hans or even that it is "correct" in some transpersonal, "objective" sense or that you could add up Holland's, Hattam's, and Kalfus's readings to arrive at some correct reading. My re-presentation of Graf and Hans is mine, a function of my identity, just as Graf's ideas about opera were functions of his identity. Other re-presentations are possible, like those of Hattam and Kalfus, indeed necessary, since they make possible a dialogue essential to the continuing exploration of an identity. This essay proposes, therefore, not a final reading of Little Hans or Herbert Graf but the usefulness of a theme-and-variations concept of identity for exploring the continuity in a human life from childhood to its . . .

CONCLUSION

Identity theory lets us sort out the two kinds of aging.

Chaucer mingles them in a passage that has always seemed to me one of the most touching elegiacs in English poetry. It is in the Prologue by the testy, aged Reeve;

> For sikerly, whan I was bore, anon
> Deeth drough the tappe of lyf and lett it gon;
> And ever sithe hath so the tappe yronne
> Til that almoost al empty is the tonne.
> The streem of lyf now droppeth on the chymbe.

From the moment we are born, we begin to die: death has drawn the tap on the cask of life and let it run, until at the Reeve's advanced years, the stream dribbles on the rim of the cask. This is the arrow of time: unidirectional aging. It just goes on and on.

I could call this identity-aging. It is simply another form of the developmental hypothesis that is so fundamental to psychoanalytic theory and practice. As Valéry wrote,

> In every man there lies hidden a child between five and eight years old, the age at which naïveté comes to an end. It is this child whom one must detect in that intimidating man with his long beard, bristling eyebrows, heavy mustache, and weighty look. . . . Even he conceals, and not at all deep down, the youngster, the booby, the little rascal, out of whom age has made this powerful monster.[36]

In the same way, inside the world-famous opera director of sixty-eight, is the little boy worried about horses biting his widdler.

To be sure, identity-aging can involve radical change. We can switch professions or homes or spouses. As Proust says,

> The character which a man exhibits in the latter half of his life, is not always, though it often is, his original character, developed or withered, attenuated or enlarged; it is sometimes the exact reverse, like a garment that has been turned.[37]

To continue his metaphor, however, that old suit is the same cut and style even if we do wear it inside out. The basic theme or themes one traces in an identity remain the same, although the person observed can turn them upside down or inside out. "The first forty years of life," says Schopenhauer, "give us the text: the next thirty supply the commentary on it."[38]

Identity-aging begins, as we have seen with little Hans, in infancy and continues all through life. To be sure, the forward growth of a man of sixty-eight does not produce so marked a change as the development of character in a boy of four or five, but the forward growth continues.

It is this kind of never-ending growth that cumulates in the last of Erikson's eight stages of man, the stage of wisdom (or its failed opposite, despair). Erikson speaks of this last stage in positive terms, as "a com-radeship with the ordering ways of distant times and different pursuits," "the coincidence of but one life cycle with . . . all human integrity." He finds, like Shakespeare, a second childhood in old age, but, as one would expect from Erikson, he finds it in characteristically positive terms. The old person's integrity corresponds to the infant's trust. To have enough integrity, enough sense of the wholeness and fittingness of one's life, means having integrity enough not to fear death, and that corresponds to the child's having trust enough not to fear life.[39]

Childhood is the mirror image of age, then, and like the mirrors of folktale, infancy images old age with both the pain and the beauty of uttered truth. The mutual reflection of childhood and old age em-bodies the paradox of aging, that aging involves the same two kinds of growth as childhood.

To think of aging as Chaucer's Reeve does, as *only* unidirectional, mud-dles different aging. We can sort them out by recognizing that childhood involves two kinds of growth or aging. Old age, the mirror image of childhood, continues both those kinds of growth into the end of life. In one, we amass the experience that Herbert Graf evidences in his memoir. In the other kind of growth, we accumulate the skills that make it possible to be an adult in society.

These two kinds of growth behave quite differently. As I pass from childhood to adolescence to youth, my cultural and physiological abilities become greater and greater. In the jogger in his thirties, there is little trace of the toddler's walk, and further, one jogger is more or less like another. Abilities mature, and then after maturity, they change in nuance and expertise but not in the basics. Once we have learned those basics of walking and talking and reading and riding and running, what we can add to the basics amounts to a small percentage of the whole activity.

Growth in ability we share with most other mortals. As children we gain the physiological and cultural skills that most of the adults around us have. We may differ greatly in the speed with which we run, but otherwise we don't differ very much. The ordinary abilities of our physiology and our culture show only a certain amount of individuality.

The other pattern of growth is quite different. It leads to a cumulating self, a self that we can read as having a constancy from the earliest infancy to the end of life. We can posit for one another identity themes upon which we play a million variations but themes that remain as familiar and recurring and as individual as we do to one another. Within those constant themes or styles, we cumulate experience. We change friends, occupa-tions, milieus, or even spouses. We get new beliefs and discard old ones. We can change utterly in some respects, we can turn ourselves inside out, but (in Proust's metaphor) the suit has the same style, the same tailoring. One can hardly recognize the toddler in the jogger, but, by contrast, in my growth as an individual you can read traces of all my earlier selves. Moreover, from the point of view of identity, I am completely individual, completely different from everyone else.

It is because we have these *two* kinds of growth that our aging becomes so cruel and beautiful a paradox. We age, as someone has said, into parodies of ourselves. Or as the old adage so relentlessly puts it, "If youth but knew and old age only could." We spend the first three-quarters of our lives growing both abilities and identity. Then one becomes both less oneself and more oneself as one grows closer to the end of life. We spend the last quarter losing the abilities we spent the first three-quarters learning, *but*—and this is the hard part—growing more identity. Perhaps this is why aging is like a parody. A parody *is* the thing parodied, intensely so, but also grotesquely so.

Identity-growth goes on and on, in principle to the end of life. Ability-growth creates a set of abilities that ripen to a peak in maturity and after that can only decay. In graphic terms, identity-growth is a line that rises continuously against time, but ability-growth rises to a peak and then declines.

There is a special kind of relation between these two kinds of growth. Identity-growth *uses* the abilities arrived at by the other kind of growth. Ability-growth provides us with the abilities we need to be ourselves. Thus, Hans-Graf used his voice and his talent for direction to become and to thrive as the kind of cooperative child-adult he was.

As we age into old age, we are both more ourselves and less ourselves. The runner slows and finally falters. The skin slackens and thins, becoming transparent. The ear loses the high tones. The eye loses its ability to compensate. Our inner lenses yellow and we begin to see more green in the sky. The body's ability to heal itself weakens. After peaks of vitality, the individual begins to lose the abilities that mark the adult he or she has been for decades.

I do not need and I do not want to list the gradual deteriorations that surprise each of us as they happen yet, sadly, should not surprise us at all. In our language, Jaques's speech in *As You Like It* on the seven ages of man is the classical text for the inevitable loss of abilities in this second kind of growth. The fifth age is the justice "Full of wise saws and modern instances," the man of power and riches and the kind of smug, worldly wisdom they bring. In the sixth age Jaques begins to describe that undoing of the skills of maturity into the incapacity of infancy. Nowadays we describe the transition as from "young elderly" to "old elderly."

> His youthful hose, well sav'd, a world too wide
> For his shrunk shank, and his big manly voice,
> Turning again toward childish treble. . . .

The sixth stage, of course, is followed by the seventh, "second child-ishness," as Jaques calls it, with a sense entirely different from Erikson's. The skills we so busily built up during our lifetimes begin to return to their childish or less than childish forms. Being "old elderly" is, as Shakespeare says, "second childishness," a childishness without the joy that we associate with infancy.

Yet there is a kind of joy, a final triumph of the self against decay. All the time those skills, that youthful kind of growth, is undoing itself, the other kind of growth, aging in the Reeve's sense, keeps on inside this hollow round. Identity continues to grow (if one can speak of a construct's "growing," and why not?). Erikson spoke of this final stage in terms of integration and wisdom and rightly so. So long as the loops of mind and body can continue to act out into the world and feed back the world's replies, so long does identity continue to grow. If youth but knew, if old age only could. Age can do less and less, but age continues to know, indeed knows more and more, grows more and more in understanding, in the strong wisdom of the heart, and that is what makes the cruel and beautiful paradox of age.

As Shakespeare's dashing young King Henry V put it,

> A . . . good leg will fall, a straight back will stoop, a black beard will turn white, a curl'd pate will grow bald, a fair face will wither, a full eye will wax hollow; but a good heart, Kate, is the sun and the moon, or rather the sun and not the moon; for it shines brighter and never changes, but keeps his course truly.

Herbert Graf seems to have been spared the undignified deteriorations of being "old elderly." He was still working as a distinguished director of opera when he died. Yet the happy accident of his having been Freud's Little Hans allows us to unmix the two kinds of growth that go into the gradually ebbing flow of "the streem of lyf." One, which Shakespeare's Henry images as straight back, black beard, curl'd pate, or full eye, waxes to a maturity and then, in old age, wanes. It becomes, first, "young elderly," then "old elderly." What Henry calls a "good heart" I would call character or, more properly, identity, and it goes on to the end. Indeed, since Herbert Graf's identity finally consists of my or your interpretation of that identity, it goes even beyond.

Notes

1. Margaret Mahler, Fred Pine, and Anni Bergman, *The Psychological Birth of the Human Infant: Symbiosis and Individuation* (New York: Basic Books, 1975), p. 102.

2. Marcel Proust, *Remembrance of Things Past*, trans. C. K. Scott Moncrieff, Terence Kilmartin, and Andreas Mayor (New York: Random House, 1981), III, p. 714.

3. Their distinction corresponds, very roughly, to the one I am proposing in the text between identity and the psychophysiological loops of perceptual and motor activity. See their "Infants' Social Perception: A Constructivist View," in *Perception of Space, Speech, and Sound*, Vol. II of *Infant Perception: From Sensation to Cognition*, Leslie B. Cohen and Philip Salapatek, eds. (New York: Academic Press, 1975), pp. 101–48.

4. For a more detailed account, see Part II of my *The I* (forthcoming from Yale Univ. Press).

5. Norman Holland, "Identity: An Interrogation at the Border of Psychology," *Language and Style*, 10 (1977), pp. 199–209, and Holland, "What Can a Concept of Identity Add to Psycholinguistics?," in *Psychoanalysis and Language*, ed. Joseph H. Smith, Psychiatry and the Humanities, Vol. 3 (New Haven: Yale Univ. Press, 1978), pp. 171–234. For general accounts by brain physiologists, see, for example, Ragnar Granit, *The Purposive Brain* (Cambridge and London: The M.I.T. Press, 1977) and John Zachary Young, *Programs of the Brain* (Oxford: Oxford Univ. Press, 1978).

6. See Part III of *The I*.

7. See Heinz Lichtenstein, "Identity and Sexuality: A Study of Their Interrelationship in Man," *Journal of the American Psychoanalytic Association*, 9 (1961), pp. 179–260, and Lichtenstein, *The Dilemma of Human Identity* (New York: Jason Aronson, 1977). For a list of some of the works using this concept of identity, see Norman Holland, *Laughing: A Psychology of Humor* (Ithaca: Cornell Univ. Press, 1982), p. 207, n. 12.

8. Sigmund Freud, "Analysis of a Phobia in a Five-Year-Old Boy" (1909), *Standard Edition of the Complete Psychological Works of Sigmund Freud*, trans. and ed. James Strachey (London: Hogarth, 1955), X, pp. 3–149.

9. See, for example, Samuel J. Keyser and Paul M. Postal, *Beginning English Grammar* (New York: Harper and Row, 1976), or Roderick A. Jacobs and Peter S. Rosenbaum, *English Transformational Grammar* (Waltham, Mass.: Blaisdell Publishing Co., 1968).

10. Herbert Graf, "Memoirs of an Invisible Man: A Dialogue with Francis Rizzo," *Opera News*, 36 (1972), No. 1, pp. 25–28; No. 2, pp. 27–29; No. 3, pp. 27–29; No. 4, pp. 26–29.

11. Mr. Melvin Kalfus, President of the International Psychohistorical Association (P.O. Box 418, New York, N.Y. 10024), has embarked on just such a study, as yet unpublished, "The Man Who Was Little Hans." He has interviewed Graf's co-workers and researched accounts of Graf's stagings, of which more below.

12. Herbert Graf, *The Opera and its Future in America* (New York: Norton, 1941), *Opera for the People* (Minneapolis: Univ. of Minnesota Press, 1951), and *Producing Opera for America* (New York and Zurich: Atlantis, 1961).

13. Graf, "Memoirs," No. 1, p. 26, p. 27.

14. Graf, "Memoirs," No. 3, p. 27.

15. Graf, *Opera for the People*, p. 6.

16. Graf, *Producing Opera for America*, p. 70; Graf, *Opera for the People*, p. 12.

17. Graf, *The Opera and Its Future in America*, p. 139.

18. Graf, "Memoirs," No. 1, p. 27.

19. Graf, *Producing Opera for the People*, p. 270.

20. Graf, *The Opera and Its Future in America*, p. 143.

21. Graf, *The Opera and its Future in America*, p. 79.

22. Graf, *Opera for the People*, p. 21.

23. Graf, "Memoirs," No. 1, p. 25; Graf, "Memoirs," No. 4, pp. 27–28.

24. Graf, "Memoirs," No. 1, p. 25.

25. The unpublished study by Melvin Kalfus describes several of Graf's productions. From the point of view of identity theory, these descriptions would be more telling if they were in Graf's own words, but they are nevertheless most interesting.

26. Graf, *The Opera and Its Future in America*, p. 83.

27. Graf, *The Opera and Its Future in America*, p. 15, p. 16.

28. Graf, *Producing Opera for America*, p. 193; Graf, "Memoirs," No. 3, p. 29; Graf, "Memoirs," No. 4, p. 29; Graf, *Opera for the People*, p. 231.

29. Graf, *Opera for the People*, p. 269; Graf, *Producing Opera for America*, p. 207.

30. Graf, "Memoirs," No. 1, p. 25; Graf, "Memoirs," No. 2, p. 29; Graf, "Memoirs," No. 2, p. 29. Victoria Hattam, "Identity Theory and the Case of Herbert Graf," unpub. paper, Dec. 1978.

31. Graf, "Memoirs," No. 3, pp. 28–29.

32. See for example, D. W. Winnicott, "Ego Distortion in Terms of True and False Self" (1960), in his *The Maturational Processes and the Facilitating Environment* (New York: International Universities Press, 1965), pp. 140–52.

33. Graf, "Memoirs," No. 4, p. 28.

34. Graf, "Memoirs," No. 4, p. 28; Graf, "Memoirs," No. 2, p. 29.

35. Graf, "Memoirs," No. 1, pp. 25–26.

36. Paul Valéry, *Analects*, trans. Stuart Gilbert (Princeton, N.J.: Princeton Univ. Press, 1970), p. 402.

37. Proust, *Remembrance of Things Past*, I, p. 468.

38. Arthur Schopenhauer, "Vom Unterschiede der Lebenslater," in *Aphorismen zur Lebensweisheit, Sämtliche Werke*, ed. Arthur Hübscher (Wiesbaden: Eberhard Brockhaus Verlag, 1946), 5, p. 523.

39. Erik Erikson, *Childhood and Society*, 2nd ed. (New York: Norton, 1963), pp. 268–69.

LIGHT AND THE WISDOM
OF THE DARK
Aging and the Language of Desire
in the Texts of Louise Bogan

***

John Muller

In 1983 Steven Spielberg's film *E.T.* drew crowds in Europe just as it did here. According to a reviewer in the *Times Literary Supplement*, the basis for "the extraordinary hold *E.T.* has on the young and old" is "a mythic quality [that] stirs subliminal currents—appealing to powerful, albeit often inarticulately expressed religious cravings." And yet it is a simple story about an alien creature who, marooned on Earth for a few days, is sheltered by a ten-year-old boy and his family. But embedded within this simple story is the peculiar way in which the boy and the creature get on. Our able reviewer tells us only this much: "A bond naturally develops between the child and extraterrestrial."[1] Yes, but the nature of the bond is extraordinary; it is one in which the boy and the creature are identified totally in their thoughts, feelings, impulses. Both fatigue concurrently. When E.T. gets drunk, the boy Eliot experiences symptoms of inebriation. When E.T. is stirred by television images of a dashing romance, Eliot, the camera shows us, clutches his girl friend and insists on a kiss. Their identification continues until the near-end of the film when both are ill, when E.T. "dies," and Eliot, at his side, says: "I don't feel anything anymore." That their bond is "natural" clearly deserves exploration. Perhaps some Lacanian notions can be useful here.

What is E.T., if not the quintessential example of the other? Out in space exists an other consciousness: is this not our persistent fantasy? In *E.T.* we are confronted with such an other, who makes his entry by coming out of the light. Both E.T. and Eliot, before their mutual and hesitant recognition, emerge from the place of light rather than darkness. In the film light heralds the other's presence, the other's consciousness and look; light is pregnant, or ominous, with the gaze of the other, harboring the desire of the other, confirming our expectation, our wishes to be recognized. Once this other (E.T.) is met, the central character (the boy Eliot) identifies with him so that E. T.'s desire becomes Eliot's desire. There is no better way to describe the nature of their bond than by calling it identification with the desire of the other. This may be helpful in understanding the way a particular poet aged over her lifetime.

Louise Bogan was a lyric poet who often worked within the constraints of the sonnet form. For thirty-eight years she reviewed poetry for *The New Yorker*, and was still doing so at the time of her death in 1970 at age seventy-two. When asked by W. H. Auden why she wasn't better known, she replied, "because I wasn't respectable."[2] Bogan, an Irish-Catholic of lower middle-class origins, had dropped out of college, was divorced, drank a lot, and had been a mental patient. Born in Maine and raised in Massachusetts, she drew on the weather of New England in her writing. But the most insistent image in both her poems and journals is that of light, and I will explore here the changes in this image across fifty years of her published texts.[3]

Bogan chose "A Tale," first published when she was twenty-four, as the lead poem in her first collection of poems in 1923 and, except in two books of new poems, she placed it first in all subsequent published collections of her poetry.[4] At the exact center of this poem, which presents a young man in search of what will endure, the poet introduced her own voice in a couplet that describes the youth as: "Seeking, I think, a light that waits / Still as a lamp upon a shelf."[5] The interpretation of these lines offered by Jacqueline Ridgeway is not surprising: "The imagery of light suggests the light of the mind, of inspiration, of knowledge or larger meaning—a significance beyond the daily and the mutable."[6] This is fair enough, but I want to argue that light and its associated objects (lamps, windows, and so forth) have a very different and distinctive function in Bogan's texts, a particularity deriving from the nature of her desire as lured by the gaze of the Other. This theme is sounded in that same keynote sonnet which closes with a view of the other whose gaze forbodes a fearful intimacy, and the knowledge that nothing does indeed endure save this:

> But he will find that nothing dares
> To be enduring, save where, south
> Of hidden deserts, torn fire glares
> On beauty with a rusted mouth,—
>
> Where something dreadful and another
> Look quietly upon each other.

In Bogan's poetry, light, I will propose, is a metonymy of the other; light bears a relationship by way of contiguity to the other's gaze, and the other's gaze, in turn, suffuses the world with desire, presenting to us the Other as desiring.

Let us begin by noting Bogan's references to light in her journal entries from 1935 and 1936, written when she was approaching forty.[7] For her, light is intimately associated with the landscape and the look, and with the world of writing, with beauty and art. We read: "Santayana's classic world—the people of Chekhov 'seen against the sky'; this is what I knew in childhood and had no word for: this is 'the light falling down through the universe,' the look and feeling of which has haunted me for so long. . . ." In Turgenev's work, she remarks, "the effects of light and shadow on the scene" are "as beautiful as anything I have ever read." She speculates on how the "changes of light that the day brings" were, for prehistoric humanity, "the only thing that approximated art" and perhaps "all that mankind had to delight in." Perhaps more significantly, Bogan experiences light as a look, a look that touches her in her desire, as we see in her description of an earlier mood:

> The excessive boredom and even unhappiness that used to assail me on country journeys with R. [Raymond Holden, Bogan's second husband] can now be experienced, elucidated, as the landscape, the sounds, the light, giving me a clear unpremeditated, unclouded-by-sentiment-or-passion-or-nonsense look and expecting (and not, for the dullest of reasons, getting) a clear look back.

She senses the landscape as looking at her and desiring: but who or what is this other in the light of the landscape that looks at the subject, desiring?

Light not only attests to an object's existence but, Lacan tells us, it is also experienced by us as linked with the gaze of "the Other." Light, which permits us to see, also allows us to be seen by the Other, and we project our own seeing onto the Other and imagine, even desire, that we are seen by the Other. This projection Lacan calls "le regard," the gaze or attention of the Other from which the desiring subject hangs suspended and receives his illusory substance. Lacan's notion of the Other's gaze owes much to Sartre's treatment of this problem in what Lacan calls "one of the most brilliant passages of *"L'Etre et le Néant."*[8] Lacan, however, claims to stress what was overlooked by Sartre, namely, "the subject sustaining himself in a function of desire." That is to say, Lacan's critique of Sartre rests on the difference between making consciousness the foundation of the *cogito* (as Sartre does) and making the unconscious (and unconscious desire) subvert the conscious subject of the *cogito* (as Lacan does). For Sartre the Other is a consciousness that objectifies: "If someone looks at me, I am conscious of *being* an object."[9] But for Lacan, the Other is not an actual person but a structured field (largely unconscious) on which one projects the light of consciousness and desire:

> I must, to begin with, insist on the following: in the scopic field, the gaze is outside, I am looked at, that is to say, I am a picture.

This is the function that is found at the heart of the institution of the subject in the visible. What determines me, at the most profound level, in the visible, is the gaze that is outside. It is through the gaze that I enter light and it is from the gaze that I receive its effects. Hence it comes about that the gaze is the instrument through which light is embodied and through which . . . I am *photo-graphed*. [p. 106]

Note the hyphenation and italicization of the last word: for Lacan, one is graphed by light, that is, delineated, outlined, given one's bearings by light. But Lacan is not referring to how other people *actually* see me; he is referring to a projection, a fantasy:

In the scopic relation, the object on which depends the phantasy from which the subject is suspended in an essential vacillation is the gaze. . . . The gaze is that underside of consciousness. . . . The gaze imagined by me in the field of the Other. [pp. 83–84]

The gaze, then, can be viewed as the projection of the light of one's own consciousness, in the sense of "die Leuchte" as Freud and later Erikson called it,[10] the light of self-awareness. It is projected so that I can experience myself as being seen, as being recognized. Just as Hegel presents self-consciousness as arising only in a desiring relationship to another self-consciousness, each desiring to be recognized by the other,[11] likewise the conscious ego—always prone to project its imaginary attributes of unity, substance, and coherence onto things to fashion discrete entities of them—projects its "light" onto the Other in order to feel recognized as a subject, for vision is, for Lacan, "the original subjectifying relation" (p. 87).

But where, in Bogan, does vision play this original, subjectifying function structuring her desire in the field of the Other? It will come as no surprise that this origin has to do with the mother, whom Erikson calls "the primal other."[12] Erikson tells us that one becomes an "I" through eye-to-eye contact with the mothering one who, in eyeing us, recognizes us, whose eye lights up in our presence, thereby giving us the sense that we are desirable, that we are, for her, an object of desire.[13] To satisfy such a desire becomes then our desire, and we learn to search out the desire of the other. But how is mother linked with light? Rilke, whom Bogan quotes as an epigraph to *The Blue Estuaries*, her collected poems, tells us that the mother is the light around the "familiar intimate things that are there without afterthought, good, simple, unambiguous,"[14] which suggests that the mother is usually associated with light by contiguity, by being there when the child has these familiar, intimate, and unambiguously positive experiences. But such tranquil intimacy was missed by Bogan as a child, who as an adult looks back on the stormy relations and separations between her parents. Her mother, "careless . . . about the order of a

room," could "deal out disorder and destruction."[15] Bogan especially
recalls one violent scene:

> It is in lamplight with strong shadows and an open trunk is in the center of it.
> The curved lid of the trunk is thrown back, and my mother is bending over
> the trunk, and packing things into it. She is crying and she screams. My
> father, somewhere in the shadows, groans as though he has been hurt. It is a
> scene of the utmost terror. And then my mother sweeps me into her arms and
> carries me out of the room. She is fleeing; she is running away.

Light in Bogan's world becomes associated, then, not with calm familiarity, but with the mother's desire, passionate and erratic.

For Bogan, whose life, as she wrote in a letter to Rolfe Humphries at the
age of twenty-seven, was "blighted" by her mother (*Letters*, p. 12), there
was no easy way to have access to the mother's desire, in part because her
mother was by nature dissembling:

> Secrecy was bound up in her nature. She could not go from one room to
> another without the intense purpose that must cover itself with stealth. She
> closed the door as though she had said goodbye to me and to truth and to the
> lamp she had cleaned that morning and to the table to be laid for supper, as
> though she faced some romantic subterfuge, some pleasant deceit.[16]

Moreover, Bogan's place in her mother's desire was crowded out by her
mother's narcissism: "How she loved herself!" Bogan wrote; "I have seen
her come home from church and go straight to the mirror and there
examine her face in the minutest detail, to see how she had looked in other
people's eyes." With her mother thus intent upon pursuing her own
reflection, it would have been difficult for the daughter to find herself
reflected in her mother's gaze. But, compounding this obstacle, it was also
clear to the daughter that the desire of her mother, whom she remembered
as a "big strong dominating [woman] with crowds of admiring gents in
tow," focused on other men.[17] When her mother got dressed and adorned
herself with perfume, it was not for her father, or for Louise: it "meant
going to the city; it meant her other world; it meant trouble. . . ." Certainly, her father was not an object of her mother's desire: Bogan's parents
did not sleep together (it was rather Bogan who slept with her mother),
and her mother rarely called her father by name. Bogan relates one of the
"crudest shocks" of her life in a recurring recollection: "The door is open,
and I see the ringed hand on the pillow; I weep by the hotel window as she
goes down the street, with *another*. . . . The chambermaid tells me to stop
crying. How do we survive such things?" (Significantly, at one point in her
childhood, following a year of "secret family angers and secret disrup-
tions," Bogan went blind for two days, but does not remember what had

been too unbearable to look at. She does recall, however, that the first thing she saw when sight returned was the forked light of the gas lamp flame.)

Nonetheless, that Bogan did identify with her mother's desire, there is no doubt, for her fears become identical with her mother's (here we may recall E. T. and Eliot) as when she writes, "The flume cascaded down the rocks, with bright sun sparkling on the clear, foamy water. My mother was afraid of the flume. It had voices for her: it called her and beckoned her. So I, too, began to fear it." But what she had to dread perhaps even more was the threat her mother's desire held for the place of the father. To identify with her mother's desire would mean to desire to treat him the same way her mother apparently did. Although her father was no competitor for the place Louise held in her mother's desire, to disregard or even hurt him would be to threaten what he represented: certain limits, regularity, frugality, economic sustenance, and form, without which there would have been only psychotic chaos.[18] Thus to identify with her mother's desire, now that it excluded her father as an other, would be to also desire the overturning of his place, and this Bogan could not do, even though she remains with her mother. Mother and daughter flee to a place where:

The woman goes ahead with a lamp. . . .

Then I see her again. Now the late sun of early evening shoots long shadows like arrows, far beyond houses and trees: a low, late light, slanted across the field and river, throwing the shade of trees and thickets for a long distance before it, so that objects far distant from one another are bound together. I never truly feared her. Her tenderness was the other side of her terror. Perhaps, by this time, I had already become what I was for half my life: the semblance of a girl in which some desires and illusions had been early assassinated: shot dead.

The solution to the dilemma, therefore, is to appear *not* to desire, or to postpone desire, or to try to withdraw identification with her mother's desire in order to protect the place of the father. But desire must then somehow be anchored in an other, other than the mother. But for a child, as Bogan the adult realized so well, the desires of others are not easily discerned: "people can only be put down as they were *found* by the child, misunderstood and puzzling to the child; clumsy beings acting seemingly without purpose or reason." Soon enough, however, she finds that houses, what goes on in them, and what desires others have, these now become associated with light and the promise of the gaze of the other: ". . . these fronts of buildings, with afternoon light flowing upon them with such terrible, dramatic effect—these certainly were important. Within them, life burned, a life in which I as yet had no part. I believed this; from my soul I believed it. . . ." Looking back at age sixty-two, she shows us how

she searched for ways to determine the desires of others (and by identification, therefore, her own):

> I came [to the city] at the age of the impossible heart, when the mind flew
> out to inhabit with warmth and compassion the rooms behind shut windows
> and drawn blinds . . . when one watched the play of people's eyes and
> mouths, as though expecting enchanting glances, magical words, to come
> from them. . . .

The windows, blinds, signs, and faces all held clues, were all potential
revelations of the desire of the Other.

Bogan's first look inside someone else's house occurred when she was
seven and her family rented a room at a boarding house. Upon walking
into the daughter Ethel's room, she was struck by "the order, the white-
ness, the sunlight, the peace, the charm." This experience marks the
beginning of a profound shift in the articulation of Bogan's desire. No
longer captivated by the gaze and desire of the mother, she now makes a
place for the desire of others and for the objects of their desire—literally
their objects, those, such as for example, in Ethel's room—"the little
objects which are the most precious part of my memory. . . ." In her
journals she devotes nine paragraphs to these objects: bed, bureau, mirror,
linen embroidery, pincushion, brooches, scissors, file, nail buffer, pin-tray,
brush, comb, buttonhook, nail polish, handkerchief box, ring tree. "I can
only express my delight and happiness with the Gardners' way of living by
saying that they had one of everything," she wrote, "*One of everything* and
everything ordered and completed. . . ." She is even more precise about
how these objects covered over any gaps: "Order ran through the house.
There were no bare spaces." In other words, these objects now fill in the
gap opened by her growing inability to identify with her mother's desire.
They serve to structure, organize, and give order to her desire; her desire is
secured in them, thereby providing her a sense of substance as desiring
subject. And the objects are desirable because they so unambiguously
serve as objects of the desire of others. So this is what went on inside
houses, this is how, and what, the other desired. So much had remained
unknown to her. Up to that age she had lived almost exclusively in a hotel.
"I had seen normal households only on short visits;" she wrote, "I had no
idea of ordered living."

Bogan's growing appreciation of order, of order as defining and setting
limits on desire, of an order outside her own whims and those of her
family, culminated in a moment when at age eleven she visited her mother
in the hospital:

> My mother was lying in bed in a pretty lace-trimmed nightgown, her hair in
> two braids. She looked young and happy and was in one of her truly loving

moods, when affection rayed out from her like light. Someone had sent her a long box full of pink roses. Who could this have been? Not any of us.

When she saw the roses sent by an unknown "other" to her mother, making her feel "that touch of 'the other' world," she said, looking back at age fifty-seven, "I found myself moving away from my mother's bed toward the fireplace, on the opposite wall." As she withdraws from her mother, willy-nilly making room for "the other world," for the roses from "the other," and for another to be the object of her mother's desire, she finds her own desire captured, channeled, by the sight of a vase of marigolds:

> Suddenly I *recognized* something at once simple and full of the utmost richness of design and contrast that was mine. A whole world, in a moment, opened up; a world of design and simplicity; of a kind of rightness, a kind of taste and knowingness that shot me forward, as it were, into an existence concerning which, up to that instant of recognition, I had had no knowledge or idea. *This* was the kind of flower, and the kind of arrangement and the sense of arrangement plus background, that, I at once realized, came out of impulses to which I could respond.

Whereas only moments before she had found the afternoon "rather frightening and forbidding" and the roses chilling, she now regards these marigolds as "mine, as if I had invented them." "I saw the hands arranging the flowers and leaves . . . : they were my hands." What a clear transition by means of substitution! The marigolds for the roses. The objects situated in a pattern where she could find a place for herself as desiring subject substituted for the experience of disorder, for the object from "the other" world, the other in her mother's desires, displacing her, sending her on to channel her desire elsewhere in the Other.

We should at this point step back for a moment and ask: who or what is meant by "the Other"? We have seen that the primal other is the mother, whose desire the child discerns and with which she identifies. When this dyad is breached and lack appears, desire shifts to others—concrete objects desirable because others desire them, and concrete individuals whose regard is sought. But soon enough another level of the Other appears: the framework that gives order to the objects, the social system that structures the desires of individuals. In Bogan's case, this took the form of the order in the homes of others and in their objects. In addition to this process of widening experience, there is yet another level of the Other that engages us, a level grounding all earlier ones, and this level of the Other is the structure of language, or what Lacan, following Lévi-Strauss, calls the symbolic order. This level makes possible every sort of differentiation, including the basic one implied in the self-other dyad, because the symbolic order functions always as a third term, as a perspective, as an anchoring point making it possible for there to be a relation between terms and not simply a fusion between self and other. Thus, strictly speaking, whenever there are two, there is always a third that functions as the framework holding the two together, providing the space between the two, marking the time of their history, serving as the context for truth spoken, what Lacan calls, "the guarantor of Good Faith," what John Berger calls language as listening judge, and what Czeslaw Milosz points to as poetry witnessing us.[19]

The *Other* is often hidden. Akin to Heidegger's notion of Being as Logos, it tends to become obscured by the *others*—objects with their claim on desire, people with their seductive masks and alluring charms. Since, as Hegel teaches, the only proper object of human desire is another human desire, there is nothing like being desired to stir up desire. We are therefore vulnerable to visual cues, especially those of the face and eyes, that tell us we are the completing object of the other's desire. Thus Lacan tells us that desire is always desire of the Other. By this he seems to mean that we desire to be desired, that in so desiring, our desire becomes identified with the other's desires and takes on its contours; moreover, that the articulation of our desire addressed to an other in language always means that desire is subject to the play of signifiers that channel desire, giving it structure and movement; and that this process of identification and signification of desire is largely unconscious and thus an other for the consciousness we take ourselves to be.[20]

What I am proposing is first, that the journey of desire from primal other, to others, to the Other, by which I mean to signify the symbolic order, constitues the *only distinctive psychoanalytic characteristic of aging*; and, secondly, that the wisdom of elders rests on recognizing and warning others of the lures involved in the gaze of the Other. For the visual domain is the sphere of illusion wherein individuals mirror, mask, and lure one another's desire, where narcissism is invested in the visual image and in how I appear to others, where the series of mutual, distorting reflections troubles our love life, as Laing notes in *Knots:* "Jack falls in love with Jill's image of Jack, / taking it to be himself."[21] Discerning these lures of what Lacan calls the imaginary register may be the chief contribution of aging to personal knowledge, for as Bogan wrote about desire and the course of a human life: "First [we require that life] be romantic, exciting; then, that it should be bearable; and, at last, that it should be understandable! These are the stages which we go through, in forming our desires concerning life."[22] It is through such understanding of visual lures that the elders of any society have struggled to make their *decisive contribution* to future generations. But the young, enthralled by the fascination of the gaze, of luring and being lured, resist the wisdom of the elders.

When we left Bogan, we saw how at age seven she first delighted in the objects ordered by others and then, at age eleven recognized she could have a place in creating design itself. Both of these moments in her life articulate with her growing involvement in a more penetrating order (the Other as symbolic order) and with her engagement in even more complex design patterns—those of the domain of language. Her attraction to the ordered house of the Gardners anticipates her pleasure in ordered, printed words. Bogan, who could not yet read at age seven, regarded their house as her "book." Shortly thereafter, her family moved to a house across the street in Ballardvale, Massachusetts; Bogan recalled at age sixty-two, "Why do I remember this house as the happiest in my life? I was never really happy there. But now I realize that it was the house wherein I began to read, wholeheartedly, and with pleasure." She describes her involvement in the new world of words with elation: "they were the beginning of a new life. I had partially escaped. Nothing could really imprison me again. The door had opened, and I had begun to be free." Thus the objects, inchoate symbols of the other's desire, genuine transitional objects, now give way to genuine signifiers opening up the vast resonances of the symbolic order whose endless combinations and substitutions will henceforth channel her desire.[23] A few years later we find a foreshadowing of her active engagement with the design and arrangement of language known as writing. Recalling her childhood and adolescence marked by her parents' poverty, social isolation, and "temperamental disabilities of a near-psychotic order," Bogan writes: "Surely all this agony has long since been absorbed into my work. Even then, it was beginning to be absorbed. For I began writing—at length, in prose—in 1909 [when 12 years old]; . . . I began to write verse from about fourteen on. The life-saving process then began." This "life-saving process" we can understand as the channelling of her desire into language, based on a discerning of "the desire of the Other" in the largest sense, including all the emotional resonances of language and the unconscious. Such discernment always involves what Lacan calls a "total distinction" between the register of the mask (the captivating visual lure of the scopic register) and the evocative field of speech, poetry, and symbol.[24] In the invocatory field the subject is open, its possibilities for articulation are as vast as the near-infinite permutations of the combinatory play of the signifiers; in the scopic register, on the other hand, the subject is caught, snared, determined by the effects of the gaze of the Other.

But besides her mother, who were the others in Louise Bogan's life? At age nineteen she gave up a Radcliffe scholarship to marry a soldier, and at twenty she gave birth to a daughter. Two years later, realizing the marriage was a mistake, she left her husband: "All we had in common was sex. Nothing to talk about. We played *cards*." A year later he died, and she supported herself and daughter by working as a clerk in New York City.

Her first book of poems appeared when she was twenty-six, and two years later she married Raymond Holden, a minor poet; their stormy marriage ended in their separation when she was thirty-seven. Her first psychiatric hospitalization, apparently for depression, occurred at age thirty-four and her second two years later. When she was thirty-eight she began an intense sexual relationship with Theodore Roethke and they remained friends until his death. When she was thirty-nine her mother died at the age of seventy-two. Three years after her mother's death, she wrote to Edmund Wilson that her mother "was an admirable person, even if she nearly wrecked every ordinary life within sight. . . . she loved beauty and threw everything away, and, what is most important, she was filled with the strongest vitality I have ever seen" (*Letters*, p. 185). At forty-four she wrote in a letter to Allen Tate, "I never cared for the Bogans. My mother . . . always held them in a certain amount of scorn; and all my talent comes from my mother's side. The only Bogan I ever really cared about was my brother, Charles," who was killed in 1918 just before the end of World War I (*Letters*, p. 34n). We see, then, that a large part of her desire remained identified with the desire of her mother.

At age forty Bogan's third book of poems was published, she and Holden were divorced, and she began what she called a "successful love affair" with a man she met on a cruise; it lasted until she was forty-eight and was marked by "perfect freedom, perfect detachment, *no jealousy* at all—an emphasis on joy."[25] When she was fifty-four, her father died (he was ninety). She wrote: "the poor gentleman looked v. noble, and very much at peace" (*Letters*, p. 275). At sixty-one, she wrote: "*No one* has *no love*, ever; even my poor father, who had a v. bad deal all around, was finally *adored* by my daughter" (*Letters*, p. 314). When Bogan was sixty-six Roethke died (he was fifty-four) and two months later she wrote in a letter: "It is sad to think that all that incredible energy is now 'undone.' The nearer one comes to *vanishing*, the stranger it seems" (*Letters*, p. 354). She was hospitalized for the third time when she was sixty-eight, and she died alone in her apartment at the age of seventy-two (the same age as her mother when she died), having continued to write, lecture, teach, receive awards and honors, and write letters whose list of recipients reads like a *Who's Who* in American literature (her published letters have been called "a stunning commentary on the arts and letters of her time" and "a stylish, clear, and entertaining literary history of the fifty years from 1920 to 1970").[26]

But for her the most important Other was poetry. The poetry of Louise Bogan, whom Richard Wilbur calls "a poet faithful to the theme of passion,"[27] voices her desire with a terse conviction. The year before she died she wrote: "You will remember, I'm sure, in dealing with my work, that you are dealing with emotion under high pressure—so that *symbols* are its only release" (*Letters*, p. 92n). Her early poems, whether they present the grief of separation, the disillusionment of faded love, the scars of jealousy, all give us the subject as desiring. Even in the attempt to still desire, its gaping abyss is left uncovered, as in "The Alchemist," published when she was twenty-six. The poem opens with the following lines: "I burned my life that I might find / A passion wholly of the mind. . . ." And it closes: "I had found unmysterious flesh— / Not the mind's avid substance—still / Passionate beyond the will." But the subject as desiring, knowing it is vulnerable, tries to camouflage its weakness. In the same remarkable first set of poems we find "Music in the Granite Hill":

> Men loved wholly beyond wisdom
> Have the staff without the banner.
> Like a fire in a dry thicket
> Rising within women's eyes
> Is the love men must return.
> Heart, so subtle now, and trembling,
> What a marvel to be wise,
> To love never in this manner!
> To be quiet in the fern
> Like a thing gone dead and still,
> Listening to the prisoned cricket
> Shake its terrible, dissembling
> Music in the granite hill.

Writing during her first hospitalization, she realizes that one source of vulnerability is the visual domain, namely, how the scopic field lures desire. Quoting Yeats, she explains: " 'Love comes in at the eyes'—A pretty pass for one of my stiff-necked pride, don't you think? It comes in at the eyes and subdues the body. An army with banners. My God, every poet in the world knew about it, except me" (*Letters*, p. 57).[28] By age forty, she has gained further perspective on how the mask and the lure make love duplicitous. I quote her poem "Heard by a Girl" in its entirety:

> Something said: You have nothing to fear
> From those long fine bones, and that beautiful ear.
>
> From the mouth, and the eyes set well apart,
> There's nothing can come which will break your heart.
>
> From the simple voice, the indulgent mind,
> No venom breeds to defeat your kind.
>
> And even, it said, those hands are thin,
> And large, well designed to clasp within
>
> Their fingers (and O what more do you ask?)
> The secret and the delicate mask.

And she exposes, relentlessly, the narcissism of the other that seeks only its own reflection in love, as we see in her poem "Man Alone," also quoted in full:

> It is yourself you seek
> In a long rage,
> Scanning through light and darkness
> Mirrors, the page.
>
> Where should reflected be
> Those eyes and that thick hair,
> That passionate look, that laughter.
> You should appear
>
> Within the book, or doubled,
> Freed, in the silvered glass;
> Into all other bodies
> Yourself should pass.
>
> The glass does not dissolve;
> Like walls the mirrors stand;
> The printed page gives back
> Words by another hand.
>
> And your infatuate eye
> Meets not itself below:
> Strangers lie in your arms
> As I lie now.

Two years earlier Holden had written a novel, Bogan writes in a letter to Roethke, "in which a sort of deBoganized Bogan goes through some paces I once went through, in the full flush of my youth and pride, and that made me very mad, and I sent the book back" (*Letters*, p. 98). Ruth Limmer, the editor of Bogan's letters, comments: "It is hard for the outsider to see what in this continously adoring portrait could have brought LB to invective," but Limmer gives the clue herself when she notes that "He turned the poet into a woman whose only desire was to fulfill the hero's needs ('. . . at once hull, anchor, sail, ocean and wind to the vessel of his being')" (*Letters*, p. 100). It is clear that Bogan had already come to reject the mutual narcissism inherent in mirroring the desire of the other, while perceiving that Holden had not moved beyond that position.

But in moving beyond the illusion of mirrored desire and the lure of the eyes (a frequent feature in her poems), Bogan does not moralize, idealize, or deny desire, even though it cannot be satisfied. Rather, as Elizabeth Perlmutter puts it, Bogan surrenders "to the grain and savor of finality and limitation."[29] Her final poem, published at age seventy and placed at the end of *The Blue Estuaries*, Bogan herself referred to as "a fairly old erotic

song" (*Letters*, p. 372). The eight-line poem alludes perhaps to "The Demon Lover," an old Irish ballad, and to the Harlequin complex:[30]

> Before I saw the tall man
> Few women should see,
> Beautiful and imposing
> Was marble to me.
>
> And virtue had its place
> And evil its alarms,
> But not for that worn face,
> And not in those roped arms.

The poem deals with the wish for the ultimate object and other of desire,
for death as the lover beyond all bounds and limits. But as she typically
does with her carefully chosen titles, Bogan undercuts this scheme by
titling the poem "Masked Woman's Song," thereby placing it in the scopic
register of visual beguilement and disguise, the seductive masquerade of
the sexes. We are thus made to realize the fundamentally unrealizable
nature of the wish for the completing object.

In his recent book Erik Erikson proposes there may indeed be such a
completing object: his very title—*The Life Cycle Completed*—suggests it.
Erikson makes the conscious I the numinous center of existence, but
understands the self to be comprehended only in the light of the Other,
whose initial representative is the mother as primal other. Drawing parallels between the first stage in his schema of the life cycle and the eighth
and final stage, between the primal other and what he calls the ultimate
other, he concludes that just as in the first stage when eye-to-eye contact
with the primal other leads to feeling recognized and to basic trust, so in
the last stage the recognition and regard of the ultimate other sustains faith
and integrity. This ultimate other we will see face-to-face and, presumably,
its totality will complete our lack, a crowning end to the journey through
the life cycle, stages of crises whose outcomes yield the useful virtues of
trust, autonomy, initiative, industriousness, fidelity, intimacy, gener-
ativity, and integrity. Such a perspective, stressing as it does the sense of I
as a numinous, certain center, is not only very American, individualistic
and optimistic, but also takes on the form of a twentieth-century morality
play, a kind of contemporary *Pilgrim's Progress*. But, it must be said, it bears
no resemblance to the life of someone like Louise Bogan, or to millions of
aging people whose primary task is to sustain food supply and shelter, and
who are useless by-products in an economy based on conspicuous con-
sumption.[31] Likewise we must wonder how, in a psychoanalytic framework, the Other as ultimate, wished-for totality can be posited, given the
power of projection and the nature of human desire.

I do not mean to say that such matters cannot be examined in a religious or philosophical context, or even in a personal context. But even in a personal context one would have to be, as Bogan was, suspicious of the ego. Furthermore, the very structure of desire and its enmeshing, its articulation, in language, is founded on lack: lack in oneself as well as lack in the Other. It is unclear what place there is in the "ultimate other" for such a lack.

What does Louise Bogan do with such lack? She puts it into her poetry. At age sixty-five she had some direct advice for her younger colleague, the poet May Sarton: "Get all the *bear* into your work! Get all the bitterness too. That's the place for it. —And twenty years doesn't seem such a tragic length of time, to me, dear May. I have been writing since 1912, the year of your birth" (*Letters*, pp. 346–47). When she was seventy, she wrote from an ocean voyage to her editor: "I have a feeling you'd hate everything. But when one old lady after another—who have ended up either in Hamburg or Heidelberg or Oakland, California—tell you the story of their lives somehow it is soothing to listen. For those stories come from the v. center of the middle . . . and are often filled with unexpected moments of pathos" (*Letters*, pp. 372–73). A year later, she wrote to Rolfe Humphries: "Maidie [her daughter] I see about once a week; and I visit a literate youngish psychiatrist twice a month. But I get pretty lonely. This is a new feeling, for I have always been pretty vigorous and self-sufficient. A slight failure of nerve, no doubt. . . . But I hate it, and wish it would go away" (*Letters*, pp. 374–75). But to readers of her poems, this recognition of limited personal existence never seems far away. We find, indeed, that in giving voice to her desire, Bogan's poems seem to enable her to contain her lack, her want, and to do so precisely by affirming it as unsatisfiable.

What has become of the theme of light in these later years? While not emphasized in her letters, it remains in her poetry. At thirty-eight she published "Evening Star," a poem in which we find light cast as the metonymy of the desire of the Other, for she attributed desire to this light, a desire that is met by her own silent desire: "Light, lacking words that might praise you; / Wanting and breeding sighs only." Some twenty-odd years later she remains caught (as we all are, Lacan reminds us) by the projection of the Other's gaze, for at age sixty she writes about the uncertainty of what "March Twilight," the title of the poem, will bring. I quote the entire poem:

> This light is loss backward; delight by hurt and by bias gained;
> Nothing we know about and all that we shan't have.
> It is the light which presages to the loser luck,
> And cowardice to the brave.
>
> The hour when the oldest and the newest thoughts begin;
> Light shed for the most desperate and kindest embrace.

A watcher in these new, late beams might well see another face
And look into Time's eye, as into a strange house, for what lies within.

The search for clues to the Other's desire persists, even to the point of its old link with what goes on inside of houses. But what is added is a certain sense of mystery, and it is perhaps such thoughts brought by impending death that lead one to reach for the mystery. At sixty-four she notes in her journal, "The light that would return, over a lifetime of autumns . . . / At a certain hour, a look of terrible mystery and silence . . ." and she reaches out to what she calls "the mystery of the ordinariness. . . ." She envies Robert Phelps, "who runs his life by the stars! What a pleasure and relief to have a faith or supersitition of any kind! I should think that believers would dance with joy in the streets." And yet she allows herself an interest in her horoscope and in psychical research. "Why not?" she asks, "The mystery draws in. One needs the help of the imagination to die. . . ."

In a poem entitled "Night," published when she was sixty-five, she writes:

> The cold remote islands
> And the blue estuaries
> Where what breathes, breathes
> The restless wind of the inlets,
> And what drinks, drinks
> The incoming tide;
>
> Where shell and weed
> Wait upon the salt wash of the sea,
> And the clear nights of stars
> Swing their lights westward
> To set behind the land;
>
> Where the pulse clinging to the rocks
> Renews itself forever;
> Where, again on cloudless nights,
> The water reflects
> The firmament's partial setting;
>
> —O remember
> In your narrowing dark hours
> That more things move
> Than blood in the heart.

Here she invokes the panorama of the cosmos, star light and life pulse, and within this waiting and restless "partial setting," she finds a place for her desire. Rather than distort the Other through her own projections, or merely find in the Other a reflection of her own desire, or attempt to induce her desire to mirror the other, she finds (and recollects) her desire as embedded in the larger lack, as part of the larger unfinished pattern.

And this can serve as one way to view her work, the "panacea," as she called it, that she maintained with integrity. All her critics agree on this: she was not corruptible in her judgment, her sensibility. She was fierce to some, to others honest and fair. We perhaps were not fair with her in finding her not quite respectable. As Theodore Roethke stated, she is "one of the true inheritors . . . [whose] best work will stay in the language as long as the language survives."[32] That is to say, her limited work (and she was the first to affirm it as such) finds its place in our tradition because our tradition itself is limited, has lacks, remains incomplete, as it must if it is to include us and our children's desire. Perhaps all we can attempt, in this limited framework, is to place our lack, our want, our desire, into the larger lack of the symbolic order, whose lack makes movement, play, possible. If aging provides a place for death, if aging nourishes a wisdom rooted in a shift in relation to the desire of the other whereby we move from captivating reflection to partial symbolization, then we may speculate about the lack as an opening for the future and perhaps as necessary for the continuance of desire; lack of being makes possible further being, where complete being would dispel all lack, all desire, all future.

Our perduring illusion, however, if we agree with what I understand Lacan to be saying, is that we project the light of our consciousness onto this field of the Other, this symbolic surrounding and supporting frame-work, and that we experience this light as the gaze of the Other signalling the desire of the Other, whose intentions we strive to read so that we can identify with its desire, so that we can be affirmed as ego-identities and illusory substances of desire. We seek the desire of the Other as the moving cause of our desire: we imagine being seen, we want to be seen as being a certain way, we impute a desire that we be seen as being a certain way, and then we think we will be happy if only we can get ourselves to conform, to mirror, or to be mirrored.

Now, perhaps if we strip away the narcissistic components of the attempt at mutual reflection, we may place our desire, claimed as our want and lack, in the larger lack, finding a fit place for it. This point has been articulated in many different ways. For St. Paul his sufferings "complete what is lacking in Christ's afflictions."[33] For the Buddhist, my egolessness enters me into that non-Being that is the foundation of Being. For Heideg-ger death means the passage to the "shrine of the Nothing" that shelters the mystery of Being itself.[34] But if we conceive of the Other as without lack, then death can only be an annihilation in the face of impenetrable fullness.

In most traditions light has played the positive role of announcing truth, and has been associated not just with consciousness but also with what is good and masculine, while darkness belongs to what is evil and feminine as, for example, in Mozart's *The Magic Flute*.[35] But perhaps we find the truth in darkness, in the opacity wherein consciousness and its light have no function.[36] Perhaps we touch the truth rather than see it or become seen by its light. We grope. We establish contiguous relations. Or perhaps it is better to say we are touched by the truth. In any case, the truth is always for us humans metonymic, partial, inevitably a process of displacement and unfinished movement, not an ego-directed pursuit to a conclusion. Writing to Roethke at age thirty-eight, Bogan rejected an "ego"-based view of identity: "I must say, I get terribly sick of novels that go along, riding a hidden or ostensible *I*, in a straight line, with some bumps, from start to finish" (*Letters*, p. 117). A year later she wrote: "I also think that our unconscious (Uncs., in Freud's charming phraseology) knows more about us than we know about it" (*Letters*, p. 138). Our egos, therefore, are not to be trusted, for, as she writes at age forty-one: "we are all self-lovers to an almost complete degree" (*Letters*, p. 180). This, however, does not lead her to become a cynic. That would amount to denying or trivializing desire, which she never does. At age sixty-five, she commented on Katherine Anne Porter's *Ship of Fools:* "What is it that is lacking? Pity and tenderness, I guess. It is not so much *fools* that human beings are, but creatures incompletely wise. Or so I prefer to think" (*Letters*, p. 344). She herself came to affirm a degree of wisdom, as we read in her poem "After the Persian," written when she was fifty-five. I quote the final two sections:

> IV.
> Ignorant, I took up my burden in the wilderness.
> Wise with great wisdom, I shall lay it down upon flowers.
>
> V.
> Goodbye, goodbye!
> There was so much to love, I could not love it all:
> I could not love it enough.
>
> Some things I overlooked, and some I could not find.
> Let the crystal clasp them
> When you drink your wine, in autumn.

Notes

1. S. Schoenbaum, "Botanist in the Manger," *The Times Literary Supplement*, 7 Jan. 1983, p. 13.

2. Louise Bogan, *What the Woman Lived: Selected Letters of Louise Bogan, 1920–1970*, ed. Ruth Limmer (New York: Harcourt Brace Jovanovich, Inc., 1973), p. 221. All further references to this work, which is abbreviated as *Letters*, are cited in the text.

3. The theme of light in Bogan's work has been noted by few critics. Robert B. Shaw remarked how Bogan "loved to chronical changes in light; in the poems the shadow is an image of transience, a token of mortality and of the inward and outward obscurities that attend our lives" ("The Life-Saving Process," rev. of *Journey Around My Room: The Autobiography of Louise Bogan. A Mosaic*, by Ruth Limmer, in *The Nation*, 27 Dec. 1980, pp. 710–12).

4. This was noted by Jacqueline Ridgeway in her essay "The Necessity of Form to the Poetry of Louise Bogan," *Women's Studies*, 5 (1977), p. 141.

5. Louise Bogan, *The Blue Estuaries: Poems: 1923–1968* (New York: Farrar, Straus & Giroux, 1968), p. 3. All of Bogan's poems quoted in this essay are collected in *The Blue Estuaries*.

6. Ridgeway, p. 142.

7. Louise Bogan, *"From* The Notebooks of Louise Bogan (1935–36)," edited by Ruth Limmer, *Antaeus* (Autumn 1977), pp. 120–29. All references in this paragraph are to this piece.

8. Jacques Lacan, *The Four Fundamental Concepts of Psycho-Analysis*, ed. Jacques-Alain Miller, trans. Alan Sheridan (1973; New York: Norton, 1978), p. 84. All references to Lacan in this paragraph are taken from this book.

9. Jean-Paul Sartre, *Being and Nothingness: An Essay on Phenomenological Ontology*, trans. H. Barnes (1943; New York: Philosophical Library, 1956), p. 271. See "The Look," pp. 252–302.

10. Erik H. Erikson, *The Life Cycle Completed: A Review* (New York: Norton, 1982), p. 86.

11. See John P. Muller, "Ego and Subject in Lacan," *The Psychoanalytic Review*, 69, No. 2 (1982), pp. 234–40.

12. Erikson, p. 40. Freud himself used the phrase "prähistorischen unvergesslichen Anderen." See *Aus den Anfängen der Psychoanalyse: Briefe an Wilhelm Fliess*, Abhandlungen und Notizen aus den Jahren 1887–1902 (1896; London: Imago, 1950), p. 192.

13. D. W. Winnicott writes in an earlier paper about "the child's seeing the self in the mother's face." See Winnicott, "Mirror-role of Mother and Family in Child Development," in *The Predicament of the Family: A Psycho-Analytical Symposium*, ed. P. Lomas (London: Hogarth Press, 1967), p. 32.

14. The Rilke text quoted by Bogan is: "Wie ist das klein, vomit wir ringen; / was mit uns ringt, wie ist das gross . . ." (What is this little with which we contend; what wrestles with us, how great it is.). Rainer Maria Rilke, *The Notebooks of Malte Laurids Brigge*, trans. M. D. Herter Norton (New York: Capricorn Books, 1958), p. 70.

15. Louise Bogan, "From the Journals of a Poet," *The New Yorker*, Jan. 30, 1978, pp. 39–70. Unless otherwise noted, all prose quotations from Bogan are to this publication.

16. Louise Bogan, *Journey Around My Room: The Autobiography of Louise Bogan: A Mosaic*, by Ruth Limmer (New York: Penguin Books, 1981), p. 19.

17. Mary Lydon has observed that Bogan's revelation has violated one of our last taboos, as elucidated by Kristeva, namely, that Mothers do not sexually desire.

18. Bogan writes in her journals, later published in *The New Yorker*, about "meals which often appeared at irregular intervals. . . . Sunday dinner and the evening meals could be counted on to appear on time" (because of father's attendance?). Writing very sparingly of her father, she went on to say: "My father had his job, which kept him in touch with reality; it was his life, always. My mother had nothing but her temperament, her fantasies, her despairs, her secrets, her subter-

fuges. The money—every cent of it earned by my father, over all the years—came through in a thin stream. . . ."

19. Jacques Lacan, *Ecrits: A Selection*, trans. A. Sheridan (New York: Norton, 1977), p. 173; John Berger, rev. of *Missing* by Ariel Dorfman, trans. E. Grossman, *Voice Literary Supplement*, Sept. 1982, pp. 12–13; Czeslaw Milosz, *The Witness of Poetry* (Cambridge, Massachusetts: Harvard Univ. Press, 1983).

20. For elaboration, see John P. Muller and William J. Richardson, *Lacan and Language: A Reader's Guide to Ecrits* (New York: International Universities Press, 1982), pp. 281–83.

21. R. D. Laing, *Knots* (New York: Pantheon, 1970), p. 31.

22. Bogan, "*From* the Notebooks of Louise Bogan (1935–36)," p. 122.

23. In an excellent (and critical) overview of the Lacanian framework, Monique David-Menard in "Lacanians Against Lacan," *Social Text*, 2, No. 3 (1982), writes: "The child's desire gains social currency, catapulted through language into an unconscious dialogue with others that breaks the psychic hegemony of the family" (p. 93).

24. Lacan, *The Four Fundamental Concepts of Psycho-Analysis*, p. 118.

25. Bogan, *Journey Around My Room*, p. xxx.

26. Barbara Grizzuti Harrison, "A Troubled Place," rev. of *What the Woman Lived*, by Louise Bogan, *Ms.*, 8 Nov. 1974, p. 90; Katie Loucheim, "A True Inheritor," rev. of *What the Woman Lived, Atlantic Monthly*, Feb. 1974, p. 90.

27. Richard Wilbur, quoted in William Jay Smith, *Louise Bogan: A Woman's Words* (Washington: Library of Congress, 1971), p. 18.

28. The line is from William Butler Yeats's "A Drinking Song" (1910), in *Selected Poems and Two Plays*, ed. M. L. Rosenthal (New York: Macmillan, 1962), p. 34.

> Wine comes in at the mouth
> And love comes in at the eye;
> That is all we shall know for truth
> Before we grow old and die.
> I lift my glass to my mouth,
> I look at you, and I sigh.

29. Elizabeth P. Perlmutter, "A Doll's Heart: The Girl in the Poetry of Edna St. Vincent Millay and Louise Bogan," *Twentieth Century Literature*, 23 (1977), pp. 157–79. Paul Ramsay, in "Louise Bogan," *Iowa Review*, 1, No. 3, p. 116, also notes "the grief which persistently and profoundly underwells her poems."

30. In "The Demon Lover," the woman is reclaimed by her former lover who is revealed to have a "cloven hoof," and the ballad ends (at least in one version) with these stanzas:

> And aye when she turned her round about,
> Aye taller he seemed to be;
> Until that the tops o' that gallant ship
> No taller were than he.
>
> He struck the topmast with his hand,
> The foremast with his knee;
> And he broke that gallant ship in twain,
> And sank her in the sea.

See *Ballads and Ballad Poetry*, ed. Edward Everett Hale (1902; New York: Globe School Book Company, 1906), p. 18. The Harlequin complex deals with "the theme of death as a lover, as a mysterious dark figure who comes and takes a woman away to her death." See David C. McClelland, "The Harlequin Complex," in *The Study of Lives: Essays on Personality in Honor of Henry A. Murray,* ed. Robert W. White (New York: Atherton Press, 1966), pp. 94–119.

31. In the United States, old people are often figured in economic terms as "represent[ing] the U.S. government's largest liability" as we read in Paul Hawken, "Not Taking Care of Old People," *CoEvolution Quarterly,* No. 37 (Spring 1983), pp. 132–33. We have nothing in our language or our culture that still names elders as do the Sioux in Lakota: *wicasa hcaka* or *winuhcala,* "real" *man* and "real" or "very" *woman.* See Eugene Buechel, S. J., *A Dictionary of the Teton Dakota Sioux Language,* ed. Paul Manhart, S. J. (Pine Ridge, South Dakota: Red Cloud Indian School, 1970). The vestigial "grand"-father and "grand"-mother may have once played this role.

32. Theodore Roethke, "The Poetry of Louise Bogan," *Critical Quarterly,* 3 (1961), p. 150.

33. St. Paul, The Oxford Annotated Bible, Col. I, 24, (p. 1427).

34. Quoted in Bernard Welte, "Seeking and Finding: The Speech at Heidegger's Burial," *Listening: Journal of Religion and Culture,* 12, No. 3 (1977), pp. 106–09.

35. See, for example, J. Eric S. Thompson, *Maya History and Religion* (Norman, Oklahoma: Univ. of Oklahoma Press, 1970).

36. Distortions arising from the primacy given to sight are discussed for example by Eugen Herrigel in *Zen in the Art of Archery,* trans. R. Hull (1953; New York: Vintage, 1971), p. 80; and by Jane Gallop in *The Daughter's Seduction: Feminism and Psychoanalysis* (Ithaca, New York: Cornell Univ. Press, 1982), p. 58. The psychology of perception uses the pertinent term "visual capture" for the phenomenon that when sense modalities conflict with each other, vision tends to dominate, even when erroneous; see Lloyd Kaufman, *Perception: The World Transformed* (New York: Oxford Univ. Press, 1979), pp. 221, 371–72. For an outstanding overview of the "metaphysics of light" and the perennial link made between light and truth, see Hans-Georg Gadamer, *Truth and Method* (New York: Seabury Press, 1975), especially pp. 439ff.

THE MIRROR STAGE OF OLD AGE

***

Kathleen Woodward

I

Every table of values, every "thou shalt" known to history or ethnology, requires first a *physiological* investigation and interpretation.

—Nietzsche, *Genealogy of Morals*[1]

Having a body constitutes the principal danger that threatens the mind.

—Marcel Proust, *The Past Recaptured*[2]

AFTER SOME YEARS in a sanatorium located outside Paris, Marcel, a neurasthenic dandy acclaimed by society for his literary gifts (although he has published only a few sketches), returns to the capital to attend a reception at the home of the wealthy Guermantes. The memorable psychological drama that takes place that afternoon in the closing pages of Proust's *The Past Recaptured* can be read as a parable of aging in the twentieth-century Western world. Like other more familiar psychological dramas of initiation (we might take the witnessing of the primal scene as an example, or the drama which gave Freud inspiration for his theory of the Oedipus complex), it is structured as a scene of recognition, followed by blindness—or repression. But this drama of aging and its discontents turns more importantly on the character's relation to future time than it does to past time. His insight into his future is doubled over into two paradoxical and contradictory scenarios about what he can achieve in terms of work. On the one hand, the man who is tormented by doubts about his own talent and disillusioned about the institution of literature itself, finds his faith in both himself and literature restored on the afternoon of what he calls the most beautiful day of his life. On the other hand, as he is confronted face to face with his advancing age, he is assailed by new doubts, and despairs that he will ever finish the very work he has now resolved to accomplish.

As with the narrative of Oedipus, the moment of recognition of his own aging is preceded by a series of delays which can be understood as a form of unconscious denial. I will mention only three, the first of which is buried deep in the past. It takes the shape of a prophetic text—Balzac's *The Girl with the Golden Eyes*—which Marcel not only did not bother to read many years before but whose significance he fails again to recognize when in the opening pages of *The Past Recaptured*, his memory returns to his first dismissal of it. A few details bear mentioning here. It should not escape our attention that the young Marcel had been urged to read *The Girl with the Golden Eyes* by the young and beautiful Gilberte, his first love, since his encounter with the now aged Gilberte will figure prominently in the closing pages of *The Past Recaptured*, a title whose irony is not often enough remarked. Those of us familiar with Balzac's gruesome tale of an incestuous love triangle will remember that the contrast between the loveliness of youth and the hideousness of age is central to this strange story of doubling and mirror images. In the words of Balzac's narrator, the two together form a "fantastic union of the mysterious and the real, of darkness and light, horror and beauty, pleasure and danger, paradise and hell."[3] In the context of the story, the relation between youth and age is perverse, not romantic or sentimental: the presence of decrepit age, figured as a voyeuristic handmaiden, serves to heighten the erotic pleasures of youth. This mother of the ineffably beautiful girl with the golden eyes is as ugly and vulgar as her daughter is lovely. She is a grim portent of corruption, death, and the macabre murder to come; she is present in the scene "like a suggestion of catastrophe and represented the horrid fish's tail with which the allegorical geniuses of Greece have terminated their chimeras and sirens, whose figures are so seductive, so deceptive" (p. 325). If in Balzac's story it is old age which is repressed for a fatal moment by the disarming presence of self-enthralled youth (so that "all this phantasmagoria of rags and old age disappeared," p. 326), the horrid fish tail of decrepit age will surface at the end of *The Past Recaptured* and threaten to eclipse the future.

By not borrowing this story of desire circumscribed by old age, Marcel neglects to acquire a certain form of knowledge about his own future. For the story enacts in a depraved guise the conflict he will face in his final pages. Long wishing to begin in earnest his literary career, he finally feels ready to do so. But the fact of his age (he is around fifty and has always been sickly) depresses him and he quite appropriately worries that he may die before he finishes his work. Just as in the story by Balzac therefore, his meeting at the reception with what he understands to be his destiny is a combination—sometimes paradoxical, sometimes contradictory—of hell and paradise, danger and pleasure. It is a *combination*, never quite a perfect union, because Marcel himself is split in terms of his relation to time. The ecstatic psychic moments of what he calls perfect knowledge—of the past recaptured, of indeed youth—connect his past with his present, giving him a sense of a productive future. His new and grim knowledge of old age, however, threatens to separate him from that ideal union of time, projecting him into a future aborted by old age.

If Marcel does not read the signs of the coming catastrophe of old age when he is younger, he also remains unaware of its meaning for himself up to the very moment that he confronts the fact of his own age. I take the following incident as my second example of his unconscious denial of old age. Lingering on his way to the Guermantes so as to postpone his arrival (this dallying is certainly not only for the sake of making a fashionable entrance), Marcel notices an old man "with staring eyes and bent shoulders [who] was sitting, or, rather, was placed and was making greater effort to sit up straight, like a child who has been told to behave properly" (p. 182).

By comparing Marcel's reaction to this sight with the way he responds soon after to the elderly guests at the Guermantes, we can gauge the degree to which he is as yet unable to see into the mirror of his own future. The narrative of this small scene rehearses in part the narrative of the scene at the reception: lack of recognition is followed by a shock of recognition. The old man whom Marcel at first takes to be just any old man suddenly assumes an identity in Marcel's eyes, revealed to be none other than a longtime acquaintance, the Baron M. de Charlus. But the scene differs importantly from the one to be played later that afternoon. In a very real sense it involves only two major characters—the nameless old man and M. de Charlus. Marcel stands to the side. He does not implicate himself in this scene, as he will be forced to later that day when the drama will assume the proportions of a doubled double, a triangle in which Marcel oscillates between two positions depending upon whether he contrasts himself with the others or finds himself reflected in their eyes. This structural variance between the two scenes is clearly revealed in the difference between Marcel's rhetoric about old age here and his rhetoric later at the Guermantes. Here he is too far removed from the realities of his own age to correctly interpret the painful nature of the old man's condition. He remains clinically detached, fascinated to detail the physical characteristics of the frail M. de Charlus (he has suffered a stroke) and to record the evidence of his loss of social status. Even more telling, Marcel sentimentalizes the old man's physical infirmities, musing for example that he preferred to see in his limited gestures "an almost physical gentleness, a sort of detachment from the realities of life" (p. 183). Later he will find himself repelled by old age—because he is dangerously close to it—and will resort to satire.

The space of the final pages of *The Past Recaptured* can be thought of as divided into two domains—the private and the public—which are related to each other complexly and correspond to Marcel's ambivalent relation to his new sense of the future. It is in solitude, when he is isolated from the gaze of others or oblivious to it, that his belief in literature is renewed and that he recaptures the past, experiencing precisely what he had felt at certain precious moments long ago. For Marcel, this form of doubling is elating. It unites the past and the present by insisting on their sameness, their identity. During these brief moments which are occasioned by involuntary memory (they cannot be willed into being), time as change, as limit, and as death is banished. Marcel feels himself a "timeless person, consequently unconcerned with the viscissitudes of the future" (p. 197).

If Marcel associates the private with what is authentic and is located deep within the self, then for him the most valuable literary work would represent that experience and the most contemptible would be concerned with the appearance of things. He thus concludes that literature is furthest from "reality" when it merely gives "a miserable listing of lines and surfaces" (p. 213). It is ironic of course that one of Marcel's greatest talents is for satire, for parodic description of the appearance of things, and that he exercises this talent when he crosses the divide between the private and public, stepping from the solitude of the small library where he has been waiting for the concert to end into the main drawing room. I might remark here that Marcel's entrance into the social world is preceded—or we might say further delayed (this is my third example of unconscious denial)—by a long and eloquent meditation on art and literature. It is immediately followed by the most trenchant and sustained satirical description of the elderly in Western literature. Proust appropriately uses the metaphor of the theater, for it is in the very nature of the theater to question what is real and what appearance. Marcel's first impression (he calls it a *coup de théâtre*) is that he has unaccountably found himself in an oddly unsavory masquerade ball at which the guests are bizarrely costumed and are playing pathetic roles. Marcel first wonders if these people have purposely made themselves up into old people. He peers into their faces, trying to see back into time in order to discover the identity of the person by reconstructing their "successive facial stages." As with his solitary magical moments, the past has surfaced involuntarily. But these double exposures, these palimpsests of time, are deeply troubling.

Let us take first the example of M. d'Argencourt. Having succeeded in identifying this man as M. d'Argencourt, Marcel at first thinks he has put on a disguise, that he "had turned himself into an old beggar who no longer inspired the least respect and [that] he put so much realism into his character of a driveling old man that his limbs shook and the flaccid features of his unusually haughty face smirked continually with a stupidly beatific expression" (p. 255). We should observe that by assuming that M. d'Argencourt is only acting old, Marcel is able to deny the physical realities of old age. At the same time however, by ascribing old age to M. d'Argencourt—and to the other guests—he is able to deprive them of power and distinguish himself from them. It is significant that the man who had long been a personal enemy of Marcel is portrayed as a "beggar" who requires no special attention. By relegating d'Argencourt to old age, Marcel renders him impotent.

Attracted and repelled simultaneously by this theater of old age, Marcel details the grotesque spectacle of the physical appearance of his old friends and acquaintances, describing them in metaphors drawn from the animal kingdom and the mineral world as if to suggest that they are less than human. At times the theater is that of the exotic absurd: the Duchesse de Guermantes is likened to "an ancient sacred fish," her "salmon-pink body barely emerging from its fins of black lace" (pp. 260–61). At others, it is menacing and threatening, a gothic melodrama. The stiff body of the aged actress Berma, for example, is described as a tomb that imprisons what remains of her life: "Her hardened arteries being already half-petrified, long, narrow, sculpturesque ribbons of mineral-like rigidity could be discerned traversing her cheeks. Her dying eyes lived relatively by contrast with the horrible ossified mask and shone faintly like a serpent asleep among the rocks" (p. 343). Elsewhere also he dwells on the texture of the skin in old age, itemizing the irregularities he finds revolting, implying that the normal condition of the skin is to be smooth (that is, young) and that thus the flaccid, wrinkled skin of old age is abnormal. But old age is not just a breach of social manners or merely aesthetically unappealing. Marcel describes M. de Cambremer, for instance, as having developed "huge red pouches on his cheeks, which hindered him from opening freely his mouth or his eyes with the result that I stood there stupefied, not daring to look at the carbuncles, so to speak, which it seemed to me proper he should mention first" (p. 268). As Marcel stares surrepetitiously at the carbuncles (those painfully purulent inflammations of the skin, symptoms of a severe and deep infection of the flesh), as he scrutinizes the skin of the other guests, he is sickened to discover "a multitude of fatty splotches" under everyone's skin. Old age, in other words, is perceived by Marcel as a dangerous disease which may infect him as well.

Interestingly enough, if one has grown older but does not *look* older, that too Marcel finds disquieting and strange. There is no way one can avoid old age: it is signified by the absence of its telltale marks as well as by their presence. Madame de Forcheville, for example, is an oddity in whom the signs of old age—what today we refer to as age spots—at first seem an asset, a fantastic new growth, but at second glance they are confirmed to be a liability, symbols of barrenness, as we see in this description of her appearance: it "was so miraculous that one could not even say she had grown younger but rather that, with all her carmines and russet spots, she had burst into new bloom. She would have been the chief curiosity and principal attraction in a horticultural exhibition of the present day. . . . Moreover, just because she had not changed, she scarcely seemed to be alive. She looked like a sterilised rose" (p. 289). It is of course Madame de Forcheville who is the mother of Gilberte, who was once so adored by Marcel. As we know, many daughters age in the image of their mothers. This uncanny doubling is perhaps the cruelest of all for it calls into question the passion of youthful love and the very notion of the continuity of an identity. Our knowledge of this doubling is for the most part abstract. Rarely is it foreseen by the young or even the middle aged. For the most part we persist in carrying into old age images of our first loves as they were when they—and we—were young. Marcel is not spared this shock at the reception. When he is greeted by a "stout lady," he finds he must struggle to remember her and then mistakes his first love for her mother. He is doubly blind to her. She has vanished into the past, or the future—it is difficult to know which. As Proust so perfectly puts it, "A name is frequently all that is left to us of a human being" (p. 308).

While Marcel reflects on the distorting power of time on others—on their masks and disguises, it comes to him with a shock that he too has been subject to the law of time. It is only by seeing himself in the eyes of others that this truth is made clear to him. For Marcel, the drawing room of the Guermantes is a dizzying hall of mirrors where each person possesses the dangerous potential of reflecting the aging Marcel: "Then it was that I, who from my early childhood had lived along from day to day with an unchanging conception of myself and others, for the first time, from the metamorphoses which had taken place in all these people, became conscious of the time that had gone by for them—*which greatly perturbed me through its revelation that that same time had gone by for me*. And, though of no importance to me in itself, their old age made me desperately sad as an announcement of the approach of my own" (p. 260, italics mine). Moments later the old people surrounding him force him to acknowledge that he too is old.

What I find fascinating is that for the remainder of *The Past Recaptured* Marcel vacillates between the rhetoric of unbridled enthusiasm for the future and his new work and the rhetoric of anxiety and physical vulnerability, between blindness to his age and insight into it. After the initial shock that he has in fact aged, he "forgets" that perception in his eagerness to get his work under way. Like an adolescent, he intoxicates himself with the ambitiousness of his project and what it will require of him: he will "endure it like an exhausting task, accept it like a rule of conduct, build it like a church, follow it like a regimen, overcome it like an obstacle, win it like a friendship, feed it intensively like a child, create it like a world" (p. 384). These images of strength, discipline, tenacity, perseverance, and power alternate with those of weakness, debilitation, impotence, and senility. Proust is as successful in expressing the latter as he is the former. Marcel worries that he may have a stroke, or a car accident on the way home, or that he may contract the same illness which befell his grandmother. He recalls with foreboding that only recently as he was going down a flight of stairs, he almost fell three times. He broods that lately he has been exhausted to the point of paralysis. He fears that his forgetfulness is a sign of old age. Tellingly, he compares his anxiety to the condition of an elderly man: "Strictly speaking, I had no particular illness but I felt as though I had become incapable of anything, as frequently happens to an old man, who, active the day before, breaks his hip or has an attack of indigestion and may for some time to come lead a bedridden existence which is now only more or less long preparation for the now inevitable end" (p. 392).

The Past Recaptured comes to an end with these thoughts. As readers we cannot follow Marcel into his future. But perhaps it is just as well that Proust closes his book with the problem posed by Marcel's double discoveries that afternoon, for the lack of conclusion raises the important question of whether indeed it is wise in personal terms to recognize oneself as old. Should in fact one accept one's mirror image of old age as reflected in the eyes of others, the social world? Or is it more productive to deny it? Should one acknowledge a lack of time when, like Marcel, one has the desire to achieve something important? Perhaps for Marcel or anyone else with ambition, blindness to one's own old age is the most profound insight. Perhaps the future should remain concealed. As Anthony Wilden has put it, explicating Jacques Lacan, "Truth for the subject is not knowledge but recognition. . . . But a certain *méconnaissance*—which we might call sublimation—is essential to health."[4] Or, perhaps, indeed, we have no choice.

Yet the fictional world of *The Past Recaptured* prompts us also to ask if it is not precisely the relation between the two kinds of knowledge gained by Marcel that renders each insight possible. This would be paradoxical but not untenable. It does seem to me to make sense that on a conscious level one struggles against limitations only when one is acutely aware of them. Certainly such a view of the relation between literature and life processes was held by Proust. As he wrote not too long before he died, creativity and illness are often linked, and often indissolubly so.[5]

II

Look at my face
you have aged me you have aged me
. . . .
        you did this!

you do this and don't remember
telling me

you do it to me
do it to yourself

—Anne Waldman, "Mirror Meditation"[6]

With these pages from Proust's *The Past Recaptured* in mind as a paradigm, I should like to advance the possibility of a mirror stage of old age, observing first that the image of the mirror dominates literary representations of the aged body. This is not surprising. The horror of the mirror image of the decrepit body can be understood as the inverse of the pleasures of the mirror image of the youthful Narcissus. As we age we increasingly separate what we take to be our real selves from our bodies. We say that our real selves—that is our youthful selves—are hidden inside our bodies. Our bodies are old, we are not. Old age can thus be described as a state in which the body is in opposition to the self, and we are alienated from our bodies. This is a common psychological truth. Ask people in their sixties, seventies, perhaps eighties if they feel old. They will insist that they feel the same way they did when they were thirty or forty, that *they* haven't changed, although their mirror image has. Or they will maintain that their body—now a *foreign* body—has betrayed them (one is never so aware of one's body as when one suffers from it). They will assert that the body is the oppressor and that they are hostage to it, or in the words of the Duke of York in Shakespeare's *Richard II*, "prisoner to the palsy" (II, iii, 104).[7] As Marcel observes, "It is in the moments of illness that we are compelled to recognise that we live not alone but chained to a creation of a different kingdom, whole worlds apart, who has no knowledge of us and by whom it is impossible to make ourselves understood: our body."[8]

We may feel ourselves to be young, but others perceive us as old, perhaps even ancient. As we have seen, this is marvelously dramatized in *The Past Recaptured*. "We did not see ourselves or our own ages in their true light," reflects Marcel, "but each of us saw the others as accurately as though he had been a mirror held up before them" (p. 265).

In Simone de Beauvoir's important book on old age published in English under the misleading title *The Coming of Age*, she explains this phenomenon by suggesting, following Sartre, that old age belongs to the category of the "unrealizables." *We* are not old; it is the Other, the stranger within us who is old. We cannot say simply that if we feel young, then we are young because age is socially as well as biologically determined. As de Beauvoir concludes, the recognition of our own old age comes to us from the Other, that is, from society. We study our own reflection in the body of the others, and as we reflect upon that reflection—reflection is of course a metaphor for thought—we ultimately are compelled to acknowledge the point of view of the Other which has, as it were, installed itself in our body. De Beauvoir explains the complex truth of old age this way: "for the outsider it is a dialectic relationship between my being as he defines it objectively and the awareness of myself that I acquire by means of him. Within me it is the Other—that is to say the person I am for the outsider— who is old: and that Other is myself."[9]

To see, like Marcel, one's own aged body with the shock of recognition is to experience the uncanny in Freud's sense. Freud describes the uncanny as belonging to "all that is terrible—to all that arouses dread and creeping horror" and "unpleasantness and repulsion."[10] He hypothesizes that the origins of the uncanny lie in the infantile stage of the psychological development of the individual and in the primitive phase of the development of the human species when mankind believed the world to be populated by the spirits of the dead. In terms of the uncanny, then, ontogeny recapitulates phylogeny. Freud further describes the uncanny as something "familiar that has been repressed." Thus he concludes that "an uncanny experience occurs either when repressed infantile complexes have been revived by some impression, or when the primitive beliefs we have surmounted seem once more to be confirmed" (p. 157). He associates the uncanny with a fear of castration and a feeling of "morbid anxiety" (p. 148) as well as with the image of the double. Following Otto Rank, Freud observes that whereas in the early stages of human history the double was an assurance of immortality and a powerful weapon against death, it later became a harbinger of death which it has remained to this day. This theory of the double is particularly interesting in light of our subject of aging and I will return to it momentarily.

But first I should like to pursue Freud a bit as he inscribes himself in his essay on the uncanny. Freud presents his essay as a tentative exploration of the phenomenon rather than a definitive study. He protests in the opening pages that he has had little personal experience of the uncanny and thus must turn to literature for evidence. In his customary self-deprecating manner, he asserts that "the writer of the present contribution, indeed, must himself plead guilty to a special obtuseness in the matter where extreme delicacy of perception would be more in place" (p. 123). He insists that "it is long since he has experienced or heard anything which has given him an uncanny impression and that he will be obliged to translate himself into that state of feeling" (p. 123).

These demurs are curious in two respects. First, this is the only instance in the essay where Freud refers to himself in the third person. Elsewhere he writes with ease in the first person, both singular and plural. Here, appearing discomfited, he finds it necessary to create, as it were, another character and refers to himself as "he." Secondly, later in the essay Freud does in fact recount a personal experience of the uncanny drawn from his own life, an incident which occurred presumably some time ago in a small Italian town. There he found himself in the red light district, and trying to escape, returned involuntarily to the very same piazza, not once, but twice.

Far more significant, however, is another personal experience of the uncanny—no doubt a much more recent one—which finds its way into a footnote appended near the end of the essay. Here Freud describes the shock of recognition of meeting his double who is "elderly" (Freud was sixty-three when the essay on the uncanny was published). It is as if Freud could not incorporate this experience into the body of the text and the main line of his speculations on the uncanny. But like the uncanny itself, what one desires to remain concealed does indeed surface. Freud found it necessary to relegate it to the margins, repressing his own experience. Although the passage is lengthy I quote it in full:

> Since the uncanny effect of a "double" also belongs to this class, it is interesting to observe what the effect is of suddenly and unexpectedly meeting one's own image. E. Mach has related two such observations in his *Analyse der Empfindungen* (1900, p. 3). On the first occasion he started violently as soon as he realized that the face before him was his own. The second time he formed a very unfavourable opinion about the supposed stranger who got into the omnibus, and thought "What a shabby-looking school-master that is getting in now."—I can supply a similar experience. I was sitting alone in my *wagon-lit* compartment when a more than usually violent jerk of the train swung back the door of the adjoining washing-cabinet, and an elderly gentleman in a dressing-gown and a travelling cap came in. I assumed that he had been about to leave the washing-cabinet which divides the two compartments, and had taken the wrong direction and come into my compartment by mistake. Jumping up with the intention of putting him right, I at once realized to my dismay that *the intruder was nothing but my own reflection in the looking-glass of the open door.* I can still recollect that I thoroughly disliked his appearance. Instead therefore, of being terrified by our doubles, both Mach and I simply failed to recognize them as such. Is it not possible, though, that our dislike of them was a vestigial trace of that older reaction which feels the double to be something uncanny? [p. 156, italics mine]

Freud's mirror image of himself as an old person is that of the trespasser, the interloper in the private domain of narcissism, the material of the unconscious having risen through the open door into the conscious. Freud says that he was not "terrified" by his double but he also says that he was "dismayed" by it, that he "thoroughly disliked his appearance." That appearance represents the future absence of Freud himself, "nothing" (it "was nothing"), his own death. It is the image of the Other, to use de

Beauvoir's terminology, an image Freud would prefer not to recognize. The mirror image is uncanny because it is something familiar that has been repressed—Freud's own old age. Here we might observe that to this day in Germany, Austria, and Yugoslavia, the superstition that one will die within a year if one sees one's double, still flourishes.[11]

By interpreting everything in terms of infantile psychology and the primitive stage of the development of the human species, Freud was unable to even formulate the possibility that there could be a psychoanalytic state of development and conflict associated with old age, with the knowledge (whether conscious or repressed) of the biological condition of having grown old and the prospect of decrepitude and decay. The one psychoanalyst who has dealt in some detail with psychosocial stages of development over the course of a life is of course Erik Erikson. He does propose a final phase of development in old age (the eighth in an interdependent sequence) characterized by the self confronting his own death. For every stage, each of which Erikson believes has its own particular tasks, he postulates a fundamental conflict between two opposing attitudes from which one emerges strengthened or weakened. In the eighth stage, that conflict is between the basic attitudes of integrity or despair in the face of death. For Erikson, integrity implies, among other things: "the ego's accrued assurance of its proclivity for order and meaning—an emotional integration faithful to the image-bearers of the last and ready to take, and eventually to renounce, leadership in the present. It is the acceptance of one's one and only life cycle and of the people who have become significant to it as something that had to be and that, by necessity, permitted of no substitutions."[12] If integrity is the final integration of the ego over time, despair is the absence of such integration; "fate is not accepted as the frame of life, death not as its finite boundary" (p. 140). This is not the appropriate place to discuss in any detail Erikson's theory of the psychosocial development of the person. I should note however that his theory rests on his predilection for a psychology of health—what he considers positive and normal behavior and what he believes serves the evolution and survival of the human species. Not surprisingly, his conception of the final stage of life evokes the image of the wise old man or the wise old woman, and Erikson is thus open to the charge of romanticizing old age. For, as Proust suggests, we must ask if it is always wise for an old person to accept death and renounce leadership, to believe that life has not permitted you to do other than you did. By asking this question, we will also be calling into question Erikson's conception of the ego as strong and adaptive. I will come back to this later at the end of this essay.

Erikson's insight that old age is a distinct phase in a human life is a very important one, however. If we accept this contribution to psychoanalytic theory—or more accurately, psychosocial theory—and if we borrow one of

Freud's basic methods, which is to read in pathological behavior those basic conflicts to which we are all subject but that remain largely hidden, then we can postulate the mirror phase of old age.

At least one study of clinical research lends support to this theory. Robert Butler's seminal essay "The Life Review: An Interpretation of Reminiscence in the Aged" contains a fascinating report of clinical cases of pathological disturbances in elderly people involving mirrors. Although Butler refers to the "apparently common phenomenon of mirror-gazing" only in passing, his remarks are provocative and suggest the fruitfulness of further research along these lines, as the following clinical summary reveals:

> Another patient, eighty-six years old and periodically confused, often stood before the mirror in his hospital room and rhythmically chanted either happily or angrily. He was especially given to angry flareups and crying spells over food, money, and clothes. When angry he would screech obscenities at his mirror image, so savagely beating his fist upon a nearby table that the staff tried to protect him by covering the mirror. But in contrast to the first patient he denied that the image was himself, and when an observer came up beside and said, "See, this is me in the mirror and there you are in the mirror," he smiled and said, "That's you in the mirror all right, but that's not me."[13]

This patient's radical rejection of his mirror image would be the pathological expression of Freud's failure in the *wagon-lit* to recognize his own mirrored double.

In *The Coming of Age* de Beauvoir chronicles countless instances from the cultural record of this obsession of the elderly with their mirror images. The weight of their testimony is impressive and thus I will repeat here some of their words, all of which record their despair at their images. Michelangelo: "I am betrayed: my mirror image is my traitor and my fleeting days" (p. 763). Gide at eighty: "Oh, come now, I really must not meet myself in a mirror—those eyes with bags under them, these hollow cheeks, this lifeless blood. I am hideous and it depresses me terribly" (p. 443). Wagner, on seeing his reflection in a store window: "I do not recognize myself in that grey head: can I possibly be sixty-eight?" (p. 443). Madame de Sévigné at sixty-one: "if at the age of twenty we were given the position of the eldest member of the family and if we were taken to a mirror and shown the face that we should have or do have at sixty, we should be utterly taken aback and it would frighten us" (p. 424). And Madame de Sévigné at sixty-three: "It appears to me that in spite of myself I have been dragged to this inevitable point where old age must be undergone: I see it there before me. I have reached it; and I should at least like so to arrange matters that I do not move on, that I do not travel farther along this path of the infirmities, pains, losses of memory and the disfigurement" (p. 427). For "inevitable"—"I have been dragged to this inevitable point where old age must be undergone"—we might read instead "invisible." This invisible point is also the point of visibility. What was invisible, what she did not recognize—her own old age—is now made painfully visible. This denial of one's image is also dramatized in Louis Aragon's novel *La Mise à mort* in which the hero, incapable of conceiving of himself as old, literally does not see his own reflection in the mirror. (We should not forget that Aragon himself refused to appear in public without a smooth mask that covered his wrinkled face.)

Although de Beauvoir maintains that we respond to our mirror image in accordance with whether our attitude toward old age is basically positive or negative, her evidence points toward the latter: we inevitably despair in so far as old age "is summed up by the words decrepitude, ugliness, and ill-health" (p. 60). She believes that to so respond is natural, that "we must always have some cause for uneasiness before we stand and study the reflection offered us by the looking-glass" (p. 425).

Is the obsession with mirrors a symptom of this stage—old age—or is this stage triggered by one's mirrored image, by the reflections of others, that is by the values held up to us by our society? Although I believe knowledge of old age can come to us from our infirmities (our own bodies can speak to us of old age), I would want to argue that old age is in great part constructed by any given society as a social category, as is, for example, adolescence. The mirror our society holds up to the elderly reveals the image of death. This is why Freud did not at first recognize himself in that image of an elderly gentleman and why that image aroused the "dread and creeping horror" he associates with the uncanny, for the Other was indeed the self and uncannily prefigured the coming years of suffering which Freud was destined to live out.

Psychoanalysis insists of course on the alienating effects of identification with an image. This insistence is perhaps strongest in the work of Jacques Lacan which can be useful to us here. By now in fact it will have become clear to many readers that we can hypothesize the mirror stage of old age as the inverse of the infant mirror stage proposed by Lacan.[14] Observing that an infant from six to eighteen months is fascinated by his mirror image, Lacan theorizes that the infant perceives the image of his body as a harmonious whole and ideal unity while simultaneously experiencing his body as uncoordinated. It is this discrepancy between the visual image of unity and the lived experience of fragmentation that gives rise to the ego and to the subject forever split, to joyful anticipation of wholeness in the future as well as to alienation. The mirror stage ushers the subject into the domain of the imaginary, a domain prior to language and largely dominated by images.

Lacan has stressed elsewhere that in the "matter of the visible, everything is a trap."[15] In old age we might say that all mirrors are potentially threatening. As in the mirror stage of infancy, in the mirror stage of old age the subject identifies with an image and in so doing is transformed. If in the case of the former the infant enters the imaginary, in the latter the subject enters the social realm reserved for senior citizens in the Western world. But the point is that the subject resists this identification rather than embraces it because what is whole is felt to reside *within* the subject and the image in the mirror is understood as uncannily prefiguring the disintegration and nursling dependence of advanced age. If according to Lacan the infant holds his mirror image in an amorous gaze, the elderly person wishes to reject it—and thereby to reject old age for himself. If the mirror image in infancy is a lure in the Lacanian sense, we might say that in old age we desire our mirror image to function as does *trompe l'oeil*, to reveal itself not as what it so shockingly presents to us as ourselves. As Freud pointed out long ago, "the ego is first and foremost a bodily ego . . . the projection of a surface."[16] The I or ego which is developed in the mirror stage of infancy is structured precisely to resist the anxiety of bodily fragmentation. In old age, with one's position reversed as it were before the mirror, the ego finds it more difficult to maintain its defenses. The ambivalence one has felt all one's life before mirrors—the constant checking and comparing—is exacerbated to an almost intolerable point. Like one of Robert Butler's elderly patients, one may turn the face of the mirror to the wall. Or like Marcel at the reception at the Guermantes, one may resist any identification with the images of one's social counterparts. This too is a reversal of the trajectory of development in infancy. After the infant identifies with its mirror image (its ego image, if you will), Lacan notes that there is a "deflection of the specular *I* into the social *I*"[17]: the child identifies—literally at first—with the images of others. In the mirror stage of old age, the narcissistic impulse directs itself *against* the mirror image as it is embodied literally and figuratively in the faces and bodies— the images—of the old people who surround us. If then the mirror stage of infancy initiates the imaginary, the mirror stage of old age may precipitate the loss of the imaginary, with the result that identification becomes a real and perhaps impossible problem that can only be "solved" on a personal level as it is in the fictional world of *The Past Recaptured*, by blindness, by repression.

As Lacan conceives it, the mirror stage of infancy is primarily a biological and psychological phenomenon (interestingly enough, he refers to experimentation with other species—the pigeon, the migratory locust— which suggests that development is contingent upon the presence of an image of one's own species). Basically the mirror stage is prior to socialization and prior to language, although the role of the mother is crucial and we can only understand the phenomenon of the mirror stage retrospectively through language; the mirror stage enacts the formation (Lacan uses the vivid term "precipitation") of the "I" before "it is objectified in the dialectic of identification with the other, and before language restores to it . . . its function as subject" (p. 2). In contrast, the mirror stage of old age is more obviously rooted in the social and economic theater of a given historical moment (I understand of course that *any* moment is historical, even the moment of the mirror stage of the infant). We might further speculate that if the mirror stage of infancy is distinguished by the perception of binary opposition, the mirror stage of old age is more problematic. First, it is inherently triangular, involving the gaze of the Other as well as two images of oneself. Secondly, one understands—consciously or unconsciously—that there is a relationship between the two terms—the two images of the self—such that one is incorporated within the other. It is not so much a matter of either-or as it is a matter of both-and. This was clearly dramatized in the last pages of *The Past Recaptured.*

What may be resolved if only temporarily on the personal level, however, cannot be so resolved in the social world. The mirror stage of old age is played out in a social arena, and one's personal responses have important social consequences. Whereas it might very well be healthy on the personal level to reject one's image as old, we must also ask what the social consequences are of perceiving the elderly as alien to ourselves. If our vision is fundamentally narcissistic, our gaze at others functions to protect ourselves. We deny full humanity to an aged person so as to preserve our own illusion of immortality. As Christopher Lasch points out in *The Culture of Narcissism*, our dread of old age has its origins not in a cult of youth but in a cult of the self.[18] It is important to stress here the relationship between narcissism and aggression. When one's narcissism is wounded, the result is aggression. The observations of the psychoanalyst Gregory Rochlin, who has written on aggression as well as the psychology of loss in old age, are particularly useful in this context: "No experience brings out the effect in self-esteem more immediately than when it is associated with the body. The integrity of one's shape and bodily function holds the deepest and perhaps longest-standing investment in respect to self-esteem."[19] But hostility borne toward others is also feared from them through projection, and aggression can complete its return in the form of self-destruction.

Perhaps most significant, our gaze allows one to reject the elderly as a class more easily—as an alien species or, as in *The Past Recaptured*, as unreal, a mere illusion, a grotesque and transitory spectacle, a piece of theater that will soon be over, covered by the fall of the curtain. To preserve psychological health on a personal level requires one to regard the decrepit and infirm elderly as an inferior class and thus reinforce and perpetuate oppression of the elderly on the level of society. (I am here conflating old age and decrepitude which, although they are by no means identical each to the other are for the most part equated in our cultural imagination.) For like sexism and racism, ageism is prejudice rooted in physical difference as well as in discrepancies in social power. As we know, throughout Western history the elderly have been rejected as a class which consumes more than it produces. And worse, the elderly have been forgotten and hidden from sight in nursing homes and hospitals by the narcissistic younger social body, by those in power. Ernest Becker's argument in *The Denial of Death* lends support to this view. He maintains that a culture is built primarily on the repression not of sexuality as Freud believes, but on the repression of death, whose symbol is the human body, the "curse of fate."[20] Old age in our culture may very well be characterized by a double bind, by personal and social conflict as intense as the oedipal conflict that arises in childhood. This helps us to understand Simone de Beauvoir's disillusioning statement in *The Coming of Age:* "whatever the context may be, the biological facts remain. For every individual age brings with it a dreaded decline. It is in complete conflict with the manly or womanly ideal cherished by the young and fully-grown. The immediate, natural attitude is to reject it, in so far as it is summed up by the words decrepitude, ugliness, and ill-health. Old age in others also causes an instant repulsion. This primitive reaction remains live even when custom represses it; and in this we see the origin of a conflict that we shall find exemplified again and again" (p. 60). Old age may very well be constructed as a social category but it has a biology as well which she believes the young cannot help but reject. Her words echo those of Nietzsche with which I opened this paper: "every table of values, every 'thou shalt' known to history, requires first a physiological investigation and interpretation." In old age, then, we may encounter yet again another form of the battle between civilization and its discontents.

Notes

1. Nietzsche, "On the Genealogy of Morals," in *Basic Writings of Nietzsche*, trans. and ed. Walter Kaufmann (New York: Modern Library, 1968), p. 491.

2. Marcel Proust, *The Past Recaptured*, trans. Frederick A. Blossom (New York: Modern Library, 1959), p. 387.

3. Honoré de Balzac, "The Girl with the Golden Eyes," *The Works of Honoré de Balzac: The Thirteen, Father Goriot and Other Stories* (Philadelphia: Avil Publishing Company, 1901).

4. Anthony Wilden, trans., *The Language of the Self: The Function of Language in Psychoanalysis*, by Jacques Lacan (Baltimore: Johns Hopkins, 1968), p. 166.

5. Diana Festa-McCormick refers us to Proust's *Chroniques* (Paris: Gallimard,

1927), pp. 216–17, in her "Proust's Asthma: A Malady Begets a Melody," in *Medicine and Literature*, ed. Eric Rhodes Peschel (New York: Neale Watson Academic Publications, 1980).

6. Anne Waldman, "Mirror Meditation," *Journals & Dreams* (New York: Stonehill, 1976), p. 141.

7. See Terrance Brophy Kearns, "Prisoner to the Palsy: A Study of Old Age in Shakespeare's History Plays," Diss. Indiana Univ. 1978.

8. Marcel Proust, *The Guermantes Way*, trans. C. K. Scott Moncrieff (New York: Modern Library, 1952), p. 408.

9. Simone de Beauvoir, *The Coming of Age*, trans. Patrick O'Brian (New York: Warner Paperback Library, 1973), p. 420.

10. Sigmund Freud, "The Uncanny," trans. Alix Strachey, in *On Creativity and the Unconscious: Papers on the Psychology of Art, Literature, Religion* (New York: Harper Torchbooks, 1958), p. 122, p. 123.

11. Otto Rank, *The Double* (1925), trans. Harry Tucker, Jr. (Chapel Hill: Univ. of North Carolina Press, 1971), p. 50.

12. Erik Erikson, *Insight and Responsibility* (New York: Norton, 1964), p. 139.

13. Robert N. Butler, "The Life Review: An Interpretation of Reminiscence in the Aged" (1963), in *Middle Age and Aging*, ed. Bernice L. Neugarten (Chicago: Univ. of Chicago Press, 1968), p. 489.

14. Jacques Lacan, "The Mirror Stage as Formative of the Function of the I" (1949), in *Ecrits*, trans. Alan Sheridan (New York: W. W. Norton, 1979), pp. 1–7.

15. Jacques Lacan, "The Line and Light, in his *The Four Fundamental Concepts of Psycho-Analysis*, ed. Jacques-Alain Miller, trans. Alan Sheridan (New York: W. W. Norton, 1978), p. 93.

16. Sigmund Freud, *The Ego and the Id* (1923), trans. Joan Riviere, rev. and ed. James Strachey (New York: W. W. Norton, 1962), p. 16.

17. Lacan, "The Mirror Stage," p. 5.

18. Christopher Lasch, *The Culture of Narcissism* (New York: W. W. Norton, 1978).

19. Gregory Rochlin, *Man's Aggression: The Defense of the Self* (Boston: Gambit, 1973), p. 243. I also refer the reader to Rochlin's excellent *Grief and Discontents: The Forces of Change* (Boston: Little, Brown, 1965).

20. Ernest Becker, *The Denial of Death* (New York: Free Press, 1975), p. 96.

THE PHENOMENON OF AGING IN OSCAR WILDE'S *PICTURE OF DORIAN GRAY:*
A Lacanian View

✳✳✳

Ellie Ragland-Sullivan

OSCAR WILDE'S ONLY NOVEL, *The Picture of Dorian Gray* (1891), is so rich in what has been termed "pathogenic" material that it has evoked a large amount of psychoanalytic commentary. I shall argue that the appeal of the novel does not inhere in its pathology, but in its dramatization of the dynamic structure of a superego. In the novel superego effects are metaphorized by extreme sentiments regarding physical beauty and normative aging, as well as by graphic caricatures which mix physical ideals with affective torments. Such an interpretation obviously contradicts Wilde's own contention that art and life were separate domains.

Wilde introduces the theme of art versus life at the start of the novel. Dorian Gray, a handsome young aristocrat, is having his portrait painted by Basil Hallward. At the last sitting he meets Lord Henry Wotton, who sets forth several of the principal themes developed in the novel. "Nothing can cure the soul but the senses," Lord Henry tells the innocent, young Dorian. A bit later Lord Henry admires Dorian's beauty, telling him that "beauty . . . is higher, indeed, than Genius as it needs no explanation. It cannot be questioned." To this Dorian responds with a *cri de coeur:* "I would give my soul if the picture would age, and I stay young. Youth is the only thing worth having." Later Basil confesses that in the portrait he has revealed "the secret of my own soul," thereby defining art as a union of soul and body.[1] Thus although Wilde proclaims *Dorian Gray* a novel about the transcendence of art over life, its fictional message is that life spills over into art.

That art and life are not separate domains will constitute one of the principal themes of my essay. "The fictional is not to be understood as the opposite of the real," Peter McCormick has argued. "Literary truths are not what *would* be true in the real world, but what in fact *may* be true in the real world."² We can apply his characterization of the interface between life and art to *Dorian Gray*. But while McCormick distinguishes the real from the fictional, I will go further, viewing the fictional as one category of what the French psychoanalyst Jacques Lacan calls the Real.

As we know, Dorian gets his wish. It is not to the "magic" of wish-fulfillment that the novel owes its enigmatic power, however, but to the strange transformation of the picture. Dorian's portrait does not simply age, it changes into a picture of a grotesque, hideous, gnarled old man with blood stains on his hands and feet. The picture is said to register the passage of time through a depiction of Dorian's soul: "It held the secret of his life, and told his story. It had taught him to love his own beauty. Would it teach him to loathe his own soul?" (p. 184). Despite such obvious moral tones, Wilde wrote in the preface to the novel that there is no such thing as a moral or an immoral book. Years later Wilde admitted in a letter that there was a moral to *Dorian Gray:* "All excess brings its own punishment."³ Asked if this were an artistic error in the novel, Wilde replied: "I fear it is. It is the only error in the book."⁴

Ironically, this "error" gives the book its power, making it a classic. For the torture of sin and guilt—the more than art in art—makes it a story about the dynamic interplay of Desire and Law in their capacities for shaping and tormenting the human psyche. By looking to the teachings of Jacques Lacan (1901–1981), I shall claim support for the idea that literary art has universal resonance only insofar as it repeats something already "known" by the artist or reader, something "known" at the level of the Real and the "true" of human life. From this perspective, literary art would be a privileged domain in which unconscious (past) knowledge imposes itself on conscious life within the realm of present time through two powerfully evocative modes: the affective resonance of language and its capacity to call forth visual imagery. But were literature only an imagistic mirror, it would be, as Wilde says of all art in his preface to *Dorian Gray*, "quite useless."⁵ More than a static system of signs or a set of encoded messages, literary art uses the materiality of language to permit the *moi* (in Lacanian terms, the *moi* is the fictional voice standing between a social *porte-parole*—the *je*—and the alien Desire of the Other) to reconstitute itself identificatorily (Imaginarily) by means of the text. Unconscious representations would provide each person with the specific references constituting a subjective text of their own. Such text is the means by which humans perceive at all.

I

Although Lacanian principles may illuminate first causes underlying some of the "truths" portrayed by Wilde in *The Picture of Dorian Gray*, Lacan did not invent these truths any more than did Wilde. Wilde's fiction reverberates with the "knowledge" *(connaissance)* gleaned from a dissection of the Real *(savoir)* of the human psyche (soul). In the novel Dorian seeks one kind of knowledge: the pleasure of the senses. His sexual and drug experiments become the underside of a commendable deployment of the senses in his role as art connoisseur. By the novel's end he has attained the kind of knowledge he sought and learns that he cannot escape the deeds of his past, that illicit sensual experiences do not lead to immortality, but to death. As Bruce B. Clark comments: "Dorian discovered that, although things may seem relative, there are absolutes in the world of ethics and the spirit" (p. 243).

Unlike Clark, I would not place the source of such knowledge within the realm of traditional religion. Such absolutes are, rather, the limits on human behavior which derive from unconscious requisites in their inter-play with social conventions. From a Lacanian perspective, one can break "knowledge" down into various kinds, and place it on different planes. At the conscious level knowledge is imparted by codes and social conventions, and by theories or systems of thought. "Truth," on the other hand, refers to unconscious knowledge: a *savoir* which directs human Desire and inten-tionality from an invisible source. In conscious life such knowledge is expressed indirectly within language. Genre, affect, rhetorical device, and innuendo all imply a source of meaning *(sens)* beyond meaning *(significa-tion)*. Intentionality becomes a matter of positioning oneself in reference to public authority, or within any context where knowledge becomes linked to narcissism and power. Desire points to the fact that human beings are questing (motivated) creatures who pursue multiple substitutes for the lack which is, in fact, inherent within psychic structure itself. In contrast to factual information or various theories, unconscious knowledge has the effect on conscious life of being a *connaissance* (recognition) of something else. It is, thus, unquantifiable.

How can a Lacanian picture of unconscious knowledge tell us anything about the magic of immortality and the ugliness of aging in Wilde's novel? In Clark's opinion, "Wilde's horror of growing old probably accounts for the theme of the magic preservation of youth in *Dorian Gray*. As he approached forty, he accelerated his activity to a frenzy in order to enjoy life before it was too late" (p. 229). This answer demands a further ques-tion: why did Wilde seek to destroy his own life and his family's reputation at the pinnacle of fame and success? I believe *Dorian Gray* dramatizes Wilde's own conflicts in bits and pieces. The novel thus tells the personal "truth" of one man's *unconscious* guilt. Five years after he had written the preface to *Dorian Gray*, Wilde expressed his guilt consciously. Learning of his mother's death while he was in prison in 1896, Wilde confessed in a letter, "I feel that I have brought such unhappiness on [my wife Constance] and such ruin on my children that I have no right to go against her wishes in anything." Later he wrote, "[My mother's] death was so terrible to me that I . . . have no words in which to express my anguish and my shame. . . . She and my father bequeathed me a name they had made noble and honoured. . . . I had disgraced that name eternally. I had made it a low byword among low people. I had dragged it through the very mire."[6] While the particular shame of which Wilde speaks—his imprisonment for homosexuality, his experimentation with drugs—would perhaps not be shocking to us today, from a universal perspective Wilde's graphic portrayal of a growing horror finds a resonance in a reader's recognition of having "known" both guilt and anxiety, however unconscious that recognition may remain.

Dorian's wish to stop time removes us from the realm of linear narrative and places us squarely in front of Lacan's theory of the gaze: that which deceives the eye by stopping time.[7] While the eye is an organ which ages, and sees others aging as well, the gaze is separable from the eye. The gaze is first perceived by a newborn baby, and introjected as if it were one more object among others. The gaze is, therefore, an object *a*. In Lacanian terms this means that it has the property of being separable, and is linked to lack. Beyond the four primordial *objects* of Desire—the breast, the gaze, the voice, excrement—Lacan named the four supports which later announce themselves as the cause of Desire: the gaze, the voice, the void, and the Phallus.[8] The gaze exists even prior to its own symbolization as a *perceptum*, then, in an irrecuperable network of perceptual equipment, knowable only by its effects. As one element that makes Desire functional—both as a specific symbol and as essential to the dynamics of recognition—the gaze interacts with the unconscious structures of Desire and Law, thus subjectivizing the Real order of seeing (eye).

Lacan has theorized that at the scopic level, we are no longer at the level of the demand [for love], but of desire, of the desire [shown] to the Other:

> It is even at the level of the vocatory drive [*la pulsion invocante*], which is the closest to the experience of the unconscious. In a general sense, relationship of the gaze to what one wants to see is a relationship of lure. The subject presents himself as other than he is, and what one gives him to see is not what he wants to see. It is in this way that the eye can function as object *a*, that is to say at the level of lack (*Sém.* XI, p. 96).

In other words, the eye and the gaze are joined in a function of lure (*méconnaissance*). What we see is seen subjectively, rendered such by the gaze that Lacan called "that underside of consciousness" (*Sém.* XI, p. 79). Put another way, both the Imaginary and Symbolic orders are enmeshed in a deception that blocks out the "truth"—the knowledge—of the unconscious. The system of language and a person's sense of identity work in tandem to distance humans from the impersonal truths and desires recorded in the unconscious. Let me suggest that *The Picture of Dorian Gray* is a metaphorical rendering of the power of the gaze in its relationship to the superego. The picture's gaze distorts time, making it an effect of unconscious "truth" rather than a fact of aging. One manifestation of such truth in the novel lies in Dorian's dying an untimely death. Even though the picture appears aged, he in fact was only thirty-eight years old. The sense of being old comes, then, from a dual linking of his own ideal image of "self" to the gaze of the other/Other (a narcissistic function). It comes, as well, from the link between narcissistic dreams and the sense that thwarted desires are somehow connected to deception of or by a Father (a superego function). "If beyond appearance, there is no thing in itself *(chose en soi)*," Lacan said, "there is the gaze" *(Sém.* XI, p. 95).

Beyond the icon lies what Lacan called the Name-of-the-Father. These form a pact beyond any image *(Sém.* XI, p. 103). Put another way, the superego gives shape and meaning to any drama of identification. One might say, then, that both Dorian and the portrait of him are masks which serve to hide what lies beyond them: the gaze of the other/Other *(Sém.* XI, p. 99). Here it is useful to recall that Freud, in one well-known formulation, defined guilt as the tension between the ideal ego and the superego.[9] The murders of Basil and of his own portrait give tacit witness to the unbearable tension Dorian feels. The novel's climax is attributable, then, to Dorian's final realization that it was impossible to sustain his own narcissistic ideal image in light of the harsh judgments meted out by the social order. The picture becomes the ultimate proof that outer voices find an inner resonance within Dorian himself.

The Picture of Dorian Gray is about aging in reverse, about eternal youth. And it is revealed to be a damning state. Dorian's sad life is not about sensual pleasure, but about emotional sterility. When the body itself becomes the object of Desire—as well as its source—a certain normative sexual evolution is attenuated. To live life by substituting the body for psychic lack requires that aging cease. The sexual pleasure that normally accompanies aging is fleshed out by relationships of intimacy, if not concerns of maternity and paternity. Dorian Gray, much like Tirso de Molina's Don Juan, is driven to flit from body to body. Sexuality is split off from bonding. Desire is separated from Law. And Dorian, like Don Juan before him, must finally give his body over to the ultimate Master.

Lacan has spoken about the process of identification by which a person assumes the Other's Desire in an Imaginary tripod where being the Phallus and having the Phallus take on meaning only in the Symbolic order (or in terms of the law of the signifier). In other words, identity only *means* in reference to the Name-of-the-Father. When a question of lack itself is in play, "being" the Phallus and "having" it can become physically confused as mutually exclusive postures.[10] A confusion between identity (secondary narcissim) and body image (primary narcissim) does indeed reify Lacanian Desire at the level of lack during the time when normative aging renders the body a less desirable object. That is, if the body itself is taken as the measure of Desire, then the body becomes the Phallus (the desired object in the Other). Normative options are excluded. A man usually identifies himself as the Phallus (desirable) because he possesses the male sex organ. A woman generally sees herself (at the level of the gaze) as desirable because she is allied to some phallic principle (a lover or husband) or represents phallic authority herself. But when Desire gets stuck on body beauty, and confused with sexual desirability as the measure of worth, then the ideal ego can no longer value itself once some zenith of physical perfection is passed.

Thus the grotesque portrait of Dorian Gray is a caricatured picture of old age, seen from the slant of a skewed narcissism. The picture Wilde paints of Dorian's early years shows him as identifying with feminine desire against the patriarchal order (as we will see later, this finds a parallel in Wilde's life). Dorian was the child of a worthless father—a man rejected by the mother's family—and an extraordinarily beautiful mother. When his mother left her aristocratic home to marry a penniless soldier, her father decided to end the marriage, hiring an adventurer to insult his son-in-law, who in turn engaged in a duel which killed him within a few months of the marriage. Although the daughter returned home, she never spoke to her father again and died within the year, leaving only a son who bore her exquisite beauty. Dorian grew up longing for the mother with whom he identified, and hating his aloof grandfather.

Without any "father" he can fully trust, Dorian seems an emotional orphan. Basil is too smitten by him to counsel him, and Lord Henry's advice leads him astray. Body narcissism becomes a compensation for a psychic lack: a Father's name to which he can happily entrust his identity. Vacillating between a prayer that his demise will be stopped and a rebellious curse to anyone who dare try, Dorian—despite Wilde's disclaimers—is *not* driven by a pleasure quest. Beyond the pleasure principle Lacan found only repetition. More than mere neurotic compulsion, repetition is, according to Lacan, the principle of identity. He equated repetition with *moi* fixations, and *moi* fixations with the death drive. And in *The Picture of Dorian Gray*, death symbolizes punishment for not bowing to social law (or convention), as well as the necessity for joining Desire to Law in some inner psychic balance.

One of the compelling themes in the novel is Dorian's constant dream of redemption. When Basil finally sees the hideous monster that has replaced the beautiful portrait he had painted, Dorian kills him, not only to protect his secret, but also to maintain his illusion of hope. In a discussion of the intersubjective relation, Lacan theorizes that what counts in the dialectic of the gaze "is not that the other see where I am, it is that he see where I am going, that is to say, that he see very exactly, that he see where I am not. In any analysis of the intersubjective relation, the essential thing is not what is there, what is seen. What structures it is what is not there."[11] Dorian does not murder Basil just because his soul has been "seen." Insofar as Dorian's deeds are discussed by one and all, near and far, the picture itself is not needed to disclose his character. Instead, Basil's death testifies to Dorian's growing fear that the future is closing in on him. To allow Basil to live would attenuate the dream that the picture will revert to its pristine state, that Dorian's nonsexual love of a pretty country girl will save him. Indeed Dorian never accepts the truth that Wilde dramatized: a soul cannot escape its own destiny. When Dorian stabs the portrait instead of himself, he still dreams that such an act will free him.

At the novel's end Dorian says, "it was an unjust mirror, this mirror of his soul. . . Was he always to be burdened by his past? Its [the picture's] mere memory had marred many moments of joy. It had been like conscience to him. Yes, it had been conscience. He would destroy it" (pp. 252–53). Wilde describes what psychoanalysts know: that the guilt and anxiety caused by superego (conscience) dicta can destroy a life leading at the limit to suicide. Dorian's conclusion was that youth had destroyed him. "What was youth at best? A green, an unripe time, a time of shallow moods and sickly thoughts. Why had he worn its livery? Youth had spoiled him" (p. 252). But as we know, youthful sexual adventures (with women) would be forgiven any young English aristocrat.

Thus *The Picture of Dorian Gray* portrays the human tragedy of "seeing" one's own truth—at the level of the gaze—(*l'instant terminal de voir*) without really understanding what has been "seen." Lacan used the expression, *l'instant terminal de voir*, to describe the primordial nature of artistic painting, the act of deposing the bits and pieces of one's own imagistic structuration on a piece of canvas. Even though Dorian gradually sees himself from the perspective of others, he feels a victim of the portrait's gaze. Never is he a beneficiary of its "truth." The picture symbolizes the hidden, the repressed. First hidden behind a screen in his bedroom and then in the half light of the attic where he had been exiled to play in an unhappy childhood, the picture is never equatable with "insight" (*l'instant de voir*). That Dorian places the picture in the attic where his grandfather had forced him to play is significant. The attic becomes a kind of metaphor for the Lacanian unconscious. Full of remnants and traces of Dorian's childhood, it is not easily accessible. Not only is it physically distant within the house, it is also dusky, dusty, and eerie just as the Lacanian unconscious, with its archaic accounts of the past, is opaque. Only occasionally does it surface into view—into the light—and just as quickly it shuts back on itself. Dorian is haunted by the knowledge that his picture bears secrets he would rather deny; Dorian nonetheless continually creeps to the attic to look at the picture, thus taking in "truth" in spurts. But these moments of illumination are just as quickly shut out, shut up in the dark of the attic.

Although Dorian cannot analyze the "truth" the portrait speaks, he does realize that it metaphorizes his own anxiety (according to Lacan, the role of anxiety in any person's life trajectory is that *it* does not deceive[12]). But while Wilde's story borders on insight, it never enters the realm of light which characterizes Lacan's *le temps pour comprendre*. That is, the moment in clinical analysis when a person begins to piece together the meanings of various gaps in his own life story. In the time of such understanding, the future is seen to flow necessarily from past history.[13]

Daniel Schneider has dicussed what Freud named in *Beyond the Pleasure Principle* as "the protective barrier defending the vital processes."[14] Schneider calls this barrier the "paraconscious monitor," which I would risk equating with the Lacanian *moi*, the source of narcissistic cohesion which blocks unconscious messages. Although psychic freedom—the ability to control one's own Desire—can only occur when the *moi* has come to "see" the sources of its own structuration, the *moi*, nonetheless, protects the subject from the impersonality of unconscious truths. Schneider concluded that an "injury neurosis" such as the abrupt forcing of insight can impair vitality and herald death; such a breakdown in vitality was described by Freud as "an inner overplus of pain."[15] Freud listed anxiety and then obsessive compulsive repetition as protective shields against injury neuroris.

Both anxiety and compulsive rituals fail to protect Dorian from his efforts to separate soul from body. As he finally stabs his picture in the heart, he falls dead, becoming the monster in the picture. Reverting to its original state, the picture becomes art: that which re-presents representations. The moral to the novel, then, is that one cannot cut the past off from the present. Indeed, if Lacan is correct, the past has always already structured the probable shape of the future. Within a Lacanian purview, freedom comes in degrees. It lies in gaining psychic distance from *moi* fictions, in taking responsibility for one's Desires, in squaring Desire with pertinent structures of Law. Lacan has described such a process as a de-being of being. Indeed the Greek word "psychoanalysis" means melting, dissolution, and death.[16]

II

In *The Picture of Dorian Gray* death and age are put in suspension until the final reckoning when art, in fact, uncannily prefigures Wilde's own destiny. Dorian's "moral" disobedience could be taken as a metaphor for Wilde's own disobedience. By pursuing his homosexual loves at the cost of the well-being of his wife and children, Wilde disobeyed implicit social conventions, as well as breaking a law against sodomy instituted in 1885. Four years after the publication of the novel Wilde was put on trial for his homosexuality, and accused of corrupting a circle of young men. Six years after this time, and three years after his release from prison, Wilde died an untimely death at age forty-six (by "untimely" I mean that his death was induced by "self" destruction and grief, instead of by normal aging). We are therefore entitled to conclude that Dorian Gray embodied Wilde's own fixation on what Lacan has called the death signifier.

Many critics have written about Wilde's obsession with death in *Dorian Gray*, but none have suggested that Wilde's destructiveness lay, at least partly, in his inability to bend to the requisites of the Symbolic order. In Lacanian terms, the Symbolic order of language and social conventions is inherently neutral and a-thematic. But through the course of History, any social order evolves certain legal codes and Imaginary preferences, punishing (castrating) those who flout such conventions and ideals. Wilde's inability to conform would be attributable, within a Lacanian purview, to the structure of his own unconscious knowledge, put in place long before adult life.

Indeed, it is not surprising to note that Wilde's art and his life were both characterized by his subversion of the Symbolic order. In the artistic domain such "subversion" is called irony and paradox, and it won him the fame and money accorded a great writer. But in his private life, such subversion was only tolerable when kept discreet. When the Marquess of Queensberry accused Wilde of sodomy, Wilde insisted, against advice, on prosecuting the Marquess for criminal libel.[17] After his release from prison Wilde, seeking refuge in a Catholic retreat, was refused this courtesy. He was also shunned by friends, wife, and children. Yet despite his own guilty torments, one senses that Wilde could never comprehend how such dire consequences could follow from his pursuit of sensual pleasures and his practice of a kind of love shared by great artists of the past. In Lacanian terms one might say that he never understood that his real crime was to have elevated Desire above Law. (Lacan's Name-of-the-Father is that which demands submission to the laws of a given social order, however inhumane and arbitrary they might be.)

Here we will do well to recall that frustrated desires are linked to deception of or by a Father. Wilde's first deception by a father must have been painful, for it was *his* father. From the moment of his birth, Wilde was subjected to his father's rejection of him. His father (and his mother), wishing that he had been born a girl, treated him as if he indeed were a girl until his sister was born three years later. We see that the Lacanian identity quest—the who am I in my parent's discourse?—was problematic from the start of life. Wilde's early sense of "self" was confused between masculine and feminine images, while the pain of social disapprobation descended upon him through, as it were, the sins of the father during his adolescent years.

Wilde's father, Sir William Wilde, was a successful eye and ear surgeon in Dublin. Not only did he found a hospital and write a text on aural surgery, he also held the post of Surgeon Oculist in Ordinary to Queen Victoria and was knighted for his work on the medical statistics of the Irish census. He was also known as a compulsive womanizer. When Mary Travers accused Sir William of having chloroformed her in order to rape her, Lady Wilde wrote the girl's father, detailing the daughter's complicity. As a result Miss Travers sued the Wildes for libel, the scandal becoming the sensation of the 1860s in Dublin. Miss Travers won (minimally), but Sir William never recovered his reputation. When he died many years later, his prodigal spending had left his family almost destitute.

Given his own early feminization, in tandem with the effects of his own father's degradation, Wilde's Desire evolved in the identificatory pattern labeled as homosexual. He identified strongly with his sister and indeed, he never really recovered from her death, which occurred when he was ten years old. A childhood history such as Wilde's would have been sufficient to place his Desire on a feminine slope (perhaps Wilde would have never given rein to his homosexuality if his second child had not been a son, thus repeating the disappointment he had brought his parents). Many psycho-analytic critics have regarded Wilde's homosexuality as the fuel behind the narcissism portrayed in *Dorian Gray*. Homosexuals desire youth above all, they say, because they are pathologically narcissistic. They can only love an ageless beauty. But such a theory does not acknowledge that primary narcissism (body narcissism) is taught as the basis of femininity to hetero-sexual women who presumably love others not cast in their own mold. Nor does it problematize narcissism as Lacan has done by making it the cornerstone of all identity. Primary (corporeal) and secondary narcissism are interwoven, although secondary narcissism is characterized by the projecting of one's ideal image in relations with others (ego ideals). Perhaps we can extrapolate from Lacan the theory that one source of human tragedy lies in the injustice that shapes every person's identity *(moi)* from mirror-stage or Oedipal experiences. Early in life, these effects situate persons within a social masquerade where, as male or female, they are required to adhere to certain roles and fictions. The myths and desires that go together to fabricate a human subject have already begun to define that person's destiny even before his or her birth.

In Lacan's view, the Real object of the homosexual's desire is not simply the pleasure of male beauty or sexuality (a displacement), but the desire to defy the Desire of the fathers.[18] Such subversive Desire, thus, takes knowledge of the unconscious into account, while paradoxically denying the existence of the unconscious. Beyond the prohibitions attributed to the fathers lies the dream of eternal *jouissance*. Such an illusion of mirror-stage bliss—or immortality—requires that Castration (psychic separation from the mother) be denied, and submission to the father rejected. But such a psychic ploy is impossible. Constant psychic perfection is unattainable. We remember Basil's utopian definition of art as "a union of soul and body." When Dorian ceases to pose for him, Basil's art loses soul. Lord Henry—the champion of verbal art—by breaking up Basil's mirror-stage dream, makes himself an agent of Castration. Yet, he is no more a representative of social norms than is Basil. By introducing Dorian to a lawless universe—one without morals—he also places himself on the side of ejecting ordinary social limits.

Since the normative is the kernel of social structure—that around which power and recognition revolves—a person "out of step" with norms is doomed to suffer. Wilde later drew a parallel between the characters in this novel and himself: "Basil Hallward is what I think I am, Lord Henry what the world thinks me, Dorian what I would like to be."[19] Basil and Dorian could well represent splits in Wilde's own ideal ego. At the level of primary narcissism, he would like to be ever young and beautiful (Dorian). At a secondary narcissistic stage, he would be morally pure and responsible, and divinely inspired (Basil). What the world sees—the *je* as social representative of the subject—is the Master of verbal wit and pithy paradox. Given the importance of public approval for psychic well-being, in opposition to the already conflictive nature of the splits within himself, Wilde could not hope for any oedipal resolution to bring *moi* ideals, *je* façades, or unconscious Desire into harmony with each other, and with social dicta.

The mirrors in Dorian Gray exist merely to amplify a lie: to reflect Dorian's façade. In the conclusion Dorian looks at himself in the mirror Lord Henry had given him: "He loathed his own beauty, and, flinging the mirror on the floor, crushed it into silver splinters beneath his heel" (p. 252). In this novel, then, fascination does not point to mirror doubles, nor to a "true" versus "false" self. The picture is not a symmetrical mirror, but an allegorical depiction of an ethical state. Similarly, Dorian's portrait metaphorizes Wilde's own self-hatred—he could not forgive himself for his homosexuality—as reflected in the eyes of the fathers he paradoxically disdained. The gaze of the Other as depicted in this novel is not the gaze at the moment of its introjection as a part object, a moment prior even to its own representability. Instead, the gaze is attached to the eye of the others in their Imaginary power to catalyze the voice of the superego. The gaze cast by Dorian's loathsome picture represents Phallic disapproval, that which exists in relation to one's ideal ego.[20] If Wilde sought to deny

Castration, then it would make sense that he would deify the cessation of aging. For Castration is on the side of Thanatos, bringing with it intimations of mortality. This helps us understand the relationship between Dorian's youth and beauty, and the aging portrait of the evil Dorian in the attic. According to Lacan, the power of beauty lies in its being an antithesis to death, the principle signifier around which all life is organized.[21] In consequence moral virtues are attributed to beauty—in itself neutral—because it suggests life, hope, love (Eros). "But you, Dorian, with your pure, bright, innocent face, and your marvelous untroubled youth—I can't believe anything against you," says Basil, in face of contradictory evidence (p. 216). Beauty serves not only as a mask screening out death, but as a denial of Castration.

In *The Picture of Dorian Gray*, Wilde sought to deny Castration. But his own unconscious guilt was so strong that creating an idyllic eternity of Peter Pans not only would not suffice. As the novel's conclusion tells us, it was also impossible. Wilde's own life was at stake. The father's name was too much with him. In Lacanian terms, acute anxiety induced by unconscious guilt can affect the *moi* so as to unravel the *moi* unity which gives the illusion of a "self" cohesion. When guilt and thwarted dreams oppress the *moi* to the point that it can no longer "see" in itself the source of good, can no longer offer itself to the world as a symbol of worthy exchange, then affective "death" is but a short step from the emptiness which takes over, literally stopping life. After his three years of exile, poverty, and alcohol, disappointment finally sapped Wilde's vitality.

As autobiography, then, I view *Dorian Gray* as a narrative sliding toward the author's own unconscious truth. The truth at issue here is recorded by Wilde's metaphoric transformation of a sense of guilt into an externalized image of growing old which represents his inner sense of being old. The outer person is but a *trompe l'oeil* while the soul never ceases to keep its corrective accounting. From a nineteenth-century point of view, Wilde hints at the religious myth of a record in God's heavens. From a Lacanian viewpoint, Wilde's fiction reveals the Real presence of unconscious effects, portraying the intimate and fragile link between a person's ideal image of "self" and the superego. The price of a severe imbalance is death, a falling out of the Symbolic order into a horror-house of unbearable Imaginary lures.

The very forces which Wilde claimed gave him vitality also robbed him of it within a ten-year period. In this sense, Wilde's death becomes a form of tragic suicide. In Wilde's life, as in Dorian's, sensual pleasures gradually came to dominate. Finally, he offers his body to death in a kind of symbolic exchange between Desire and death. "I do not seek happiness, but pleasure," wrote Wilde, "which is more tragic."[22] Condemned for his kind of pleasure, Wilde lacked the kind of philosophical stance from which emotional sustenance can be drawn (at one point he wrote in a letter: "When I think about Religion at all, I feel as if I would like to found an order for those who cannot believe"[23]). If the fiction of *Dorian Gray* demonstrates the psychic power of unconscious Desire and Oedipal Law as the organizing principles of each human identity, the course of Wilde's life reveals that he had no freedom from the tyranny that constituted his soul, and in this he magnifies the propensity of all human beings to suffer. In *Dorian Gray* the unfolding of Dorian's story dramatizes Lacan's idea that the ideal ego gives timing to a discourse in reference to the Father's Name as inscribed in the unconscious. Far from a mere conflict between impersonal "instincts," we are confronted with the timing which punctuated Wilde's own life trajectory.

Wilde's life, and his art, bear out Lacan's contention that unconscious truth is not buried, but floats at the surface of life—or text—as an enigma to be deciphered. In the preface to *Dorian Gray* Wilde wrote that "to reveal art and conceal the artist is art's aim" (p. 138). In fact, Wilde does the reverse. He reveals the artist so poignantly that the pain of Dorian's shame and guilt as told by the picture completely overshadows the overt theme: that Dorian has sold his soul in order to stay young forever. Both youth and old age become states of mind, rather than chronological periods. Time is the subject of the novel. But the time at issue concerns the judgment meted out by the social order as it finds a resonance in the place of timelessness: Wilde's unconscious. Indeed Wilde bears out Lacan's contention that unconscious knowledge shows up in the order of present time, giving shape and coherence to the unfolding of each person's subjectivity. Diachronic time punctuates synchronic time with meanings that have nothing to do with adult life. Indeed, childhood history structures adult life in its interaction with the Real of social events. Given such an interface between Lacanian theory and Wilde's text, I would go so far as to suggest that the story narrated in *Dorian Gray* is itself secondary. The source of the novel's power resides at the point where the reader meets Wilde in a field of Imaginary resonance. All the dreams that go into longing for a second chance, the fear induced by anxiety, the ache caused by guilt: these bind reader and author by Real sentiments which need not attach themselves to any specific cause.

III

Erik Erikson's model of eight developmental stages from birth to old age has been criticized by Lacan insofar as it depicts the ego as a whole entity.[24] As we have seen, for Lacan the ego and the superego are multiform networks of interacting parts, and every human subject is inherently divided between conscious and unconscious levels. Thus simplistic attributions of sickness or health are less easy to sustain in a Lacanian reading, as our reading of *The Picture of Dorian Gray* has shown.[25] Indeed Dorian himself "used to wonder at the shallow psychology of those who conceive the Ego in man as a thing simple and permanent, reliable, and of one essence. To him, man was a being with myriad lives and myriad sensations, a complex multiform creature that bore within itself strange legacies of thought and passion, and whose very flesh was tainted with the monstrous maladies of the dead . . ." (pp. 211–12).

Elsewhere I have offered another interpretation of the birth to death cycle based on Lacan's theory that the unconscious can count up to six and not beyond.[26] The six numbers would unfold in the successor logic delineated by Frege in his formula where O, the number and the successor, function to constitute the series of natural numbers.[27] When applied to a logic of the evolution of human subjectivity, Frege's mathematical logic shows the conscious subject being produced as effect, rather than already there as cause. Like his mathematical formula in which every number implies something before it and something after (n + 1), the functioning of subjectivity means that both anticipation and retroaction are always in play. In terms of the history of the human subject, "time is discontinuous and reversible."[28] Since everything in the history of a subject ultimately comes out from the Other, the historization of one's life always places the Other in advance of one's own conscious suppositions. In Lacan's words: "What is realized in my history is not the past definite of what was, since it is no more, or even the present perfect of what has been in what I am, but the future anterior of what I shall have been for what I am in the process of becoming."[29]

In my view, the six numbers denote the logic of mirror-stage and Oedipal effects as recorded in the unconscious. These are the referents around which societies organize themselves, moving individuals along a blind signifying chain where they represent themselves to one another as objects of love or Desire. Insofar as human subjects are only *represented* in the Symbolic order, they are not tethered to a totalized identity, but to the object (a/A).[30] Thus, the future anterior ultimately refers to the diachronic aspect of a person's life: what is recorded in the unconscious is the history of childhood. These effects punctuate a life and a discourse, structuring them in a synchronic retroactivity.

I have argued that Lacan's six unconscious numbers mark the structuring of perception in a kind of identificatory evolution which organizes human subjects as objects of their own Desire, and their own *moi* repetitions. At zero a neonate identifies with the images of the surrounding world during the first six months of life, by a kind of perceptual fusion or identificatory merger. From six to eighteen months of age a baby passes from the boundarilessness of 0 to No. 1, gaining a sense of stability by identifying with its species, with a *Gestalt*. Following the assumption of a body image in the mirror stage, a child identifies at No. 2 with its own name. That is, the mirror stage is brought to a close by the perceptual awareness of otherness. Lacan called this the intervention of the Oedipal structure. So powerful is the event that Lacan called the division of an originary sense of Oneness between mother and child a Castration. From about eighteen months of age to five or six years of age, a child is in the process of acquiring language. In this post-mirror phase, a sexual identity is acquired. At No. 3 a child learns whether it is a girl or a boy (this is not necessarily correlated with gender), and takes a stance toward father's name.

These early identificatory effects are put in place during childhood. In adult life, a recursive function sets in. Numbers 0 to 3 have structured reality perception, thus preparing the stage anticipatorily for a retroactive counting from 4 to 6 (7) as the adult subject seeks to inscribe himself in the Symbolic order. From an Imaginary perspective numbers 4, 5, and 6 would be seen as a logical progression (synchronically speaking), a symmetrical inversion of numbers 3, 2, and 1. From a diachronic viewpoint, numbers 4, 5, and 6 denote a mathematical recursion, or a shadow extension of mirror-stage effects and Oedipal experiences into adult life. But by inversion I do not mean that 4, 5, and 6 repeat 3, 2, and 1 in any one-to-one way. Desire infers lack, the number always points to the number preceding and the one following. All the same, a normative evolution from childhood to adult life means that at numbers 4, 5, and 6 individuals change their Imaginary positions on an Oedipal triangle, in the pursuit of reifying narcissism and realizing Desire. At No. 4 young adults identify with others—outside the family—in an exogamous marital-type bonding relation. At No. 5 identification with one's own children in maternal and paternal relations reverses childhood Oedipal effects. At No. 6 one identifies with family or tribal posterity (lineage) in an effort to mollify death and warm oneself with a sense of communal unity. At No. 7 (the one more inferred number) identification is with the ineffable, the mysterious, the impossible. At No. 7 one finds transcendent principles such as God. At No. 7 one might also situate the unconscious. Insofar as there is no Other of the Other, six would be the channel capacity for one-dimensional—identificatory—perception.

Within the model I have proposed no subject can ever be a total self or an essence. Instead, each subject is a set of mathematical units or unities which dramatize the perceptions and representations that constitute human mentality. There is, however, a kind of normativity. A normative Oedipal development means that a person can carry on Plato's hunt for knowledge without ending in death. For these individuals there would be no beyond the Oedipal complex at the level of "self" knowledge. I would go further and propose that normal aging (another No. 7)—three score years and ten—generally ends in normal death. The effect of the Father's name in such a trajectory—the timing to a given life—is predictable. From this perspective, Oscar Wilde's tragedy is to have become stuck between numbers 2 and 3. Wilde's adult quest became a tedious repetition of the question of sexual identity. Am I this? or that? Dorian, in a literal sense, was neither: was Gray.

If Wilde's psychic unfolding was not normative, Dorian's unnecessary death has impelled us to ask what anxieties Wilde was trying to quell in his writing. For Dorian had, in fact, beaten all odds. He had gotten away with murder. The one man who could have murdered him (James Vane) was killed in a hunting accident. Those who wished him ill died themselves. Why, then, did he confess? Why did he stab his portrait, knowing that it *was* his soul, his vitality? I have been suggesting that Dorian's death portrays Wilde's life in the future anterior. The secret of Wilde's own loathsomeness to others was never, in fact, understood by Wilde. His penultimate crime was not to have tasted forbidden fruit, not his sexual illicitness, not any Oedipal breach of some mythic incest taboo. His crime was that of arrogance, to have dared to flout social and religious mores and to flaunt his flouting in the faces of the Fathers. In another era Albert Camus's Mersault was guilty of the same crime as Oscar Wilde. Mersault, anti-hero of *L'Etranger*, also died an untimely death. And Mersault—like Wilde himself—was puzzled that his differentness could be judged so hateful by others, that it was punishable by death.

The painting in *Dorian Gray* never permits the peace Lacan found in paintings: the invitation to "lay down" the gaze. In real life an inner gaze judges each person intra-subjectively and finds an outer resonance in the gaze linked to the eye of others. But painting offers a respite from judgment, from projection of the *moi* in some ideal ego function. By contrast Dorian's picture quickly situates itself in an intersubjective realm. Following Lacan, I have argued that the picture dramatizes the fact that Wilde himself was never free from psychic tyranny. Lacan said that when demand *(demande)* [for love] disappears without repression, one has a true dissolution of the Oedipus complex. In such a case the superego reduces itself to the identity of Desire with Law. In a sense, after the dissolution of the Oedipus complex, a subject has nothing more to ask of anyone.[31] But despite his verbal wit and his philosophical nihilism, Wilde never stopped asking society for forgiveness/love. As a visual depiction of a tormenting superego, Dorian's picture evokes a sense of moral ugliness. When troubled young people sigh, "I feel so old," they do not really tell us how old people feel. They *do* tell us that Western stereotypes equate old age with sickness and pain, with psychic heaviness. Old age, in this sense, is a metaphor for being psychically burdened.

The repugnance of Dorian's picture might also stand as a reproof against the social ideal that aging and dying should occur with dignity and grace. The picture suggests that a life which steps out of the normative sequences imposed by a given social order also upsets the expectation that aging and dying should occur gradually. The novel is about the attenuation of a normal aging for someone whose inner structures cannot withstand the injustice of the collision between psychic reality (what one *is*) and social expectation. I am not so much referring to Dorian, however, for he is indeed pictured as a monster. Instead, it is the novel as it eddies up from Wilde's own unconscious gaze which interests me, the novel as a metaphor for unconscious (metonymic) truth.

In a Lacanian context, every person's death is their future project, the signifier around which a life is organized. Such a view is the opposite of Simone de Beauvoir's concept of death: "Time is carrying the old person towards an end—death—which is not *his* and which is not postulated or laid down by any project."[32] Lacan postulated an unconscious project of becoming, a dynamic infusion of repressed representations into conscious life. These play in and on language, as long as they are denied or misrecognized. Conscious "knowledge" *(connaissance)* does not recognize this *savoir*, described thus by Lacan: "The truth is invisibly this slave work."[33] The "timing"—deadline—which structures each psyche as either normative, neurotic, perverse, or psychotic derives from a particular relationship to the Father's Name. Such timing structures the unfolding of a life story as a meaningful *mise en forme* of the Real (*Sém.* XI, p. 40). Real has a double resonance here: the Real effects of the outside world in structuring a psyche, and the Real of that knowledge as it resurfaces to shape a person's life project.

The meaning attributed to a Father's Name also determines the fixations characteristic of a *moi* ideal. In Lacan's words: "The point of the ideal ego is the one from which the subject will see himself, *as seen by the other*—which will permit him to maintain himself in a dual situation satisfying for him from the point of view of love" (*Sém.* XI, p. 241). From a personal viewpoint, Wilde's novel is a rehearsal of his own pathetic *cri de coeur*, his plea for unconditional love. On a broader scale, it is a portrait of the moral structure of any social context, insofar as its organization prescribes sexual norms and certain attributes for masculinity or femininity. Philosophically speaking, the novel could be seen as a "truth-functional" proposition about the Real bonds between literary art and unconscious life. It serves as a testimonial—by antithesis—to the ideal of a gentle aging where death is earned as a peaceful exit to an ordinary life, lived in submission of Desire to social law.

Oscar Wilde never came to any harmonious balance between the forces of Desire and Law. The tragic "truth" revealed in his novel joins hands with Lacanian theory to teach that an individual's psychic structure is but a microcosm of the social macrocosm. Both are the outcome of the structure of the superego, and not the reverse. Within this purview, aging and dying (barring real accidents) evolve as particular functions of mental causality, and not as accidents of nature. Finally, *The Picture of Dorian Gray* appeals to the everyday reader as well as the psychoanalyst. The novel proves that categories such as normal or pathogenic lose their judgmental resonance when seen as structures along which human beings evolve in a more or less intense grappling with forces beyond their ken.

Notes

1. Oscar Wilde, *The Picture of Dorian Gray*, in *The Annotated Oscar Wilde*, ed. with intro. and annotations by H. Montgomery Hyde (London: Orbis Publishing, 1982), p. 148, p. 149, p. 141.

2. Peter McCormick, "Moral Knowledge and Fiction," *The Journal of Aesthetics and Art Criticism*, 41, No. 4 (Summer 1983), p. 407.

3. Bruce B. Clark, "A Burnt Child Loves the Fire: Oscar Wilde's Search for Ultimate Meanings in Life," *Ultimate Reality and Meaning*, 4, No. 3 (1981), p. 236.

4. Oscar Wilde, Letter to the Editor of the *St. James's Gazette*, June 26, 1890, in *The Letters of Oscar Wilde*, ed. R. Hart-Davis (London: Rupert Hart-Davis, 1962), p. 259.

5. As Bruce Clark has observed, Wilde was greatly influenced by his Oxford professor John Ruskin who taught that all things useful should be beautiful (p. 227). In *Dorian Gray* Wilde changes this to the idea that art is beautiful; moreover "all art is quite useless" (p. 138).

6. Wilde, Letter to Robert Ross, March 10, 1896, in *Letters*, p. 399; Letter to Lord Alfred Douglas, Jan.–March 1897, in *Letters*, p. 458.

7. Jacques Lacan, *Le Séminaire de Jacques Lacan, Livre XI: Les quatre concepts fondamentaux* (1964), text established by Jacques-Alain Miller (Paris: Editions du Seuil, 1973), p. 95.

8. Jacques Lacan, *Le Séminaire de Jacques Lacan, Livre XX: Encore (1972–73)*, text established by Jacques-Alain Miller (Paris: Editions du Seuil, 1975), pp. 96–87.

9. See Ghyslain Charron, *Freud et le Problème de la Culpabilité* (Ottawa: Editions de l'Université d'Ottawa, 1979), p. 111.

10. Cf. Jacques Lacan, "On a question preliminary . . . ," in his *Ecrits: A Selection*, trans. Alan Sheridan (New York: W.W. Norton, 1977), p. 207.

11. Jacques Lacan, *Le Séminaire de Jacques Lacan, Livre I: Les écrits techniques de Freud* (1953–54), text established by Jacques-Alain Miller (Paris: Editions du Seuil, 1975), p. 249.

12. Lacan, *Sém.* XI, P. 40.

13. Jacques Lacan, "The subversion of the subject and the dialectic of desire in the Freudian unconscious" (1960), in *Ecrits: A Selection*, p. 303.

14. Daniel E. Schneider, "Myth, Literature, and the Heart," in *Psychoanalysis of Heart Attack* (New York: The Dial Press, Inc., 1967), p. 51.

15. Schneider, pp. 48–49; Freud is quoted in Schneider, p. 52.
16. See Luigi Zoja, "Working against Dorian Gray: Analysis and the Old," *Journal of Analytical Psychology*, No. 28 (1983), p. 55.
17. In the introduction to *The Annotated Oscar Wilde*, H. Montgomery Hyde describes Wilde's three trials. In response to the Marquess of Queensberry's accusation that he was a sodomite, Wilde sued for criminal libel. In three trials lasting over a period of two months in 1895, he was found guilty of homosexuality. Wilde was given the maximum sentence of two years in prison at hard labor (pp. 16–20).
18. See Lacan, *Sém*, XI, p. 38.
19. Wilde, Letter to Ralph Payne, Feb. 12, 1894, in *Letters*, p. 352.
20. See Catherine Millot, "Le surmoi féminin," *Ornicar? revue du champ freudien*, No. 29 (April–June 1984). In discussing the relationship of the ideal ego to the superego, Millot says: "Let us note that it is a demand which is at the origin of the formation of the ideal ego for everyone: a demand of the subject addressed to the Other, and which has seen opposed to itself an end point of non-receiving. It is on the basis of this refused demand, on the basis of a privation, that the subject identifies itself with this Other which has the power to answer it. . . . The question is that of the relationship between the initial demand, at the origin of the formation of the ideal ego, and the final demand, that of the superego" (pp. 114–15, my translation).
21. Jacques Lacan, in *Le Séminaire de Jacques Lacan, Livre II: Le moi dans la théorie de Freud et dans la technique de la psychanalyse* (1954–55), text established by Jacques-Alain Miller (Paris: Editions du Seuil, 1978), p. 271.
22. Quoted in H. Person, *Oscar Wilde: His Life and Wit* (New York: Harper and Row, 1946), p. 5.
23. Wilde, Letter to Lord Alfred Douglas, Jan.–March 1897, in *Letters*, p. 468.
24. See Lacan, *Sém*. II, p. 179. Erik H. Erikson, *The Life Cycle Completed: A Review* (New York: Norton, 1982).
25. Many critics understand Dorian as representing an innate doubleness in Man, to which they attribute the novel's appeal. Certainly the theory of the double places Wilde in Victorian times. *The Portrait of Dorian Gray* is in the line of nineteenth-century novels of monstrous, fictional doubles beginning with Mary Shelley's *Frankenstein, or the Modern Prometheus* (1818) and followed by Robert Louis Stevenson's *The Strange Case of Dr. Jekyll and Mr. Hyde* (1885) and Abraham Stoker's *Dracula* (1897). Psychoanalytic studies of the double which focus on *Dorian Gray* stress a pathogenic narcissism. Harry Tucker, Jr., proposes that Dorian Gray killed his double because his own self-love makes it impossible to love another; see his "The Importance of Otto Rank's Theory of the Double, "*Journal of the Otto Rank Association*, 12, No. 2 (Winter 1977–78), p. 61. Otto Rank has suggested that the most prominent symptom of such narcissism is a powerful consciousness of guilt which forces the hero to reject responsibility for certain actions of his ego, placing it instead upon another ego, a double who is created by a diabolical pact; see Otto Rank, *Der Doppelgänger: Eine Psychoanalytische Studie* (Leipzig, Vienna, Zurich, 1925), p. 76. Such interpretations consider both the ego and the superego as static whole agencies capable of a neurotic division.
26. Ellie Ragland-Sullivan, "Counting From 0 to 6: The Lacanian Imaginary Order," in *The Annual of Lacanian Studies*, ed. Jacques-Alain Miller and Patrick Hogan (Paris: La Fondation du champ freudien, in preparation). This essay is also available as *Working Paper* No. 7 from the Center for Twentieth Century Studies,

Univ. of Wisconsin-Milwaukee. For Lacan's theory that the unconscious can count up to six, see *Sém*, XX, p. 122.

27. Jacques-Alain Miller, "Suture (elements of the logic of the signifier)," *Screen*, 18, No. 4 (Winter 1977–78), p. 27.

28. Antoine Vergote, "From Freud's 'Other Scene' to Lacan's 'Other'," in *Interpreting Lacan*, ed. Joseph H. Smith and William Kerrigan (New Haven: Yale Univ. Press, 1983), p. 207.

29. Jacques Lacan, "The function and field of speech and language in psychoanalysis" (1953), in *Ecrits: A Selection*, p. 86.

30. Jacques-Alain Miller, "Another Lacan," *Lacan Study Notes*, No. 3 (Feb. 1984), p. 3.

31. See Millot, p. 30.

32. Simone de Beauvoir, *Old Age* (London: André Deutsch and Weidenfeld Nicholson, 1972), p. 217.

33. Jacques Lacan, *Le Séminaire de Jacques Lacan*, "Entre parenthèses," June 16, 1969, unpublished.

"WHO IS THE DOUBLE GHOST WHOSE HEAD IS SMOKE?"

Women Poets on Aging

***

Diana Hume George

> Now the dead move through all of us still glowing,
> Mother and child, lover and lover mated, . . .
> Dark into light, light into darkness, spin. . . .
> As the lost human voices speak through us and blend
> Our complex love, our mourning without end.
>
> May Sarton, "All Souls"[1]

I: DOUBLE HAUNTING

I BEGAN THIS INVESTIGATION of contemporary women poets confronting the aging process (one in which I have a great deal invested) as a "daughter" looking toward "mothers" for power and authority, for answers to ostensibly disinterested questions. What do women poets in their maturity write about? What themes compel their attention? How do they deal with aging, what do they feel about it, how do they confront it? Behind those questions were others of which I wasn't aware: what can they teach me about how it's done, this mortally serious business of growing old? Will they endow me with their wisdom? Bestow blessings on me, mother to daughter? Touch holy water to my forehead? I bent over their poems as Alice bent over Gertrude: what is the answer? (What is the question?)

This, I now know, is how I read them, poets from fifty to seventy: Denise Levertov, Maxine Kumin, Louise Bogan, Elizabeth Bishop, May Swenson, Marie Ponsot, Charlotte Mandel, May Sarton, Muriel Rukeyser, Adrienne Rich, and sixteen women living in a nursing home whose poems are recorded by Kenneth Koch in *I Never Told Anybody*.[2] Writing to me about Levertov, Kumin, and Sarton, poet and feminist critic Alicia Ostriker said: "What strikes me as I think about these poems is that all these women poets are *courageous*. And their intention is to be so, to take it in, to face it out, not to be self-protective but to get themselves somehow in balance so they can *do* their aging and dying fearlessly. Or am I projecting?"[3] I answer her now, in the wake of my tracking, my tracing: you are right, Alicia, and you are projecting, as you knew you were, and as

I am. These poets are not evasive in their art, though they may be so in life, may even record that evasion in poetry. "These things of words I could have crooned or droned," writes Marie Ponsot to children in "Advice: Ad Haereditates, III," she lets "drift away as we sit here, adult, / and otherwise articulate."

The writing of women poets on aging is confrontational, angry, tender, unashamed, naked. They wish to "*do* their aging and dying fearlessly," but the project of becoming fearless is enormous; thus their poetry records the process rather than the final result. They are not yet fearless, and do not pretend to be. I find in them as much confusion as certainty, as much panic as poise, as much desperate hanging on as graceful letting go. Theirs are poems of death and loss, and no feat of wishful projection allows me to escape the fact that few of them have come to terms with their fears. But all of these poets *use* their fears in the continuing process of coming to terms with their aging, with their dying. Clothed in their courage to be, they are also naked in their fear of non-being, haunted by death. And it is, as Ostriker would say, their intention to be so.

Naked and haunted. Naked as a baby, haunted as by ghosts. And it is their intention to be so. Many writers have commented on the process of reminiscence during old age, and in almost all of the poets I read, there is a studied, intentional preoccupation with memory, loss, with personal history and the representation of it, with childhood, parents, unfinished business. Kenneth Koch's nursing home poets fill their anthology with nostalgic recreations of their distant pasts, precise vignettes of people and moments whose lineaments may also be discovered in the works of cerebral and analytic poets such as May Swenson. Margaret Whittaker, like many of her housemates, recalls a moment of her childhood:

> Kevin and Billy are eating tunafish sandwiches and Southern Fried Chicken.
> Night is like popcorn popping, or getting the butter from Grandma.
> The woman on the porch is filling a dish with homemade taffy candy.
> My mother is pickling Norwegian Salt Berries.

In "October," the simple act of peeling a pear causes May Swenson's speaker to remember her father paring fruit in the fall, while her mother boiled the jars for canning. That repeated moment provides an associational leap into her father's lap:

> Sunday mornings, in pajamas, we'd
> take turns in his lap. He'd help
> bathe us sometimes. Dad could do
> anything. He built our dining table,
> chairs, the buffet, the bay window
> seat, my little desk of cherry wood
> where I wrote my first poems.

"Where Presence—is denied them, / They fling their speech," wrote Emily Dickinson.[4] This situation is not unique, of course, to women poets or older poets, since poetry has always taken as one of its domains the representation of loss, has always attempted to incarnate, to give body to idea, to memory. I agree with Karen Mills-Courts that what she calls the "spectral power" of the written word is essential rather than incidental to poetry. If poetry is always both "haunted" and "haunting" in its effort to represent and to give body to that which is always/already lost, then how may one distinguish the particular form of haunting that the work of these poets embodies?[5] Into which silent graves do women poets concerned with aging fling their speech?

I am still puzzled by my own surprise at finding that the ghosts haunting these pages, the bodies reconstituted in work and image, are so often those of the mother and father, and their familiar and familial substitutes. What else did I expect to find? Did I think that at fifty or sixty or seventy, the poetic "self" would have washed its hands of such sacred blood? Did I think that the preoccupations of all poetry would have been magically outgrown, or outlived, when these courageous women reached what I hoped would correspond to Erik Erikson's eighth stage of psycho-social development, that tidy place called "integrity?"

Apparently, as a daughter supposing the mothers to be omnipotent, I did expect just that. Instead, what I found is the crystallization, the intensely crowded concentration of attention, of the mind upon its sources and origins, and in a context not only personal, but psychoanalytic; not only psychoanalytic, but oedipal; not only oedipal, but often pre–oedipal. Many older women poets fling their speech into the graves of mothers and fathers, intending to constitute a "self" by digging in graves, to put ghosts to rest by resurrecting them, to haunt as they themselves are haunted. In Marie Ponsot's "Late," one in a series of poems dedicated to her mother, the haunting of the dead by the living is manifestly intentional, even though it takes place in dream:

> Dark on a bright day, fear of you is two-poled,
> Longing its opposite. Who were we?
> What for? dreaming, I haunt you unconsoled.

Perhaps all poetic language is both elegiac and epitaphic, as Mills-Courts suggests. If "every linguistic gesture can be seen as a kind of speaking monument," then during the act of writing "every poet becomes, momentarily, a carver of gravestones." Mills-Courts further argues that even as one constitutes a self through writing, that self slips away at the moment of inscription, so that the haunting is always double, the gravestone carved always that of the poet as well as what he or she intends to memorialize.⁶ In the poems of women confronting the aging process, the double bind inherent in the double haunting is manifest rather than latent, realized rather than evaded. The sought self slips away, or is not yet located. What Rukeyser calls the "building" is always in process, never completed; never an object, always an activity. In "I Look At My Hand," Swenson sees that "it is also his and hers," the hand of the "Father and Mother / who dropped me" and for whom she is "repository of your shapes." Asking their forgiveness for her failure to reconstitute their images in a next generation, she "hide[s], still hard, / far down under your shades." Engaged in the creation of an identity not yet wholly achieved, she wishes not to rid herself of their "shapes," but to become both their apotheosis and her own, such that "what can make no replica / may spring from me." Throughout Swenson's late work, the poet watches the dying, the dead, the dispossessed, in the effort to discover how to "do right."

To do right is also to do *it* right: to age, to die, to complete the creation of what can make no replica, as we discover in Swenson's poem "Feel Me": "'Feel me to do right,' our father said on his deathbed."

> Had he defined his terms, and could we discriminate
> among his motives, we might have found out how to "do right"
> before *we* died—supposing he felt he suddenly knew
> what dying was.

Although the speaker cannot "feel" her father now that he is dead, "His power courses through us," and "we still seek / his meaning." To seek his meaning is to seek her own. In this poem, the speaker moves toward (but never arrives at) that meaning by touching the remembered and imagined parental body. Speaking for him as he could not in his extremity, she defines his terms:

> "Lie down with me, and hold me, tight. Touch me. Be
> with me. Feel with me. *Feel* me to do right."

So conscious and deliberate is this process of double haunting through inscription of words that Marie Ponsot writes, in "New York: Appendix of Predecessors," "Cut a first stone. / Cut, for my father's Edwardian father. . . ." Pleading with death for "ellipsis" in which to "catch up," she asks this "general please":

> Everyone stop dying
> Just for a while a week do not
> Rattle, throat sick of speech; bang
> Steady, pulse thready and thinning. . . .

She is aware that in carving a gravestone for the father who "gave / A great shout and / Rearing up died," she is both putting him to rest and disturbing his bones, both consecrating and violating his grave, and always engaging in what Wordsworth called the "tender fiction" of epitaphs— bringing the dead to life through the process of inscribing.[7] She is equally aware of that other tender fiction, by which she hopes to constitute herself through resurrecting and violating the bodies of her dear dead: "I am your triumph as phoenix / Whom I weep as pelican."

But this violation of graves is not vulgar and secular; it is, rather, holy and sacred. The exhumed body parts of parents are placed in carefully prepared reliquaries of the mind, where they are studied with the loving reverence reserved for saints, in each of whose body parts a portion of soul may inhere. The poets build their own tombs, stone by living stone, even as they invoke the spirit of life. With their ceremonies of words, they continously bury and resurrect both their parents and themselves. And although the poets turn almost always to both mother and father, the mother occupies a special place in the double haunting of the dead by the living, the living by the dead. Especially in the poems of Ponsot, Rukeyser and Levertov, womb and tomb are doubly and reversibly equivalent.

II: NURSING MOTHER

> It is true, Martin Heidegger, as you have written,
> *I fear to cease*, even knowing that at the hour
> of my death my daughers will absorb me, even
> knowing they will carry me about forever
> inside them, an arrested fetus, even as I carry
> the ghost of my mother under my navel, a nervy
> little androgynous person, a miracle
> folded in lotus position.
>
> Maxine Kumin, "The Envelope"[8]

Constrained by considerations of space to make this discussion introductory and exploratory, I raise here psychoanalytic and feminist questions germane to my reading of the women poets I have mentioned above, as I move toward a close reading of Rukeyser's "Double Ode" in section three. Here I touch on the special relation of the aging woman poet to her own mother, and the oscillations of dependency represented by the cyclic return to infancy. This discussion might serve as prologue to explicating any number of late poems by May Sarton, Maxine Kumin, or Charlotte Mandel. Here I will draw on mother/daugher poems by Denise Levertov, Marie Ponsot, and May Swenson.

Although dependency and decrepitude are not necessarily the results of (even extreme) old age, we are all afraid of it, and this fear permeates the poems that aging women write to and about their parents, and especially their mothers. Writing of their mothers' final illnesses and deaths, the poets practice for their own potential final moments, looking old losses squarely in the eye, recounting in excruciating detail the cyclic return to infancy that can accompany old age. In their roles as nurses and giants to dying mothers, Levertov and Ponsot take a hard look at the fact that if we live long enough, we may be extended back into a parody of infancy, in which the parent/child constellation reverses. In "Nursing: Mother," Ponsot "flinches" before the sacredness of her mother's exposed body, knowing that "from between those thighs,"

> I thrust into sight thirsting for air
> (So it must have been; so my children came;
> So we commit by embodying it, woman to woman,
> Our power: to set life free.
> She set me free).

Perhaps this passage explains why the aging woman poet's connection to her own mother partakes of the sacred in so distinct a manner; the power "to set life free" is the inheritance of the daughter, the legacy of the mother, whether or not the daughter uses that power. It is not duplicated in the legacy of mother to son, or father to daughter. All mothers set their daughters free, but the nature of the "embodiment" is perhaps compounded in the case of the woman poet, whose work is "to set life free" with word as well as with body. Recipient of so special a gift, Ponsot must witness the transformation of the giver from serenely self-sufficient woman to "Infant Empress" whose "Winsome dominance" is all that she has "kept of who she is." To whom, the poet wonders mournfully, "have age and injury made / This most local woman alien?" In "A Daughter (II)," Denise Levertov echoes this pensive resentment in her anger toward the "force roaming the universe, / malicious and stupid," which brings pain and dependency and powerlessness to the end of "so vivid a life."

This mourning for one's mother, and perhaps for oneself, has something of the uncanny about it. For Freud, as we know, the uncanny is something "familiar that has been repressed," something long known but forgotten.[9] How may we understand the relation between the uncanny and one's aging parents, especially one's mother? Here we may usefully recall Lacan's theory of the mirror stage of infancy, a theoretical point in time in which the "I," the sense of cohesive identity, is produced by an anticipation of wholeness through the mediation of both mirror and Mother (Other). That "I," however, is fundamentally "alienated" because of the discrepancies between the image in the mirror—whole, complete, coherent—and the experience of living while "still sunk in . . . motor incapacity," and because the image is believed by the infant to be the mother's image *of* her.[10] Can Lacan's formulation suggest anything to us about aging as well as infancy?

In her essay "The Mirror Stage of Old Age," Kathleen Woodward postulates a mirror stage of old age that is the inverse of the Lacanian mirror stage of infancy: in old age, she writes, "the harmonious whole resides within the subject, and the *imago* prefigures disintegration."[11] What mirror in old age produces not the anticipation of wholeness but the fear of what Lacan called "nursling dependence"?[12] That mirror, I suggest, is the mother. To watch one's mother, whose eyes or hands or gestures are duplicated in yours, fall into "nursling dependence," even or especially if that "nurse" is you, is to rehearse for the possibility of that same catastrophe in your own body. In her poem "A Daughter (II)," Levertov, for example, formalizes her death watch as "the witnessing" in which she sees both the mother and her relationship to the mother disintegrate; the daughter cannot have the one thing she now most wants: "one minute / of communion." Isolated from such communion, the daughter, as we read in her poem "A Daughter (I)," can only recall the "pleasure" that "goes back / to the London garden, forty, fifty years ago, / her mother younger than *she* is now." Recalling her mother's prime, the poet reaches back toward her own childhood *and* forward to the unexpressed possibility of her own infirmity: fifty years ago, the poet was a child, and now she is older than her mother was then.

As Woodward has suggested, the self gazing upon this aged Other—an Other who is an aspect of, or even constituent of, the self—gives rise to the Freudian sense of the uncanny. The daughter poets do not say so, but they are witnessing at the deathbeds of their mother things long known and repressed. Lack of mobility, lack of dignity and integrity of the most bodily kind, the helpless bid for affection from those one is dependent upon—these things are "long known," hidden in everyone's repressed memory of infancy. But in infancy, a sense of identity, however alienated, develops to salve one's wounded dignity. In the mirror stage of old age, the self embedded in a history of action and integrity disintegrates. That the giants of this insulting nursery should be one's own children—a better but in some respects more poignant fate than that the giants should be strangers—makes the return doubly familiar and familial. In her capacity as an aging woman witnessing the death of her mother, Levertov emphasizes bodily disintegration in an unflinching passage from "A Daughter (I)":

> . . . . . Now mother is child, helpless; her mind
> is clear, her spirit proud, she can even laugh—
> but half-blind, half-deaf, and struck down
> in body, she's a child in being at the mercy
> of looming figures who have the power

to move her, feed her, wash her, leave or stay
at will. And the daughter feels, with horror,
metamorphosed: *she's* such a looming figure—huge—a
                                          tower
of iron and ice—love
shrunken in her to a cube of pain
locked in her throat.

Drawing on the work of Simone de Beauvoir, Woodward also has suggested that in order to preserve our sense of ourselves as strong, we ultimately and inevitably distance ourselves from those beloved and aged parental bodies, now so utterly transformed by age, now frail and weak. Those whom we have loved over the years, those close to us, she writes, "constitute a special group within the human species, a class of immortals who do not grow older than they were when we first saw them as children and now remember them as adults. We continue to 'see' a younger version of them and close, repeated contact over the years works to preserve that ageless image. In this case, then, familiarity does not breed contempt, but a certain blindness."[13] Woodward makes her comments the center of a discussion on the dissociation and alienation of a perceiving self from the image of the aging body in a beloved other, and finally from the image of the aging body of oneself. The Other—in this case, the mother—is not identified with her aging body. The mother is, rather, trapped *in* an alien and alienating body. Attitudes toward the mother's body on the part of aging women poets offer extensive support for Woodward's thesis, and urge one qualification: the aging women poets I read here are almost without exception engaged in the difficult process of *trying* to accept the aging body. They thus constitute a special case in one respect; they fight against the alienation they do indeed feel, and do indeed express in passages such as Levertov's above. Consciously attempting to prepare for their own aging and dying, they approach rather than retreat. The mother's body is a rune for Ponsot, as we read in her poem "Nursing: Mother": "Long closed against me, now her flesh / Is a text I guess to read." May Swenson examines "my dumpy little mother's" emaciated body on the undertaker's slab in her poem "That the Soul May Wax Plump," and finds that it has "a mannequin's grace." She can contemplate the most extreme details of an aged body's death with equanimity:

> . . . . At the moment of her death, the wind
> rushed out from all her pipes at once. Throat and rectum
> sang together, a galvanic spasm, hiss of ecstasy.

I find little alienation in these startling lines. Yet even in this poem, marked so clearly by acceptance of the aging, dying and even dead body of the mother, such acceptance is won partially and hard, for the poem ends with the wish to restore the mother's youth: "On the undertaker's slab, she / lay youthful, cool, triumphant, with a long smile."

The wish to restore the mother's youth barely disguises its counterpart: the wish to restore the poet's own youth. Swenson, Levertov, and Ponsot all enact Woodward's hypothesis that parents constitute a "class of immortals" whom we "see" as younger than they are. "Where I dream," writes Ponsot in "Nursing: Mother," her mother "still walks domestic / In a peacock dress, bead-embroidered." The poet/daughter dreams her "serene, regent in her own / Diamonded mystery." For Levertov, the meaning of her wish to restore her mother's youth is no secret to be kept from herself. She acknowledges its content in "A Daughter (I)":

> the daughter knows
> another, hidden part of her longed—or longs—
> for her mother to be her mother again,
> consoling, judging, forgiving,
> whose arms were once
>   strong to hold her and rock her,
> who used to chant
>   a ritual song that did magic
> to take away hurt.

And in "Nature," May Swenson traces the wish back to its source: "Mother in hospital, I slept in her bed. / Inside a stomach great as the planet. . . ."

Such a "vision," as Swenson calls it, might be viewed as pathetic or childish. We might lament that these mature women need to hang on to the imagined forms of parents who are actually dying or dead. We might, but we'd be wrong. The process of resurrecting parents, and especially the mother, is in all these poets a means to achieve self-sufficiency through "reliving" dependency. The poets know that the search for wholeness must finally end in the self; they are aware of their reasons for participating in this form of double haunting with their texts and their dead. Through their encounters with the dead, the poets synthesize present and past, in the knowledge that the "last of our encounters [are] transformed from the first." That is Muriel Rukeyser, speaking in "Neruda, The Wine"; but it might have been any of the poets whose works I have discussed. In "Late," Marie Ponsot wears her dead mother's "fire of diamond on my hand" as she goes "talismanned / By you to find you, though I'm lost & late." What their lives together lacked, the poet's words can restore, so that the poet can get on with it:

> We meant while we were together to create
> A larger permanence, as lovers do,

> Of perfecting selves: I would imitate
> By my perfections, yours; I would love you
> As you me, each to the other a gate
> Opening on intimate gardens and
> Amiable there.

Ponsot has been an infant in relation to her mother, and a mother in relation to the infant her mother became. It is only now, after her mother's death, and as she herself ages, that poet as woman can meet mother as woman. I am reminded of the woman in her fifties who said to me, after her mother's slow death, "Now that my mother is dead, she is restored to me. And somehow I am restored to myself. How does that work, I wonder?"

III: DOUBLE DISCOURSE

> No language can sing unless it confronts the phallic Mother. . . . it must swallow her, eat her, dissolve her, set her up like a boundary of the process where "I" with "she"—"the other," "the mother"—becomes lost. Who is capable of this?
>
> —Julia Kristeva, "The Novel as Polylogue"[14]

> "Never one without the other", knowingly, lucidly to exercise *and* criticize power is to dephallicize. . . . A constantly double discourse is necessary, one that asserts and then questions. Who is capable of such duplicity? Perhaps a woman. . . .
>
> —Jane Gallop on Kristeva, *The Daughter's Seduction*[15]

In Ponsot's "Late," the double haunting of mother by daughter, daughter by mother—"each to the other a gate opening"—ends with the vision of their imagined forms wandering together in mutually intimate gardens where their ghostly forms may be amiable. My reading of these poets has suggested that an encounter with one's parents (and in the case of aging women poets, especially the mother) may permit the poetic self to move toward wholeness, even if not to achieve it. But getting to the gardens can be terrifying. As we learn in May Sarton's "The Fear of Angels," the ghosts of parents, those "angels," "strip us down to the infant gaze"; we might have to turn away, unable to "yield the last defense. / To go back." But Sarton's angel answers, "Not back but deeper." If the poet can permit her encounter with the dead parents to reach deeply enough into the psychic past, the result can be the achievement of what Jane Gallop has termed the double discourse of Kristeva's semiotic and symbolic realms. Although Kristeva does not posit that the ability to speak such a double discourse is connected to the aging process, I think the process of aging is at the very least propitious for its development. The confrontation with parental imagos that is necessary to the concept of a double discourse is characteristic of women poets coming to terms with aging. Perhaps the person capable of this is not only a woman, but also an older woman, whose concerns make her likely to inquire into the source of object relations that are also intimately connected with the emergence of the symbolic order in language. Perhaps, in other words, the form of double haunting characteristic of women's poetry on aging makes possible the "double discourse" of which Kristeva speaks. Muriel Rukeyser was sixty years old when she wrote the poem more than fortuitously titled "Double Ode."

Although Rukeyser might have found the theoretical language of Jacques Lacan and Julia Kristeva somewhat alienating, in "Double Ode" she enacts a triumphant and joyful confrontation with what Lacan calls the phallic mother, and with a father who, like the mother, inhabits that world Kristeva calls "semiotic." Kristeva distinguishes the semiotic from the symbolic, as an archaic dimension of language, "pre-discursive, pre-verbal, which has to do with rhythm, tone, colour, with all that which does not simply serve for representation."[16] The semiotic is linked to the mother's body, and exists prior to the paternal order of language as sign. Although there are differences between Kristeva's notion of the semiotic and Lacan's notion of the imaginary, both are opposed to and prior to the symbolic. From an encounter in a world under, within, and before the realm of the symbolic, the speaker of "Double Ode" returns to the symbolic realms of language, of naming, then descends into the semiotic again, so that the poem embodies the "constantly double discourse" of both the naming father and the phallic mother, the symbolic and the semiotic, the domains of both authority and dissent, of asserting and questioning.

I am using the term "phallic" here in the Lacanian rather than the Freudian sense, as an attribute of power associated with the symbolic and the father, but which belongs to neither mother nor father—nor to any speaking being. It symbolizes the unmediated power always lacking in real people, but thought by all of us to exist in the parental imagos of the imagination. That the father may be "phallic" is no surprise, but the power of the phallic mother imago is perhaps even stronger, because it is doubly veiled behind and before the power of the father. In Lacanian terms, the phallus is, as Jane Gallop writes in *The Daughter's Seduction*, "the subject presumed to know, the object of transference, the phallic mother, in command of the mysterious processes of life, death, meaning, and identity."[17]

Kristeva posits that an ethical feminism must both exercise and criticize power, must speak in the language of mastery and authority *and* the language of dissent and vulnerabillity in a permanent alteration: "never one without the other."[18] To live only in the semiotic realm is to risk both absorption by the dangerous aspects of the mother, and to remain powerless. To speak only in the language of the father, of symbolic power, is to risk co-optation and another kind of obliteration. In Gallop's dramatically staged meeting of mother and father, daughter and mother, daughter and father—both family argument and family orgy—French theorist and analyst Luce Irigaray plays the daughter who can face up to the father, but who fears her relation to the mother because the mother absorbs the daughter as well as being absorbed *by* the daughter. The daughter is the weaker one, unable to "withstand this assault on her own body boundaries." Gallop proposes, both with and against Kristeva, that "Irigaray might not be paralyzed, might be able to laugh, if she could really allow herself to be reabsorbed into the mother, quit resisting the identification, allow the distinction between speaker and interlocutor to break down. But that would mean running the risk of death—loss of self, loss of identity, beyond that—loss of the comforting belief in the omnipotent Mother who guards and can ensure the daughter's life."[19] This is exactly the meaning of Kristeva's exhortation to "swallow her, eat her, dissolve her, set her up like a boundary of the process where 'I' with 'she'—the other, the mother—becomes lost."[20]

By employing Kristeva's and Gallop's formulations as a strategic backdrop to the explication of Rukeyser's "Double Ode," I hope to have suggested my sense of this poem's imaginative achievement ahead of time. While my reading of Rukeyser will continue to point to specific parallels between her images and these feminist/psychoanalytic issues, I mean to let the poem persuade the reader, as it did me, through story and song.

The geography is dreamscape. Rukeyser's "Double Ode" recounts a dream, reads like a dream, so much that I fell asleep and re-dreamed it.[21]

> Wine and oil gleaming within their heads,
> I poured it into the hollow of their bodies
> but they did not speak. The light glittered.
> Lit from underneath they were.

In waking life, "their bodies" are two black stone figures from Mexico, statues to contain water or oil and wine. This first ritual invocation, the pouring of wine and oil, does not bring them to voice, but illuminates them. The dreamer/poet continues pouring water:

> over her face it
> made the lips move and the eyes move, she
> spoke: Break open.
> He did not speak.

The dreamer knows that the "sun and the moon / stood in me with one light." Sun and moon, father and mother, "they began to breathe and glitter." The speaker then evokes a compelling primal scene in which:

> gifts poured from their sex
> upon my throat and my breast.
> They knew. They laughed. In their tremendous games
> night revolved and shook my bed.

What did they know? That she was watching? That she had come to them for the blessing, for the unveiling of the mystery, for re-birth? The scene suggests a child hearing or even witnessing the parents making love, for she is in "her [own] bed." But this primal scene is prior to the first hearing or sight or imagining of those giants whose bodies lock in mortal loving. This is the conception of the poet herself, present at the love-making which makes her and which, in her bed sixty years later, she dreams. She wakes in a "cold morning":

> Your presences
> allow me to begin to make myself
> carried on your shoulders, swayed in your arms.
> Something is flashing among the colors.

What flashes is her own movement, her own coming into being: "I / move with the blessing of the sky and the sea." Sun and moon, sky and sea, poet and her parents: internalizing the dream of birth, she gives birth to her parents and herself.

But the movement of the poet's life has only begun. She resolves to dream again: "Tonight I will try again for the music of truth / since this one and that one of mine are met with death." Death is the spectral presence in this revivifying of ghosts. In the rest of this long and musical poem, the speaker does not actually dream another dream, but re-dreams this one over and over, returning to it in waking, making sense of the gift. She knows that "my two parents are the sun and the moon," realizes that this has been a visitation of the "strong father," who is a "bell kicking out of the bell-tower," and of the mother, who "shines and shines his light." Deliberately employing conventional imagery to suggest male and female powers—sun and sky as father, moon and sea as mother—she nevertheless subverts those connotations. This "double ghost whose head is smoke" is mother and father; but the poet is a woman of woman born, and she knows whose body she came from and must return to:

> Her thighs hold the wild infant, a trampled country
> and I will fly in, in all my fears.

Speaking of the "phantasmatic nuptials" of union with both the phallic mother and the desired, unattainable body of the father, Kristeva asks: "How can we verbalize this prelinguistic unrepresentable memory? . . . Such an excursion to the limits of primal regression can be phantasmatically experienced as the reunion of a woman-mother with the body of *her* mother.[22] What Kristeva speaks of theoretically, Rukeyser renders into this naked image. In order to be born, the poet must "fly" back into the place of birth, fearful and fearless: "Those two have terrified me, but I live. . . ." Repeatedly, she invokes both beloved parents, and repeatedly she locates the center of power, meaning, and identity in the mother:

> their silvery line of music gave me girlhood
> and fierce male prowess and a woman's grave
> eternal double music male and female,
> inevitable blue, repeated evening
> of the two. Of the two.

The father bestows fierce male prowess on the poet, but the mother's gift is "woman's grave / eternal *double* music, *male and female*" (my italics). The mother into whose grave/body she enters is the phallic mother of whom Lacan and Kristeva and Gallop speak, never "real," only "imaginary." In the analytical discourse of Kristeva, the omnipotent mother must always be what Gallop calls in *The Daughter's Seduction* a "fraud"; in Rukeyser's poem, her face, her thighs, her womb, are true.

Recalling herself from the realm of the mother in whose womb she has been hearing the strains of the "eternal double music," under whose spell she has seen and felt something "flashing among the colors," the poet reenters the symbolic order of language to take on the function of naming and of analyzing her experience:

> But these two figures are not the statues east and west
> at my long window on the river they are mother and father
> but not my actual parents only their memory.
> Not memory but something builded in my cells.

In a chain of negating signs, Rukeyser names what "these two figures" are not: not the statues they are in the secular, waking world, but rather parents; not parents but only their memory; not memory but that "something builded" into me, the union and the alternation of meaning so overwhelming as to be unrepresentable, yet meaning (temporarily) "fixed" into a chain of signifiers: figures, statues, parents, "something." And the something—suddenly, again, unnameable—brings her back to the musical realm of the dead or lost loves: sister, husband, a nameless "dark outlaw."

Kristeva: "No language can sing unless it confronts the Phallic Mother."
Rukeyser:

> The song flies out of all of you the song
> starts in my body, the song
> it is in my mouth, the song. . . .

This chant, a song in itself, ends in liquid and light, where the "pouring" with which the poem begins is resumed, "the rivers coming to confluence / in me entire."

A constantly double discourse; never one without the other; a double ode: once again the poem returns to the realm of naming, of analyzing her encounter, now adding a dimension of meaning I consider crucial:

> But that was years ago.   My child is grown.
> His wife and he in exile, that is, home,
> longing for home, and I home, that is exile, the much-loved country
> like the country called parents, much-loved that was, and exile.

Knowing that her parents are exiles in death, and she exiled from them, that to be mother is to be both "home" and "exile," she brings into play an unusually literal version of the absence of presence, the presence of absence, the always/already lost place that is both moment and body. *Exile: Separation by necessity or choice from one's native country, home; expatriation; especially, such separation imposed as a punishment; banishment; one who is so separated; to cause to leave a home.* It is the human condition to be so exiled. It is the maternal condition to be exile, exiler, country of origin, much-loved home that cannot return to its own much-loved home. To be a mother is to be the double site of loss, the site of double loss; a poignant and indwelling presence, an aching absence. You can never go home again, yet you are always going home again, from the country of exile.

The moment is crucial in Rukeyser's poem: "His wife and he turning toward the thought / of their own child, conceive we say, a child." As the poem begins with the imagined moment of her own conception, which she has brought to being by "thinking" it in dream, so it is her son's and his wife's "turning toward the thought" that engenders their child: the "conceive of" and "conceive" in the same gesture. It is precisely this conception of the grandchild, this thinking through, that "bears" her to her own rebirth: "*Now* rise in me the old dealings: father, mother, / not years ago, but in my lastnight dream . . ." (my italics). It is time, now, at this moment of conception, to confront not only her own meaning as omnipotent mother to her son, but to make the journey back to her own much-loved country of exile, which can be traveled to only in dream, and only with magic fluids to offer to these gods: water, oil, wine. Thus as she becomes grandmother, Grand Mother, she transforms herself into infant, to seek her own Grand Mother. And although she does not speak of it explicitly, perhaps she also makes this journey to prepare herself ritually for that other, less luminous infantilization that ends only in death.

For Rukeyser, the result of the journey into the underworld to speak in some long-dead and always-living language to the gods who are her parents is movement: "Moving toward new form I am—carry again / all the old gifts and wars." To move toward new form means both to accept the gifts and to engage in old wars. The poem is joyous, but also violent. The site of struggle, the scene of violence, is the mother's body, not the father's: she is the much-loved country, but she is also "trampled." This "moving toward form" is the issue of the double discourse, for it is only through alternately consuming and allowing herself to be consumed by the mother, only through dreaming and waking, hearing music and naming, dreaming of mother *and* father, that she has come to this. "Moving toward new form I am"—a new form *of* "I am" in which she gives form as poet to the double-headed ghost of her own coming into the world.

> Black parental mysteries
> groan and mingle in the night.
> Something will be born of this.

At the moment that her own child groans and mingles in the night, creating his own parental mysteries, the poet-mother delves into *her* parental mysteries. "Something will be born of this." A multiple birth: the resurrection of the mother and father, the remembered birth of the son she has exiled, the conception of the grandchild, the birth of the poet herself into "new form." Hosts of parents are at their groaning and mingling within her, a continuity differentiating itself *in* her.

But what is the nature of this "new form," this "something born?" Will Rukeyser name it for us, tell us the secret, take on the voice of authority and mastery we (or I) presume her now to possess? Instead of that much-needed answer, she repeats three times a ritual chant:

> Pay attention to what they tell you to forget
> pay attention to what they tell you to forget
> pay attention to what they tell you to forget.

To what *who* tells you to forget? And what have "they," told "you" to forget? "They" has no clear grammatical referent, and the only possible referent is the "black parental mysteries." Are "they" the parents? Or their representatives in the symbolic order, the bearers of power? She will not say, yet "what they tell you to forget" contains the sought-for truth. The poem sends "you," the reader, backward, to reread what the poet herself has "paid attention to": sex, birth, pain, loss, death, power, joy, all evoked by returning oneself to the place of origin, to that more-than-primal scene in which the self is conceived.

And this is a forbidden site, the sight that blinds, the violation of the father's nakedness and the mother's womb. The parents who are powerful enough in their imaginal form to "know" and "laugh" while their daughter witnesses their lovemaking, even while she participates in it, cannot have been so brave or so foolish in reality. Real parents and their substitutes— other people, institutions—must always "tell you to forget," to sublimate. Only the hero-poet herself can disclose the mystery in order to take on "new form." To "pay attention to what they tell you to forget" is the essence of the analytic situation and the foundation of psychoanalysis, whose purpose is to journey to the underworld so that one may take on "new form" through the mediation of "old dealings."

This psychoanalytic heroism also feminizes the traditional hero-god relationship. The poet-woman told to forget disregards the mortal dangers and undertakes the quest to the underworld to seek out the great goddess. I am reminded of Robert Graves' conviction that only those poems which celebrate the goddess, the relation of the hero to the eternal tragic cycles, only those that touch upon the theme that vivify "such common stories as they stray into" (this phrase is from his "To Juan at the Winter Solstice") are truly creative. Everything else is bloodless, imitative, reasonable, only Apollonian. Rukeyser celebrates the woman as hero who dares to encounter the ultimate, even death, for the sake of immortality of a kind; and she does so in the person of the poet who is herself an embodiment of the triple goddess at that moment when she undertakes the journey: she is herself the child, the nubile woman, the crone, in her guises as infant, mother, and grandmother.

"Double Ode" culminates in both the incorporation and the transcendence of the guardian-gods it has evoked:

> Farewell the madness of the guardians
> the river, the window, they are the guardians,
> there is no guardian, it is all built into me.

In this sequence of disclaimed signifiers, the poem moves back to that earlier chain of negations: not statues, but parents; not parents, but only their memory; not memory, but "something builded in my cells." In an almost impudent and sacrilegious moment, the poet appropriates her parental gods. "Know the mother, first take her place, thoroughly investigate her jouissance and, without releasing her, go beyond her," writes Kristeva.[23] "Irigaray might not be paralyzed, might be able to laugh," if she were willing to run the risk of losing "the comforting belief in the omnipotent Mother who guards and can ensure the daughter's life," writes Gallop.[24] Going beyond the Mother *and* the Father, "moving toward form," engaging in the constantly double discourse, has produced just that sense of freedom and integrity in "Double Ode." In a voice of mastery and authority, Rukeyser announces: "there is no guardian," which is the acknowledgment that she has become her own guardian. She has transcended the need for omnipotent mother and father, come entirely into her own.

Or has she? The final line: "Do I move toward form, do I use all my fears?" Because this is a poem based on rhythm, cyclic movement, returns, it does not answer all of its own implied questions, or those which the reader may pose to it. It answers to the desire for meaning and coherence and a fixed and firm identity—and it does not. Ending on that question, the poem both suggests answer and uncertainty; to move toward form, it implies, *requires* that one use all one's fears.

Has she used all her fears? The reader does not know, and the question the poet asks of herself seems far more than rhetorical. The end brings the reader, and the poet, back to the beginning of the dream, where the poet is first engaged in bringing these old forms to life and in being overwhelmed by them. Brought back to the beginning of the poem as the poet is brought back to the beginning of her life, I see again that only one ghost has spoken to her: the mother. The father remains silent throughout—his silence ironic, since his is the domain of the symbolic, of language. Of his dying we are given only one detail: that his feet were cut off.[25] He may have been sun to the mother's moon, sky to her sea, he may bring blessings, but he is mute. Here it is the mother who speaks in that more archaic language that Rukeyser translates into the symbolic realm; and the mother says only two words: break open. Is this what the poet has done? Has she broken open rather than closing into fixed meaning? Has she done this by breaking open her mother's body, and her own? "Do I move toward form, do I use all my fears?" Does that "form" ever take shape, or does its head, like that of the "double ghost," remain always shrouded in smoke?

Kristeva on the artist who is mother as well as daughter: "the maternal function can be the apprenticeship of modesty and of a permanent calling into question; and if a woman lives maternity and her artist's work thus, far from being a totalizing Mother-Goddess, she is rather a locus of vulnerability, of calling into question of oneself and of languages."[26] Asking that final, vulnerable question, rather than claiming to have mastered the mystery, desiring to use her fears rather than to disown them, Rukeyser remains on the trembling threshold of language and music, where "the song it is pouring the song," where the rivers are always "coming to confluence in me entire."

Even now, in her poem "Then," when Muriel lies dead with her parents, silent, "the song it is pouring":

> When I am dead, even then
> I am still listening to you.
> I will still be making poems for you
> out of silence;
> silence will be falling into that silence,
> it is building music.

Notes

1. May Sarton, *Selected Poems of May Sarton*, ed. Serena Sue Hilsinger and Lois Byrnes (New York: W.W. Norton, 1978). Throughout this paper I have chosen not to include reference to page numbers for the poetry cited.

2. Althogh I do not cite the works of all of these poets, I include here the titles of their later works for the reader's reference. Citations in this essay are all drawn from the works listed here. Denise Levertov, *Life in the Forest* (New York: New Directions, 1978); Maxine Kumin, *The Retrieval System* (New York: Viking, 1978) and *Our Ground Time Here Will Be Brief: New and Selected Poems* (New York: Viking, 1982); Louise Bogan, *Collected Poems* (New York: Noonday Press, 1954) and *The Blue Estuaries: Poems 1928–1968* (New York: Ecco Press, 1968); Elizabeth Bishop, *The Complete Poems: 1927–1979* (New York: Farrar, Straus, Giroux, 1983); May Swenson, *New and Selected Things Taking Place* (Boston: Little, Brown and Co., 1978); Marie Ponsot, *Admit Impediment* (New York: Alfred A. Knopf, 1981); Charlotte Mandel, *A Disc of Clear Water* (Upper Montclair, N.J.: Saturday Press, 1981); May Sarton, *Selected Poems* (New York: W.W. Norton, 1978); and *Halfway to Silence* (New York: W.W. Norton, 1980); Muriel Rukeyser, *The Collected Poems* (New York: McGraw Hill, 1978); Adrienne Rich, *A Wild Patience Has Taken Me This Far: Poems 1978–1981*, (New York: W.W. Norton, 1981); and Kenneth Koch, *I Never Told Anybody: Teaching Poetry Writing in a Nursing Home* (New York: Random House, 1977).

3. Alicia Suskin Ostriker's volumes of poetry include *The Mother/Child Papers* (Santa Monica, Ca.: Momentum Press, 1980) and *A Woman Under the Surface* (Princeton, N.J.: Princeton Univ. Press, 1981). Her *Writing Like a Woman* was published in 1983 by the Univ. of Michigan Press as part of the Poets on Poetry Series, Donald Hall, General Editor. Her letter to me was written on February 19, 1984.

4. Emily Dickinson, *The Complete Poems of Emily Dickinson*, ed. Thomas H. Johnson (Cambridge, MA: The Belknap Press of Harvard Univ. Press, 1958), #413.

5. Karen Mills-Courts, *Poetry as Epitaph: Representation and Poetic Language*, unpublished book manuscript. Mills-Courts teaches at the State University of New York, College at Fredonia.

6. Mills-Courts, p. 111.

7. For Wordsworth's little known discussion of epitaphic language, see his

"Three Essays upon Epitaphs" in *Literary Criticism of William Wordsworth*, ed. Paul Zall (Lincoln: Univ. of Nebraska Press, 1970), pp. 90–126.

8. Kumin, "The Envelope," *The Retrieval System*.

9. Sigmund Freud, "The Uncanny" (1919), in *On Creativity and the Unconscious: Papers on the Psychology of Art, Literature, Love, Religion* (New York: Harper Torchbooks, 1958), p. 157.

10. Jacques Lacan, "The Mirror Stage as Formative of the Function of the I as revealed in Psychoanalytic Experience," *Ecrits: A Selection*, trans. Alan Sheridan (New York: W. W. Norton ,1973), p. 2.

11. Kathleen Woodward, "The Mirror Stage of Old Age," in this volume.

12. Lacan, p. 2.

13. Kathleen Woodward, "Instant Repulsion: Decrepitude, the Mirror Stage, and the Literary Imagination," *The Kenyon Review*, V, no. 4 (Fall 1983), p. 45.

14. Julia Kristeva, "The Novel as Polylogue," in her *Desire in Language: A Semiotic Approach to Literature and Art*, ed. Leon S. Roudiez, trans. Thomas Gora, Alice Jardine, and Leon Roudiez (New York: Columbia Univ. Press, 1980), p. 191.

15. Jane Gallop, *The Daughter's Seduction: Feminism and Psychoanalysis* (Ithaca: Cornell Univ. Press, 1982).

16. This description of Julia Kristeva's concept of the semiotic is Jane Gallop's in *The Daughter's Seduction*, p. 124.

17. Gallop, p. 115.

18. This phrase of Kristeva's is found in her *Des Chinoises* (Paris: Editions des femmes, 1974), p. 44. I draw on Jane Gallop's translation.

19. Gallop, p. 115.

20. Kristeva, "The Novel as Polylogue," in *Desire in Language*, p. 191.

21. "Double Ode" first appears in Rukeyser's *The Gates* (New York: McGraw-Hill, 1976).

22. Julia Kristeva, "Motherhood According to Bellini," in *Desire in Language*, p. 239.

23. Kristeva, "The Novel as Polylogue," in *Desire in Language*, p. 191.

24. Gallop, p. 115.

25. Although this may be a diabetic detail, its inclusion in the poem places the speaker's father in the mythic company of the flawed or "castrated" gods and heroes, such as Oedipus and Jesus.

26. Kristeva, "L'Autre de Sexe," *Sorcieres*, 10, p. 40, quoted in Gallop, pp. 122–23.

L'EDEN CINEMA:
Aging and the Imagination in Marguerite Duras

***

Mary Lydon

THE CLOSING SHOT OF *Duras Filme*, a documentary made for French television of the shooting of Duras's movie *Agatha*, shows the artist looking directly into the camera and declaring with satisfaction: "Je suis en pleine régression" ("I am in full regression"). Grey-haired and bespectacled, Duras, now in her seventies, is no longer the beauty she once was—by conventional standards at least. Her face has acquired a rather Buddha-like cast with the years, but on this occasion she was grinning gleefully, the still splendid eyes gleaming with intelligence, alight with all the mischief one encounters in the bright determined glance of a little girl.

Earlier in the film, having remarked on the lack of inhibition she finds so admirable in actors ("Ils s'en foutent complètement," "They don't give a damn," she says approvingly) Duras had allowed as how she too, at last, had attained a comparable liberation from convention: the same sublime nonchalance. "Je m'en fous, je m'en fous complètement," she announced delightedly in her turn to France's television viewers, the majority of whom would not have heard of her, much less seen or read her work, except perhaps for *Hiroshima mon amour*, which they would be more likely to associate with Alain Resnais, who directed it, than with Duras, who wrote the script.[1]

"Je m'en fous" is a strong expression in French ("I don't give a damn" is a bowdlerized translation). For it to be uttered publicly on television, with obvious satisfaction, by an ordinary-looking elderly woman before an audience that even in 1984 holds strongly to certain conventions is something of an event. Translated into American terms it would be as if Eudora Welty, for example, were to say calmly, "I don't give a fuck," to Jim Lehrer or Robin McNeil.

My intention in focusing on this incident is not however to present Duras as a kind of superannuated *enfant terrible* (though she may be one), but rather to suggest that in the context of a life and work that are tightly interwoven by her own design, Duras's joyfully assumed regression as she enters old age is a logical and aesthetically appropriate development. It serves furthermore as a highly suitable introduction to a consideration of her corpus, her life's work, from the perspective of aging and imagination.

Marguerite Duras's life might be called legendary on at least two counts: not only because of its exotic beginnings and the passion with which it has been lived, but also because she has repeatedly offered it to be read in a gesture that confirms the etymology of the word "legend," which derives from the Latin, *"legenda"*: literally, "things to be read."

Though born of French parents, Duras grew up in what was then French Indo-China, now Vietnam, and the colonial experience left its mark, not, as one might expect, because she was a member of the colonial class, but because the material circumstances of her family put them on closer terms with the Vietnamese than with the French *colons*, their compatriots. Her mother, a grade-school teacher, widowed within eight years of her marriage, was ruined by the purchase of a parcel of useless land from corrupt officials. Driven mad by rage and the hopeless determination to stem the yearly flooding of her rice fields by the Pacific (an occurrence of which the vendors of the land had neglected to warn her) she would have been little more than poor white trash in the hierarchy of the French colony. Living out their childhood in the shadow of their mother's obsession (her burning desire for vengeance, her desperate effort literally to turn back the tide of injustice), Duras and her beloved younger brother, though never permitted to forget that they were white, played in the jungle with the Vietnamese children and spoke their language.

Having graduated from the French *lycée* in Saigon, Duras returned to France for her university education and published her first novel, *Les Impudents*, in 1943, the beginning of a series of quite successful, and in the light of her mature work, surprisingly conventional novels "à la Hemingway," as someone, undoubtedly French, has called them. Among these, *Un Barrage contre le Pacifique* (1950), Duras's initial account of her mother's battle against the sea, is of particular interest in the light of her subsequent artistic development.

It was in 1955, with the publication of a short novel, *Le Square*, which relates the encounter between a young housemaid and a third-rate commercial traveller in a provincial town, that the distinctive timbre of Duras's mature voice became perceptible and by *Hiroshima mon amour* (1960) it had grown to be unmistakable. Though *Hiroshima* marked Duras's cinematic debut at the same time that it announced her mature style, it was to be several years before she ventured to make a film of her own—a reticence she attributes to the hegemony of "les gens de l'image," filmmakers who jealously guard the territory of the visual against the encroachment of writers, whose stock-in-trade is "mere" words.[2] Her belated regression and the stunning films it has produced now permit Duras to express her contempt for such an attitude, to register her victory over those who said: "Let her write scripts, let her write books, but let her not try her hand any more at making images because she doesn't know how."[3]

Le Ravissement de Lol V. Stein, published in 1964, turns out in retrospect to have been the overture to what is now recognized as Duras's India cycle: a series of works that includes *Le Vice-Consul* (1965), *L'Amour* (1971), *India Song* (1973), filmed in 1975, *La Femme du Gange*, filmed in 1973 but never distributed, and *Son nom de Venise dans Calcutta désert*, filmed in 1976. Duras came into her own with the India cycle, and the assumption of a psychic heritage to which it gives aesthetic form freed her, I would argue, for the insouciant regression that has produced the even more remarkable later works. Three of these are particularly suggestive for a study of the interplay of aging and imagination, and will accordingly be invoked here: two plays, *L'Eden Cinéma* (1977) and *Savannah Bay* (1982)—Duras has been consistently active in the theater since the sixties—and a film, *Le Camion* (1977).

L'Eden Cinéma, Duras's dramatic adaptation of *Un Barrage contre le Pacifique* lends itself particularly well to this study for several reasons, both aesthetic and historical. Not only does it focus on the imagination of the aging mother (her cinema, as Duras calls it in her "Remarques générales" at the end of the play), but *L'Eden Cinéma*, since it was written twenty-seven years after the prose version, reflects Duras's own aging as a woman and an artist in the interim. The play thus represents a moment of experiential as well as imaginative juncture between the mother's text (in a generalized sense of that word) and the daughter's writing, or in the terms invoked by Duras, between *le cinéma de la mère* and *le cinéma de l'enfant*.[4]

The very title, *L'Eden Cinéma*, is a striking formula. The two words, one Hebrew (*'eden* = delight), the other Greek (*kinema -atos* = movement, from *kineo*, to move) combine in one phrase the dominant strains of our Western cultural heritage: the Judaic tradition which is aural (Jahweh *speaks* to his people) and the Greek tradition which is visual (philosophical speculation, or theory, has its etymological roots in *theoros*, spectator, from *theoreo*, to behold). Less loftily, *L'Eden Cinéma* evokes the movie-goer's garden of delights, and in Duras's mythology it stands for a real place: the cinema where her mother played the piano for ten years until the advent of the talkies: "Jusqu'à la fin du cinéma muet" (p. 15), the moment when the movies, having learned to speak, could dispense with the mother's accompaniment. *L'Eden* subsequently becomes the site of the encounter between Joseph, her son, and the woman who will separate him from her.

In a gesture reminiscent at once of the repetitiveness and the return to childhood characteristic of old age, Duras re-tells, in *L'Eden Cinéma*, the originary drama of her life, evoking the obsessional images that have haunted her art since its inception and that now, in her maturity, have been reduced to an incandescent intensity. The drama, as I have indicated already, is that of the mother's battle with the sea: her Canute-like effort to build barricades against the Pacific. Predictably, these makeshift dikes are washed away by the first high tide and the conflict between the mother *(la mère)* and the sea *(la mer)* leaves no trace save the mother's madness. The homophony in French underlines the mimetic rivalry involved in the encounter, such that the mother—whom her daughter, Suzanne, eventually calls "a ravaging monster" (p. 99)—is no less terrible than the sea, capable likewise of overflowing and swallowing up all before her, including her children.

"She was hard, the mother. Terrible. Impossible to live with," Joseph declares at the beginning of the play, as the mother looks on, listening absently, lending her presence to her children's recital of her story—or what they know of it (p. 16). According to the text, Joseph is smiling when he pronounces this verdict, his attitude indulgent as it might be towards a child. The word *"terrible"* in French is less terrible than its English counterpart, carrying overtones of "priceless" as in expressions such as *enfant terrible*, but the emphasis shifts to the darker side of the word as the play progresses. Suzanne takes up the litany: "Full of love. Mother of all. Screaming. Yelling. Hard. Terrible. Impossible to live with." And Joseph responds: "Weeping over the whole world. Over the dead children of the plain. Over the convicts of the dirt road. Over the dead horse, that evening." Suzanne concludes the sequence: "Godless, the mother. Masterless. Measureless. Limitless, as much in the suffering she garnered from all sides as in the love of the world. The forest. The mother. The ocean" (p. 17).

The attitude of the mother throughout this recital and on every occasion when the children recount her history is impassive. She listens without appearing to understand. Duras's directions are explicit and worth quoting at some length:

> The mother will remain motionless on her chair, expressionless, like a statue, distant, *separated*—like the scene—from her own story.
>
> The others touch her, caress her arms, kiss her hands. She offers no resistance: what she *represents* in the play exceeds what she *is* and she *is not* responsible for it.
>
> Whatever can be said here is spoken directly by Suzanne and Joseph. The mother—the object of the narrative—will never speak on her own behalf. [p. 12]

The mother is at once formidably present, in the flesh, and *absent-minded*, and it is this absent-mindedness (one of the most banal characteristics of old age, here turned to full psychological and aesthetic account) that allows the children, Suzanne in particular, to take over the narration of what they know of the mother's story up to and including her death.

It is in the representation of this death, on which the play concludes and in which the mother actively takes part, that the oxymoron of her absent presence throughout the play achieves its strongest expression. Again the stage directions are explicit: "The mother is still there, sitting in the bungalow, while they talk about her death," we are told, and having described how the old corporal (the mother's faithful retainer) helps her onto the camp bed at centerstage that serves as catafalque, Duras continues: "The mother thus, live, lends herself to the staging of her own death. There it is. It's done. The mother is stretched out 'dead' before the public, her eyes open" (p. 143).

It is, of course, a commonplace of the theater for actors to "play dead," but the representation of death in this scene is a sophisticated refinement on the theatrical convention, such that the live actress plays the live mother becoming a party to her own death, in obedience to the artist/daughter's scenario, or her imaginary, to use the Lacanian term: her "cinema" in Duras's vocabulary. Thus Duras accomplishes (appropriately for a writer) at the linguistic level the task that had defeated the mother: the subjugation of *la mer/e*.[5]

If the wordplay seems fanciful so much the better, since it is the mother's fancy, or imagination, that threatens to inundate her children, burying them just as the waters of the Pacific annually buried the Vietnamese children in the mud of the plain. Hence the love that Suzanne and Joseph bear the mother is as ambivalent as it is fierce. At the beginning of the play Suzanne acknowledges their growing desire to run away: "Already we were thinking of leaving the mother there. Of quitting the plain. . . . Already we were beginning to think that it would be better if she were to die," she admits (pp. 33–34). The silence following these remarks is broken by the record Suzanne puts on their ancient phonograph (soon to be replaced by a new model, the gift of her first admirer, Mr. Jo). The music, which accompanies the play throughout, had been presented initially as "the mother's story" ("Cette musique c'est aussi l'histoire de la mère," p. 13.), and is now identified as the waltz from the Eden Cinema, its tempo suggesting at this point in the play "that they were going round in circles in that place," the stage directions claim (p. 35).

The second time the record is played—this time on Mr. Jo's new phonograph—it inspires what Duras calls "the miracle" (p. 63). Joseph and his sister waltz together under the admiring gaze of the mother and the old corporal. "The dance becomes like a family resemblance, they dance together as one," Duras writes, and Suzanne's voice is heard to say:

For us it was the most beautiful thing we had
heard.
That music.
Everything became clear.
When we would leave it would be that music
we would sing. . . .
That air was the air of her death. Born of the
Delirium of fabulous cities.
The air of our impatience.
Of our ingratitude.
Of the love of that brother.
    They dance
Of my love for him, that little brother, that
dead little brother.
Such love.
The mother was looking at us. Pensive all
of a sudden.
Old.
We were dancing on her body.

[pp. 63–64]

Transformed by the mediation of Mr. Jo's phonograph, the Eden waltz
sounds the imminent departure of Suzanne and Joseph, but the melody
remains "l'histoire de la mère" (the mother's story/history: the French
word carries both connotations). Though the piano of the Eden Cinema
may be closed, the children will carry with them the mother's refrain, her
forgotten memories which she hears them repeat, without understanding
them, her cinema. Hence the "dead" mother: present and absent at once,
"gone" in the head in a parodic repetition of her departure as a young girl
from northern France in search of the unknown, anticipating that of
Suzanne and Joseph. The mother being "someone who had gone"
("quelqu'un qui était parti," p. 13) remained "Always ready to 'go'
elsewhere" ("Toujours prète á 'partir' ailleurs," p. 111). Duras stresses the
ambiguity of the verb "partir," and it seems plausible to see in the mother
the prototype of many of her most powerful women characters, all "gone"
or ready to "go," ranging from the housemaid of *Le Square*, through Lol V.
Stein, Anne-Marie Stretter and the beggar-woman of *India Song*, down to
the latest and perhaps most liberated of these wanderers: the elderly
woman hitchhiker of *Le Camion*. What are the notorious "voices off" of
India Song or *Son nom de Venise dans Calcutta désert* if not representations of
the mother's separation from her text ("La mère . . . separée . . . de sa
propre histoire," p. 12), her failing grip on her own past which her children
must play back to her, like a phonograph, in order to guarantee their own
identity.[6] Who are you, after all, if your own mother doesn't know you?

Perhaps the main reason why senility is thought to be "sad" is the blow it deals to the narcissism of those who are no longer recognized, remembered, who no longer star in the mother's cinema.

L'oubli, oblivion, forgetting, has been a dominant theme in Duras's work at least since *Hiroshima mon amour* where the failure to die of love is linked to the failure to remember, the inability to preserve the loved object from the waters of oblivion. Viewed from this perspective, the mother's dogged determination, in *L'Eden Cinéma*, not to forget the injustice that has been dealt her and the Vietnamese peasants of the plain, represents a kind of triumph over the rising tide of forgetfulness, the swell that erases a calamity of the proportions of Hiroshima as effortlessly as the features of a once-loved face. But her children as individuals tend to get lost as the mother's love extends its embrace to the whole world. When the mother becomes "Mother of all," she becomes "impossible to live with" for her own children, to whom she is "dead" before her time (recall Duras's quotation marks: "The mother is stretched out 'dead' before the public, her eyes open."), separated from them by her demented love for the downtrodden, by the violence of her desire for revenge and finally by her children's own need to forget her, to separate themselves from "the ravaging monster" she has become.

The mother, the sea, the waters of oblivion, the alienation of senility are taken up again by Duras in *Savannah Bay*, a play written specially for the great French actress Madeleine Renaud, who opened *L'Eden Cinéma* in the role of the mother.[7] In *Savannah Bay* she plays a character called Madeleine, a grandmother in her dotage from whom her granddaughter, played by Bulle Ogier in the first production and identified in the text only as "Jeune Femme" ("Young Woman"), tries to glean information about her own mother, who committed suicide soon after her birth.

In an epilogue to the play, Duras is categorical in her insistence that the part of Madeleine be played only by an actress who has attained "la splendeur de l'âge" ("the glory of age"). She writes: "The play *Savannah Bay* was conceived and written with that glory in mind. No young actress may play the part of Madeleine in *Savannah Bay*" (p. 8). And it seems to me that the spectacle of the great Madeleine, doyenne of the French stage, playing "Madeleine" is a reprise of the representation in *L'Eden Cinéma* of the "'dead' mother." "Madeleine" is also an actress, and Duras prefaces her play with a description of the character that brings out the continuity of *Savannah Bay* with *L'Eden Cinéma*. It is short enough to be quoted in full:

> You no longer know who you are, who you have been, you know you have acted, you no longer know what you acted, what you act, you act, you know you must act, you no longer know what, you act. Nor what your parts, nor who your children, living or dead. Nor which the places, the stages, the

capitals, the continents where you have cried out the passion of lovers. Only that the audience has paid and that the show is their due.

You are the theater actress, the glory of the age of the world, its accomplishment, the immensity of its final deliverance.

You have forgotten everything except Savannah, Savannah Bay.

Savannah Bay is you. [p. 1]

In the wake of our reading of *L'Eden Cinéma*, this passage hardly requires what Beckett (whom it recalls) has somewhat dismissively dubbed "the lenitive of comment."[8] It should be remarked however that the verb I have rendered as "act" is "*jouer*" in French, which means to play, in the sense of child's play, as well as to play a role. I rejected "play" as a translation on the grounds that it might be too ambiguous in English, and find that "act" is all the more appropriate in that it introduces a note of seriousness (fully warranted in Duras's view, I believe) into an occupation that might be dismissed as mere play-acting. Furthermore, translation is a powerful interpretive force (Beckett, again, is a case in point), and my English rendering of *jouer* sheds further light perhaps on the mother's complicity in the staging of her death in *L'Eden Cinéma*. Could it be that to act (to take action) may mean to lend oneself to a particular representation for which someone else has written the script?

"Savannah, Savannah Bay" is a refrain that recurs throughout the play, functioning somewhat like the Eden waltz in the earlier text, which was, as we saw, the mother's story, just as, according to Duras, Savannah Bay "is" Madeleine: "Savannah Bay c'est toi." From the point of view of her interlocutor, the "young woman," her granddaughter, this is literally true, since Savannah Bay stands for *her* mother's (Madeleine's daughter's) story. The passionate encounter of which the young woman is the result took place on the surface of a white rock, washed by the waters of Savannah Bay, and it is the story of this legendary love that she importunes her doting grandmother to tell and re-tell, jogging the failing memory which is her only link with a mother she never knew.

In this later work the site of the lover's meeting and the consummation of their love (the daughter's primal scene) is reduced to a rock that the sea uncovers only intermittently: "cette pierre blanche" (p. 32). The French "*blanche*" suggests more vividly than the English "white" the blank page, so that the rock becomes a tablet wiped clean of the lovers' inscription by every wave that breaks over it. "They met there," the young woman says, reciting what Duras calls "La légende" that she has learned from her grandmother:

He had seen her stretched out, smiling, covered at regular intervals by the swell . . . and then he saw her throw herself into the sea and swim away . . . (Pause). She cut through the sea with her body and disappeared into the

watery cleft. The sea closed over. As far as the eye could see you saw nothing
but the bare surface of the sea, she had become impossible to find, invented.
Then all at once he rose up on the white rock. He called. A cry, Not the
name. A cry. (Pause). And at that cry, she came back. From the far end of the
horizon a moving dot, her. (Pause). It's when he saw her come back . . . he
smiled . . . she smiled, and that smile. . . . [p. 33]

The grandmother, "distracted," intervenes here to finish the story: "that
smile, that particular smile . . . might have given the impression that . . .
once . . . even for a brief moment . . . as if it were possible . . . that you
[one] might have been able to love" (p. 34).

The woman in this story was very young—only sixteen—and yet there
is a resemblance between her and the mother of *L'Eden Cinéma*. Like her, in
the scene I have just quoted, the fantasmal scene of the play, she is
"stretched out" (Duras uses the same word, "*allongée*"). Like her she is
"quelqu'un qui était parti," someone who had gone, abandoning herself to
the sea so that "you never knew if she would return" (p. 33). Yet, like the
mother when it comes to the staging of her own death, she can be
paradoxically compliant, offering herself to the stranger of the rock by
simply saying to him: "If you like I can give myself to you" (p. 45), a
surrender all the more dramatic since she has never been with a man before
and acknowledges that she cannot know what the words mean. Indeed in
their French version they are rather more ambiguous than in English. "Si
vous voulez je peux *me prêter* à vous," the girl says (my emphasis), and "se
preter à," to lend onself to, does not quite extend to an outright gift,
though it promises compliance. More important however, in the context of
the present discussion is that Duras has chosen the same verb for her
description of the mother's "death" in *L'Eden Cinéma*. "La mère, donc, se
prête, vivante, à la mise en scène de sa mort," she wrote (p. 143). "The
mother, thus, live, lends herself to the staging of her death."

The association of love with death, a commonplace of the Romantic
tradition which Duras's writing takes up and elaborates, would require
lengthier discussion than space permits here. My purpose rather is to
point out how the signifiers of her text, its very *letter*, betray the repetition
of what I take to be the primal fantasy, the originary legend, the matrix of
her life's work: *la mĕr/e*.

"Marguerite Duras turns out to know what I teach without me" ("Marguerite Duras s'avère savoir sans moi ce que j'enseigne"), Lacan wrote,
impressed by the insistence of the letter in Duras's writing and paying her
homage (an unprecedented gesture for him) on that account.[9] For it is by
the letter alone, according to Lacan, that the spirit, or the unconscious,
speaks, unbeknownst to itself: the condition, precisely, of the unconscious
and of its utterance. "I do not thus wrong her genius by resting my

criticism on the power *(vertu)* or purity of her means," he wrote of Duras, adding: "That the practice of the letter converges with the custom [or savoir-faire] of the unconscious is all I will attest to in rendering her homage,"[10] a tribute whose full import may be appreciated when it is juxtaposed with the following pronouncement by Lacan, the kernel of his "return to Freud."

> Of course, as it is said, the letter killeth while the spirit giveth life. . . . but we should also like to know how the spirit could live without the letter. Even so, the pretensions of the spirit would remain unassailable if the letter had not shown us that it produces all the effects of truth in man without involving the spirit at all.
>
> It is none other than Freud who had this revelation, and he called his discovery the unconscious.[11]

That "the letter produces all the effects of truth in man without involving the spirit at all," might be taken as emblematic of Duras's repeated claims that writing is something that passes through her (*"traverser"* is the verb she uses). The writer's passion, she says to Michelle Porte, is to be exclusively oriented towards the outside ("de n'être rien qu'une sorte de mise en disposition vers le dehors"), and the result, she claims, is an extremely impoverished personal or emotional life: "On a une vie person-nelle très pauvre, les écrivains, je parle des gens qui écrivent vraiment." Paradoxically, however, writing for Duras is prompted by an internal injunction ("une injonction interne"), but this interior force (the spirit?) can be apprehended only in the text it produces: the letter, whose origin therefore, as Duras untiringly insists, must remain unknown. Not sur-prisingly then, the logic of Duras's mature works has frequently escaped a public enamored of clarity and correspondingly reluctant to acknowledge the obscurity of the unconscious in what Lacan calls "the practice of the letter." But for Duras, maturing as an artist has meant acquiring the confidence to resist and finally to ignore the demands of "logic," so that she is able to say by 1977 of *Le Camion*, for example: "For the first time in my life I didn't pay the slightest attention to a certain kind of logic" (p. 99). The works of Duras's later years are indeed exemplary of what Lacan has called "reason since Freud," and in light of his remarks quoted above, one might risk the paraphrase that the virtue of Duras's writing lies in the rigorous freedom of its associations: a practice of the letter she has achieved by a progressive shedding of conventions (social and political as well as literary), culminating in the joyfully assumed regression of her old age. Like the elderly hitchhiker of *Le Camion*, she is now prepared to tell her story, in the sequence the letter dictates, to the first comer, without trying to anticipate the response; oblivious to the ignorance, indifference, or prejudice she may encounter.

Le Camion (The Truck) may be very briefly summarized. A truck driver (played by Gérard Depardieu) picks up an elderly woman (played by Marguerite Duras) by the side of the road in the Northeast coastal region of France known as La Manche. They ride together for a certain length of time; she talks, about whatever comes into her head; he sets her down at a place on the road as deserted as where he had picked her up. The word "played" no sooner written, however, requires modification. Neither Depardieu (currently one of the most successful stars of French commercial cinema) nor Duras, whose first appearance in a film this is, "play" their parts. They *read* them, script in hand, Depardieu *for the first time*, since Duras had expressly forbidden any rehearsal. The enormity of this demand on a popular and successful actor should not be underestimated, and together with Depardieu's acquiescence to it, it is an indication not only of Duras's daring but of the confidence she inspires among the artists with whom she works.

The action of the film takes place not in the cab of the truck, as one might expect, but in a darkened room where Depardieu and Duras sit facing each other across a table: "la chambre noire" ("the dark room") or "la chambre de lecture" ("the reading room"), Duras calls it. The camera cuts at intervals to the truck itself and the changing landscape through which it moves. It is not until the penultimate shot of the film that the curtains of the dark room are opened and the viewers see the park that lies outside the bay windows and the arc light that stands there, focused on "la chambre de lecture."

Surely this must be the ultimate *réplique* to "les gens de l'image" who so intimidated Duras as she took her first hesitant steps into the world of cinema. "I couldn't have made *Le Camion* if I had the slightest modesty," Duras says to Michelle Porte, "you have to be immodest to make *Le Camion*, but immodesty is humility perhaps" (pp. 92–93). The Duras "legend" has achieved sufficient stature to allow her to dispense with "la légende" in the sense of narrative sequence, as in *Savannah Bay*, in favor of "legend" in the literal sense: things to be read.

Ezra Pound remarked that the advent of the cinema sent a certain literary narrative into the discard.[12] The effect of *Le Camion* on "realistic" cinema, or the multimillion dollar extravaganzas that currently vie with each other in pursuit of perfect illusion, is the same. On the other hand, *Le Camion*, like Duras's other films, differs from most independent or avantgarde cinema by its insistence on the word, on writing and even on "story," however vestigial or dislocated the latter may be. In the interview with Michelle Porte, published along with the text of *Le Camion*, Duras characterizes writing as the very cargo of the film: the truck transports, she says, "all the writing of the world," the accumulated lived experience that has inevitably and mercifully sunk into oblivion (p. 106). Happily we forget ninety percent of our lives, she declares, otherwise, if we had total recall of "the suffering, the passions, the joys, the moment would be bleached white, despoiled; it would no longer exist. . . . Forgetfulness ["l'oubli"] is the real memory" (pp. 106–7).

For the truck driver of *Le Camion*, a young macho manual laborer and member of the Communist party, his elderly passenger barely exists. "He doesn't ask her who she is?" Gerard Depardieu inquires, and Duras replies: "No he doesn't wonder who she is. He asks no questions. He has nothing to do with a woman who is getting on in years. His habits are definite. They are discriminatory: a woman who is no longer young is not interesting" (p. 37). Later on, Depardieu asks: "What might she be like? What is she like?" and after a pause Duras answers: "Small. Thin. Gray. Ordinary. She has that nobility of the ordinary. She is invisible" (p. 64). It is this "nobility of the ordinary" ("la noblesse de la banalité") that makes the woman of *Le Camion* universal, an effect that would have been impossible to achieve had she been played by an actress, even (or rather particularly) one as great as the Madeleine Renaud of *Savannah Bay*, or Madeleine Plon or Simone Signoret, both of whom Duras at first considered for the part. It is because she is nondescript, as Duras herself has become, with age, that we can recognize her everywhere, in those hordes of ordinary elderly women whom, if we have seen *Le Camion*, we can no longer entirely ignore. Thus, paradoxically, it is Duras's dazzling originality to star, finally, in her own cinema, by virtue of what is most ordinary about her, what she shares with all other women, the eclipse of sexual identity, the invisibility conferred by advancing years.

Towards the end of the film, just before the truck driver sets her down, the woman pronounces conclusively: "Que le monde aille à sa perte" ("Let the world go to hell," or perhaps more literally and hence more figuratively: "Let the world get lost," p. 67). Duras repeats this refrain on her own account in the first of what she calls "Textes de Présentation," which follow the play. "Let the cinema get lost," she says, "that's the only cinema. Let the world get lost, let it get lost, that's the only politics" (p. 74). The despair, even the nihilism of this statement is however alleviated, if not redeemed, by the final words of the last "Texte de Présentation" which are as follows: "The woman of the truck is not bored any more. She is looking for no sense to her life. I discover in her a joy in existing without a quest for meaning. A true regression in progress, a fundamental one. The only recourse here being the definitive knowledge that recourse does not exist" (p. 81).

We have travelled a long way from the mother of *L'Eden Cinéma* and her passionate belief in recourse against injustice, her tireless battle against a sea of troubles. Yet the sea, and the wind, figure importantly in *Le Camion* too, as Duras acknowledges:

> When I speak of the windy country, where no tree is left standing, where
> all the trees are felled, I am continuing no doubt a certain discourse, though it
> is displaced. . . . I talk about the wind all the time and the sea too, far and
> near, always strong, like a constant mental image. I think that the sea is what
> is going to come, what is going to swallow everything up in its purity. I think
> that's it, the wind and the sea, because for me, it's the wind off the sea.
> [p. 129]

The hour of the barricades, "les barrages," is past—whether against the
ocean itself or the sea of oblivion for which it serves as metaphor. As for *la
mère*, she too has undergone a sea-change. The woman of *Le Camion* has a
daughter who thinks, she says, that "poetry is the most widely shared
thing in the world. Together with love. And hunger" (p. 54). Furthermore:
"She's always talking about a counterknowledge which would infiltrate us
at every moment and that we try to keep at bay. But in vain, she says. She
says: fortunately, since otherwise we would have to expect the death of
deaths" (pp. 54–55). Clearly Marguerite Duras is that daughter too, even as
she becomes, as all women do, like her mother.

Anticipating no doubt many of the viewers, Gerard Depardieu's opening words in *Le Camion* are "C'est un film?" ("It's a film?" p. 11). Duras
answers: "C'aurait été un film. (Temps) C'est un film, oui" (pp. 11–12). I
translate: "Say it were a film. (Pause) It's a film, yes." The future anterior
("c'aurait été"), which is extremely difficult to render in English, plays a
cardinal role in Duras's later works. I have argued elsewhere for translating
it by the formula "Say. . . ."[12] Michelle Porte, commenting on the exchange I have just quoted, suggests that when Duras says "C'aurait été un
film. C'est un film," she means that it is enough for her to say so for *Le
Camion* to be a film. Duras's response to this suggestion is illuminating and
deserves to be quoted in full:

> Yes, I think it's the first film I've made, and perhaps the first film ever, in
> which the text carries everything. In Grévisse's grammar it says that the
> future anterior is the pre-ludic conditional used by children when they are
> making up games. Children say: Say you were a pirate, you are a pirate, say
> you were a truck, they become the truck; and the future anterior is the only
> tense that translates children's play: whole and entire. Their cinema. [p. 89]

The epigraph to *Le Camion* is the passage from Grévisse's *Le Bon usage*
referred to here by Duras. In English the future anterior is customarily
called the future perfect: a term that adds a further nuance to the ambiguity of a tense that embraces the past and future at once. When Michelle
Porte remarks on the despair of the statement "Let the world get lost, it's
the only politics," Duras counters by saying that the woman of *Le Camion*

"lives it with gaiety, because she lives it by inventing personal solutions to what is intolerable in the world, for example by hitchhiking every evening and inventing her life" (p. 107).

Duras, aging and in full regression like the woman of *Le Camion*, is free, like her, to invent her life's work. "C'aurait été la mère. C'est la mēr/e." The cinema that was once the preserve of the mother has become at the last child's play.

Notes

1. This essay was written before the publication of *d'Amant* (Paris: Editions de Minuit, 1984), *The Lover* (New York: Pantheon, 1985). Now everyone, on both sides of the Atlantic, must have heard of Marguerite Duras.

2. See "Entretien avec Michelle Porte," in Marguerite Duras, *Le Camion: suivi de Entretien avec Michelle Porte* (Paris: Editions de Minuit, 1977), p. 95. All translations from the texts of Duras are my own.

3. Duras, "Entretien," p. 95.

4. See Marguerite Duras, "Remarques générales," in her *L'Eden Cinéma* (Paris: Mercure de France, 1977), p. 150, for a description of "le cinéma de la mère," and "Entretien," p. 89, for "le cinéma de l'enfant." The present essay seeks to elucidate these terms and to trace the elaboration of Duras's corpus within their orbit.

5. The ⌣ symbol (the grave accent over the "e" in *mère* must be cancelled for the portmanteau word to work) has a precedent in Michel Butor's *Ou: Le Génie du lieu II* (Paris: Gallimard, 1971) where the words *ou* (or) and *où* (where or when) are collapsed and the cancelled accent *accents* the resulting undecidability.

6. In *India Song* the actors never speak while on camera. Voices, their own and others, are heard (by them as well as the viewers) accompanying the action and commenting on it. *Son nom de Venise dans Calcutta désert* uses the same soundtrack as *India Song* to accompany different images.

7. *L'Eden Cinéma* was premiered by La Compagnie Renaud-Barrault at Le Théâtre d'Orsay on October 25, 1977 in a production by Claude Régy. Her *Savannah Bay* (Paris: Editions de Minuit, 1982) was first presented by the same company in 1982.

8. Samuel Beckett, "Homage to Jack B. Yeats," in *Disjecta: Miscellaneous Writings and a Dramatic Fragment*, ed. Ruby Cohn (London: Calder, 1983), p. 149.

9. Jacques Lacan, "Hommage fait à Marguerite Duras du *Ravissement de Lol V. Stein*," in *Marguerite Duras*, ed. François Barat and Joel Farges (Paris: Editions Albatros, 1975), p. 95.

10. Lacan, "Homage fait à Marguerite Duras," p. 95.

11. Jacques Lacan, "The Agency of the Letter in the Unconscious or Reason since Freud," in his *Ecrits: A Selection*, trans. Alan Sheridan (New York: W. W. Norton, 1977), pp. 158–59.

12. Ezra Pound, *The ABC of Reading* (New York: New Directions, 1960), p. 76.

13. See my translation of Duras's *L'Homme assis dans le couloir* (Paris: Editions de Minuit, 1980) and my accompanying essay "Translating Duras: 'The Seated Man in the Passage,'" *Contemporary Literature*, 24, No. 2 (Summer 1983), pp. 258–75.

LIFE'S IAMB:
The Scansion of Late Creativity in the Culture of the Renaissance
***
William Kerrigan

RECOLLECTED IN TRANQUILLITY: this seems a promising account of the creative process for a literary critic bent on understanding the somewhat rare phenomenon of extraordinary artistic vitality late in life. We often think of the aged as sitting in the shade on the sidelines, having run their passion's heat. Wordsworth conjures up a poetry of retirement, a work of imagination linked without inherent conflict to memories of past experience, and good late art has probably been produced in just this fashion. An example would be wisdom literature, the major genre in our culture to presuppose a seasoned author, where one who has known the world, observed its ways, and suffered its ups and downs now comes forth, rich in recollection, to pass judgment on all this. "Having been there, I declare it to be worth just so much or just so little," saith preachers and sages in the awesome tranquillity of their wisdom.

Recollection in tranquillity (though Wordsworth denies this) tends to doom the creative moment to an intensity inferior to that of original experience. But another tradition speaks to us of creativity as tense fulfillment, scattering past experiences like leaves in a hurricane, rather than aftermath or addendum. I will pursue the logic of this second view of creativity with regard to the late career, and in the belief that creative acts, like the creations they leave, must ultimately be viewed in the context of history, I will coordinate this theoretical, psychological issue with certain features of the culture of the renaissance. Two great poets and one great physician constitute my examples.

But what, first of all, is the wisdom that enables important accomplishment when it is not something that we grow toward and achieve by increment, as a fruit achieves ripeness?

POSITIVE CAPABILITY

The inspiration of the poet, Socrates proposes in the *Phaedrus*, is a species of mania. Romans would later speak of a *furor*. On the one hand this madness or frenzy has traditionally been conceived as a special passivity before a supernatural agency. Metaphors for this openness or malleability, this capacity to be impressed, are often rooted in the embryonic, the inexperienced, and the youthful. Socrates notes that the Muses love to seize "a tender, virgin soul," which in the Renaissance Ficino glossed as follows:

> The poet's province is very wide, and his material is varied; so his soul (which can be formed very easily) must subject itself to God. This is what we mean by becoming "soft" and "tender." If the soul has already received alien forms or blemishes because of its ability to be formed so easily, then it certainly cannot be formed in the meantime by the divine forms; and this is why Socrates added that the soul must be completely "untouched," that is, unblemished and clear.[1]

There must be no foreign imprints in the way of the divine forms. Poetic creation, like creation itself, demands a pregnable nothing.

Keats adapts this conception of the virginal receptivity of the poet in his famous letter on negative capability. Though he subverts the Platonic and Neoplatonic stress on divine forms, substituting an ability to receive particulars for an ability to exemplify ideas, he retains the association between creative capacity and the clean slate of unventured youth. Early in the letter Keats expresses disappointment over the work of a seventy-nine-year-old painter. He "went . . . to see *Death on the Pale Horse*. It is a wonderful picture, when West's age is considered; But there is nothing to be intense upon."[2] Then, after a run of anecdotes expressing disdain for the inevitable fixities of a weathered human character such as manners and routines, habits in general, Keats describes the protean selflessness of the great poet.

The fundamental metaphor, once again, is infantile. It condemns the psyche of the poet to a militant inexperience, a selfhood without sediment, and together the threat of experience and the agony of inexperience comprise the major thematic network of Keats's poetry. The maker of the Grecian urn left in cipher the secret of its creation when he positioned lovers in pursuit, forever prior to the indelible and ever-after preconditioning fact, the lines and wrinkles etched by consummation, "For ever warm and still to be enjoy'd, / For ever panting, and for ever young." What of the poet who survives experience and, like everyone else who passes through consummations, becomes this rather than that, a character, the owner of (or in the Keatsian inflection, the property of) certain themes and voices and imaginative styles he is no longer free to choose? Where is there in our inherited wisdom about creativity an advantage suggested for *positive* capability—the ability, not to take on the character of what is initially external, but to engage the external with a character already internal?

Skill, we might reply, and turn from inspiration to a soberer tradition of literary self-reflection. Remembering, however, all the skillful verse by veteran poets in which, as Keats nicely put it, "there is nothing to be intense upon," we will remain with the enraptured fliers, the tradition of the right stuff, for which Socrates was decisive:

> But if any man come to the gates of poetry without the madness of the Muses, persuaded that skill alone will make him a good poet, then shall he and his works of sanity with him be brought to nought by the poetry of madness, and behold, their place is nowhere to be found.[3]

But must the poet come passively? There are indeed hints of another and somewhat contradictory prescription for creative intensity in the classical notion of maniacal, furious authorship.

In the *Phaedrus* Plato revised for poetry, priestcraft, prophecy, and love—for varieties of individual strife in the context of city life—the Homeric *thymos*, the wrath moving warriors to glorious combat.[4] The ancient psychology of martial competition became the second echelon of his tripartite soul, and foremost among the passions seated there stood wrath. Adapting the Homeric lesson that the warrior virtue of anger required discipline, Plato interestingly suggested in the *Republic* that passion could only be controlled by anger. This was an anger turned against the self, particularly the appetites, to produce shame: "And do we not . . . observe when his desires constrain a man contrary to his reason that he reviles himself and is angry with that within which masters him, and that as it were in a faction of two parties the high spirit [*thymos*] of such a man becomes the ally of his reason?"[5] Potentially heedless and headless, wrath as the ally of reason turns against would-be usurpers in the city-state of the soul. Conflict is inevitable: the specter of being mastered by desire prompts anger to be noble, and if the usurping passion should be anger itself, as in the case of Achilles, prompts a virtuous anger to oppose its headless twin.

Anger, and the sorts of conflict born of anger, bear somehow on the manic flights of the poet. The charioteer of the *Phaedrus* must control two horses in his inspired flight back to the transcendent source, and while Plato is not specific about the sense of his myth, the very fact that psyche is figured by a warrior trying to direct the great machine of Homeric battle-fields suggests that the two horses, obedient and disobedient, must somehow comment on the internal logic of *thymos*. Tradition, if no more helpful than Plato himself in spelling out the wrathful element in creative mania, understood the two horses in this manner. For Ficino they are wrath and concupiscence. The rational soul "reins back the irascible power with ease, but the concupiscible with difficulty; for the latter objects that it has been forced to abstain because of a clownish peasant's sense of shame." Because of its aptitude for shame-making, wrath "seems closer to reason than desire."[6] Working in the same tradition, Milton contends that, in order to prevent "the cheat of soules" by false prophets, "those two most rationall faculties of humane intellect, anger and laughter, were first seated in the brest of men"—seated, that is, in the second partition of the soul, the philosophical afterlife of Homeric *thymos*.[7]

So there are diverse pressures in the concept of *furor poeticus*. Manifestly it is presented as a deliberate effacement of the self. But in some manner or degree it is also a state of rage. In moral contexts, as we have seen, this rage gets called forth by threats to self-mastery, and is thus associated with a preservation, not a loosening or giving over, of internal psychic structure. There is something at once visionary and egocentric about wrath: it would impose the self's command on the world or on unruly elements within the psyche. Such hints in the derivation and mythology of inspired creation seem as amenable to the imagery of age as passive inspiration to the imagery of youth: rigidity, selfhood, the defense or preservation of self-hood. And the old, when not beheld in telephone commercials, are notoriously irascible—bitchers, complainers. (This is perhaps an unappreciated element in the many cultural myths linking children with the elderly: to prove that wrath is something separate from reason Plato could do no better than to point to children, "from their very birth chock-full of rage and high spirit."[8]) I think that wrath, sublime wrath, plays a central role in some instances of late creativity.

Freud could be said to have extended the ancient psychology of anger. It must be disciplined, Plato assumed, and aggression in Freud's theory is checked at the level of psychic structure by resistance and defense. It can be transformed into an urge for moral nobility, Plato assumed, and in Freud's theory aggression turned against the self produces guilt, which is to the economy of the superego what shame is to the community at large. But reason in Freud has of course lost something of its classical security. How wrong Plato was, unless he was being ironic, when he has Socrates, who is paralleling the tripartite soul with civic structure and hoping to foreclose the possibility of insurrection, turn to Glaucon with this wishful declaration: "But its [anger] making common cause with the desires against the reason when reason whispers low, Thou must not—that, I think is a kind of thing you would not affirm ever to have perceived in yourself, nor, I fancy, in anybody else either." To which Glaucon: "No, by heaven, he said."[9]

But the horse of ire is a more spirited beast than that. Whom wrath will serve, whom wrath's victim will be: such are the great issues seated in the breast of the tempestuous magus of Shakespeare's final play.

PROSPERO'S FURY

Age was everywhere encoded in Renaissance culture, and one suspects that this must be so for every period. We can scarcely consider a year, or a day, a house or car or garment, the history of our nation or the logic of the television schedule, without activating a structure of positions in the life cycle. The information about age conveyed in a poem such as *The Shepheardes Calender* would slow down a team of bright semioticians, and the same could be said, for instance, of *Rabbit Is Rich*. Surely age is a key determinant in Shakespeare's sense of individual character; it provides the rhetorical itinerary for his famous speeches about the human condition; it joins with gender, kinship, and class to make a meaningful assembly of the *dramatis personae*. It also and especially leaves a strong mark on genre, romance (with its sense of repeated action, and its absorption of devastating tragedy before delivering satisfaction to all generations, but conspicuously to the parental one) being the genre of age, as it is the genre of Shakespeare's age. But the life cycle must remain somewhat peripheral to the discourses of psychoanalysis and literary criticism, since otherwise it would be widely appreciated that *The Tempest*, Shakespeare's crowning romance, is the most forthrightly Oedipal play in the canon, free from the displacements that mask the complex in *Hamlet*. All is clear as day once we stop to consider what, really, the Oedipus complex is.

We err in thinking of it as a drama that happens once and thereafter reappears in distorted and fragmentary form. For in truth the oedipus complex happens throughout life, and not just in the sense that the past is never over; the complex evolves and this process is shaped by crises or renegotiations concentrated at some few—three, to be precise—"ages": it cannot be separated from the great transitions of the life cycle. In the way certain men inhabit this cycle, forming a pattern that (it would be interesting to ask why and to what effect) for certain purposes (doing psychoanalysis, making romances) tends to be deemed typical, the complex has three great moments—the filial drama of superego formation, in which the mother is lost to sexual desire and the father obeyed; the entrance into manhood through courtship, where youth claims its promised inheritance by winning from a father a successor to his original love object; and the paternal drama of relinquishment, where once again, as he was in childhood, the old man is the lonely corner of the triangle, losing his daughter to a suitor. The relationship of the aging father to the suitor in the third age of the complex is particularly agonized. Once, in the triumph of his youth, the father occupied the slot now inhabited by the suitor, which may favor empathy, but may at the same time intensify suspicion: for the father knows, through the remembered hyperboles of his youthful heart, how complete a victory he must now permit. Nor is this all. Within the structure of the first moment of the complex, the suitor occupies the ground once held by the father's father. For the fathers of daughters, as for the mothers of sons, at the entrance and exit to life stand dramas of inevitable exclusion. Freud called the third woman in the life of man Death, and in his psychoanalysis, death's deepest figure is borne to the man by his daughter, the last loved one who might be a wife, but like the first mother, is destined by the laws of the complex, and by the inexorable lapse of lifetime, for another. The tragedy peculiar to the third age of the complex lies in the convergence of human law (the incest taboo) with biological law (our moral destiny).

This is what *The Tempest* is all about. If we discount the spirits in the wedding masque, there is, uniquely in the canon, but a single woman on its stage. "I / Have given you here a third of mine own life," Prospero tells Ferdinand, placing "a third" in the third foot of the third line of Act IV. He returns to this fatal number when surveying his future in the third speech from the end of the drama proper: "And thence retire me to my Milan, where / Every third thought shall be my Grave" (V.i.310–11). Miranda, a third of life, the third woman in his life, is indeed his death. Of course, it does not ease Prospero's burden that he must give his daughter to the son of the man who has wronged him, thereby averting the tragic potential explored in *Romeo and Juliet*, but his most emphatic relinquishment is surely Miranda herself, whose betrothal is followed quickly by the farewell to magic and the release of Ariel, "my brave spirit," "delicate Ariel," "fine Ariel," "my industrious servant," "my delicate Ariel," "my bird," "my dainty Ariel," "my tricksy spirit." This nest of epithets smacks of the bordello; one of several nice touches in Paul Mazursky's film *Tempest* is the transformation of tricksy Ariel into Prospero's mistress. To lose the love of this woman to another means to lose the love of woman, means dying. But this fatality offers some room for play.

Who put the *sper* in Pro*sper*o? A wealthy WS went out with a play that, remembering so many others from his pen, represents the major psychological sources of male conflict, without which there would be (among a lot of other things) no Shakespearean theater. Prospero, in the beginning, calls up a tempest of wrath to avenge an ancient crime. The primal eldest curse is the rivalry between brothers. In one of the two subplots this crime is passed on, by its perpetrator, to yet another brother. "Thy case, dear friend," Sebastian declares, "Shall be my precedent" (II.i.285–86). But Antonio seems to have become coarser—and, from his point of view, more efficient—in the years since he ousted Prospero; now he will himself plunge the knife into the sleeping Alonso. Some theorists believe that sibling rivalry predates the Oedipus complex, stemming, perhaps, from what Modell has called the "primal fantasy" of limited goodness: whenever the good, as love or attention or food or what-have-you, is bestowed upon another, there is less of it for oneself.[10] It seemed the primal curse to Augustine: "I have myself seen jealousy in a baby and know what it means. He was not old enough to talk, but whenever he saw his foster-brother at the breast, he would grow pale with envy."[11] But the liveliest storms of dramatic energy in *The Tempest* emerge from the hierarchical conflict between generations, as we learn in the second and comic subplot from Caliban.

As usual, he takes us to the roots of things. Like Antonio, he lacks the "deity" of conscience in his breast, but his original crime was the attempted possession of Miranda. When Caliban, again like Antonio, passes on his first transgression to Stephano and Trinculo, it is clear that he has become enough encultured to have wised up about Oedipal strategy. Prospero must be gotten out of the way *before* seizing Miranda, which in turn becomes the motive for his murder: "And that most deeply to consider is / The beauty of his daughter" (III.ii.95–96). A male's lot is hard when he has to fend off lateral threats from brother Cain. A father's is harder still. Even if, a brother having stolen his prosperity, he lives on a deserted island, sans ducats, suitors will find him out and do him in for his daughter alone.

The usurpation of a father and sexual robbery of Miranda: these are also the harbored crimes Prospero playfully but testily indicts in Ferdinand. They are virtually interchangeable. When the suitor declares that he is "the best" that speaks his tongue, usurping his father-king in the paternal medium of language, Prospero burdens him with the punishment Caliban earned for attempted rape. Ferdinand putting himself in the place of his apparently deceased father, as if the death were exactly to his wish— Prospero knows with an almost comic precision what this must come to:

> —One word more! I charge thee
> That thou attend me. Thou dost here usurp
> The name thou ow'st not, and hast put thyself
> Upon this island as a spy, to win it
> From me, the lord on't.

> [I.ii.453–57]

In a very subtle way—indeed, in a very psychoanalytic way—Ferdinand has committed patricide in a remark, defining his worth by placing himself in the position of his apparently departed father. Prospero's bluntly literal but not uninsightful accusation constitutes a test, a weighing. The boy has the wish: they all do. But does he also know that, in some way beyond his power to decide his own virtue or vice, he is already guilty as charged and therefore in possession of a working superego? Otherwise there would be no brakes, and he would actually have to commit the crime in order to be guilty of it. Indeed—and this is the test—being treated as guilty might give him the occasion and the motive to become guilty in fact. And it does: the boy goes for his sword, and magic must stay him. But Prospero implicitly acknowledges that Ferdinand will eventually pass this test, and carry his logs without violence, when he misinterprets the boy's inability to draw his sword (and thus to commit the crime he is charged with) as a case of guilty conscience—good guilt, prevenient guilt:

> Put up thy sword, traitor!
> Who mak'st a show but dar'st not strike, thy conscience
> Is so possessed with guilt.

> [I.ii.470–72]

These are rich lines. Prospero likes to pretend that there is a Prospero inside Ferdinand telling him to put up his sword. Caliban and Antonio lack this deity within, this internal Prospero, this magical self-control that freezes swords above milky heads. One of the key roles of magic in the play is to act the part of prevenient guilt.

Prospero's exaction should in a general way be obvious by now. He wants to be the internal voice that tells Ferdinand what he can do. The second age of the Oedipus complex is a triumph for the suitor and a death for the father, but Prospero demands that Ferdinand repeat, as he wins Miranda, the first age of the complex, submitting to Prospero as father and superego—demands, that is, that Ferdinand repeat the same childhood drama that he himself, and with far less of pretense than Ferdinand, is now repeating. Made a son again by the courtship of Ferdinand, Prospero responds in kind: Ferdinand must be made a son again. Is this a wise imposition, done for the good of the young, or a compelled deference to the vanity of an abdicating old man? There is room for play in this question.

One evident difference between the first and the third oedipal moment is that the father gets to stage his loss. An authority at last, he consents, gives away, hands over. We have grown accustomed to thinking of romance as a genre of expelled negation, renewing the world in the process of transferring it to the upcoming generation. The gift is delivered in this romance, but not without overcoming, or maybe not quite overcoming, a palpable resentment. In *The Tempest*, for one thing, the element of stage-craft, of willed divestiture, has grown limitless. Prospero's magic not only restrains the propagation of crimes against Alonso and himself: it also guides to fruition the very love that costs him a third of his life. There is something begrudging about the way Prospero frees his daughter. " 'Tis

new to thee": the gift of people other than himself is not so wonderful as
the soaring victorious heart of his daughter might like to think. (Romance's
soured version, as it were, of tragedy's hopeful but deferential "we that are
young / Shall never see so much, nor live so long.") The effect of this
peevish stagemanaging is to emphasize the debt owed Prospero. Shakespeare sets this tone in the long second scene of his opening act, where first
Miranda, then Ariel, and finally Caliban are all told the story that justifies
their obligations to this marvellous father. The story enacted in the play
itself continues to stress, not so much the beauty of the gifts as the huge
charity of the giver and the wonders of his giving. We find this telling
exchange near the end of the play:

> *Alonso*   I am hers.
> But, O, how oddly will it sound that I
> Must ask my child forgiveness!
> *Prospero*   There, sir, stop.
> Let us not burden our remembrance with
> A heaviness that's gone.
>
>   [V.i.196–99]

The idea that the parental generation owes even a debt of apology to the
young need not be suffered. Prospero, in any case, is handling all the
accounts.

The ability to know tragedy and yet more than tragedy is the fundamental claim of romance. In *The Tempest* one feels that Ferdinand and
Miranda may never earn the privilege of their genre. It is as if they have
been too well provided for, heirs of too much prosperity. But at their final
appearance Prospero seems to have foreseen even this subtle diminish-
ment, and allows them a special moment of their own during which the
new generation is saved from the tragedy of being incapable of tragedy:

> *Here Prospero discovers Ferdinand and Miranda playing at chess.*
> *Miranda*   Sweet lord, you play me false.
> *Ferdinand*   No, my dearest love,
> I would not for the world.
> *Miranda*   Yes, for a score of kingdoms you should wrangle,
> And I would call it fair play.
>
>   [V.i.172–74]

This is weighty wit. It permits the seeds of tragic experience at least a
shallow hold on the brave new world. The lovers make a game of broken
vows ("you play me false"), worldly and adulterous ambition ("for a score
of kingdoms you should wrangle"), and the dangerous self-deceit that
makes foul fair (I would call it fair play"), while they play another game.
Indeed, while they play *the* game—chess, the definitive social and psycho-

logical game of European history that can only end with the killing, or more exactly with the suicide, of the King. It is the dark game played for real in the two subplots of *The Tempest*. "You'ld be king o' the isle, Sirrah?" (V.i.287), Prospero asks Stephano, and if he were to answer truly, he must, joining a line of Shakespearean characters stretching all the way back to Richard, Duke of Gloucester, answer "Yes!" In the course of the play Ferdinand, too, has been made to acknowledge this thing of darkness his. The game of chess belongs to his Oedipal inheritance.

In the plot of the drama, moving from the tempest of Prospero's rage to his deliberate self-weakening, an angry withholding seems to be gradually eclipsed by generosity. But Shakespeare invites us to understand that these two emotional postures are not mutually exclusive, but rather productive of each other. From the fury of the initial tempest we know that the necessity of being generous (of forgiving Alonso and Antonio, of giving Miranda's hand to Ferdinand, and of bearing the difficult truths implied by these acts) must enrage Prospero. Yet the sheer arduousness of being so generous seems to prompt him to perfect, down to the smallest detail, his giveaway. By the end the magus has indeed, like the good man in Plato, turned rage against his own rage: "Yet with my noble reason 'gainst my fury / Do I take part" (V.i.26–27). If we think back to his revealing misinterpretation of Ferdinand's paralyzed swordarm, we realize that ultimately Prospero too is one "Who mak'st a show but dar'st not strike," since—what other reason could there be for such magical self-control?— his "conscience / Is so possessed with guilt." He confirms Ferdinand in the happiest oedipal lesson, the same one that Luke Skywalker confirms in *The Return of the Jedi:* if you do not kill your father, your father will not kill you; he also has a superego. But the play does not want us to forget that Prospero's is a considerable fury, and that there is a considerable counter-fury brought to the mastery of it.

The magic put to such benign uses in the end is initially the brewer of a storm, the primordial instance of macrocosmic malice, and just before Prospero deliberately forfeits his power, he savors it in precisely this way. His is a "rough" magic, violent and fearful, remembered in images immemorially associated with the rage of a deity:

> by whose aid
> (Weak masters though ye be) I have bedimmed
> The noontide Sun, called forth the mutinous winds,
> And 'twixt the green sea and the azured vault
> Set roaring war; to the dread rattling thunder
> Have I given fire and rifted Jove's stout oak
> With his own bolt; the strong-based promontory
> Have I made shake and by the spurs plucked up
> The pine and cedar; graves at my command

> Have waked their sleepers, oped, and let 'em forth
> By my so potent art. But this rough magic
> I here abjure; and when I have required
> Some heavenly music (which even now I do)
> To work mine end upon their senses that
> This airy charm is for, I'll break my staff,
> Bury it certain fathoms in the earth,
> And deeper than did ever plummet sound
> I'll drown my book.
>
>   [V.i.40–57]

Because Prospero also has a superego, he can perform in his maturity this final and sublime repetition of good Oedipal resolution, turning his aggression against himself in the self-castration of acquiring a guilt-charged conscience. The extreme fates promised the instruments of his potent art show us its roughness being turned against itself. The staff, the spear that "made shake" the mountains, will be broken and buried deep. But this is as nothing to the immeasurably deep drowning to which he sentences the book. Even Caliban realized that to kill Prospero one must first disarm him of the book. Prospero is contemplating the last move left in the game. Checkmate: the magus is here stagemanaging his own decline within the metaphors of the game that is *The Tempest*, his departure from power, potency, daughter, life.

There has been an arresting substitution in the figurative logic of the play. Prospero's magic imposed on Ferdinand the vision of his drowned father. Why? It was partly a small symbolic vengeance in which Prospero "murders" an old enemy and takes his place in Ferdinand's superego as literal "second father" (V.i.196): perhaps, too, the transaction by which Ferdinand finds in Prospero "So rare a wond'red father" (IV.i.123) and Prospero finds in Ferdinand "my son" (IV.i.146) gives the old magus symbolic access to a form of succession he notably lacks—a son. And the vision of the drowned Alonso was partly a temptation, as we gather from the treatment given to Ferdinand's first declaration of his worth. The truth of someone's feelings for another will be observable when that other person is, or is believed to be, dead: Shakespearean drama offers us numerous scenes and stratagems based on this exploitable technique for eliciting true confession. One is not surprised to find, in a play so patriarchal as this, the "death test" combined with the idea that a father's authority should be interminable. Prospero is testing for undying reverence. This value can be felt in Ariel's eerie and beautiful evocation of the dead Alonso. His song envisions a sea as attuned to the majesty of a dead father as it has just been attuned to the potent art of a living one—a magic burial in which everything "that doth fade" (I.ii.398), everything that may make a father weaken and die and disperse, becomes a hardened sea treasure "rich and strange"

(I.ii.400) as the nymphs, knowing intuitively the degree of ritual this father commands, "hourly ring his knell" (I.ii.401). At the end of the play Prospero, who boasts that his magic has opened graves and resurrected the dead, brings the corals and pearls back to life. It is here that some necessity in the balance of metaphor comes into play. Something must take the place of the vision of the drowned Alonso: the vision of the drowned book. For, despite its romance ending, the play does not wish to deny that a father *has* drowned in this tempest, the victim of his own rage in the service of his noble reason. The great self-congratulating demonstration of virtue that fills this stage depends on such a loss. Survivors are tested in that someone must be dead before their true feelings about him can be known for certain. Prospero must pass a reversal of the death test: he must prove his good will to those who will outlive him. And in order to prove that he has proven that, he must somehow die. So the potent art drowns. The book of his dreams and dramas lies at such a depth that we will never be able to see whether the nymphs perform its spells.

This is an old man's play—a play about becoming an old man. There is no particular reason to fault its rage. And if the old are vain in their handing down? No one can deny that the world has been handed down stylishly. The old man steps out again, now powerless, wanting "Spirits to enforce, Art to enchant" (Epilogue 14). It belongs to the meaning of the play that he should always have acted somewhat like a ghost, an irreal fugitive from a dream feeling himself in need of special acts of sympathy in order to make his impression—so terribly concerned, for example, that Miranda, who has to be all ears, really be listening. Well pleased, we applaud. Prospero has enriched us. Except for the magic. . . . He did not want to pass on the magic. For that we are indebted to the divers who salvaged the First Folio.

I am interested in authors, in the odd chains of psychic works that result in great art, and like everyone so inclined I wish we knew more about Shakespeare. There were daughters, of course, and he is said to have contracted his fatal illness celebrating the wedding of the youngest one. Possibly, in the case of *The Tempest*, that is enough to know. This particular *furor poeticus de senectute* was in obvious ways the provision of a culture centered about fathers, their prosperity, and its inheritance. The sense of fatal abdication that attends the marriage of children belongs to what Johnson called "general nature." But the imperial magic in Prospero's self-dramatization of his metaphorical death clearly bespeaks a time when fathers could, and often did, arrange everything. (Were we to shift this analysis into social anthropology, it could easily be shown that Miranda's presence in the play, though freighted with symbolic meaning, is largely an occasion for the father-in-law to establish a relationship of ideal filial deference with the son-in-law.) This enforcing and enchanting magic is indeed a secular scripture—a right claimed, an aesthetic opportunity of social patriarchy.

Milton's late *furor*, to which we now turn, was won from an acuter suspicion of society and a profounder (though by no means total) alienation from it. He moves us toward phenomena found on the fringes of renaissance culture, particularly religious enthusiasm. His self-accusing wrath does not stem, as Prospero's does, from a vengeful aggression submissive to noble reason—from an old Oedipal resistance to death tamed by the confluence of biological necessity and one final chance to demonstrate his virtue in fatherly love. Milton steers the Oedipus complex into odd dimensions beyond its conventional three ages.

His late inspiration involved an angry retrieval of youth—a peculiar and passionate form of mourning. The shame of age: normally, and insofar as specific cultures exact this as psychological death tax, terribly, the old indict themselves for having survived their youth. Milton tapped the rich wrath of creativity by reversing the familiar structure of such mourning, and accusing his youth for having preceded his old age.

MILTON'S OLD EXPERIENCE

da DUM. In the iamb, the heartbeat of English poetry, new energy is final, and it was so in the career of John Milton. "Till old experience do attain / To something like prophetic strain," the young poet wrote, foreseeing, in "Il Penseroso." The drama Babe Ruth compressed in a single at-bat Milton drew out for a lifetime, and preserving his immense ambition through years of open preparation and secret evasion, swatted like a sultan at last, enjoying the most conspicuously creative old age in the annals of English verse. *Paradise Lost* was probably begun when Milton, blind, gouty, grieving over the death of his second wife and the eclipse of his political ideals, was fifty (about the age a presumably infirm Shakespeare left the stage to Beaumont and Fletcher), and it was published when he was fifty-eight. About seven years remained to him, and although *Paradise Regained* and *Samson Agonistes* cannot be dated with full certainty, they have usually been thought later than *Paradise Lost*, mighty afterwords to the great epic. There was no dotage. Unlike other important poets who have turned out vital work in their last years, Milton wrote virtually *all* the poetry that is his major claim on the attention of after-times during the final quarter of his life. Quite possibly—and this observation begins to suggest the size and tenacity of his ambition—Milton himself would not be pleased with his distinction as the best old poet in our language, since by his own sanguine measure he died prematurely.[12] Ever defying mortal schedule, Milton at twenty-four was but "at manhood . . . arrived so near," when traditional reckoning would place him three years past it, and later, at forty-four, considered that he had spent "ere half [his] days."[13] But the title is his nonetheless. If we adjust for the true Renaissance life expectancy, his sixty-six years was a goodly sum, and in the year he died he added fifteen lines to *Paradise Lost* and redivided its books, appropriately giving the grand masterpiece of poetic old age its final form at virtually the last minute.

New energy at the end was not only his achievement: it was also his theme. In the early Latin poem, "Naturam non pati senium (That Nature is not subject to old age)," he opposes those dour appraisers who thought the world in senile decline. "We have seen the best of time," Thomas Browne observed, echoing, among many others, Donne in the *Anniversaries* and Gloucester in *King Lear*.[14] But Milton contends that such a view projects the fate of the human body onto the cosmos. Nature, in fact, does itself as sportively as ever. The potency of the beginning reigns unabated: Phoebus blazes, Neptune smites, Flora gambols, and today's lightning-bolts are being turned out with all the zing of yesterday's. This is the theodicy of *Paradise Lost* in embryo. Eternal providence can be asserted because it asserts itself. Good, despite apparent withdrawal, overcomes evil, and creation, despite apparent exhaustion, overcomes chaos and decay.

Resurgence is everywhere in the late work. Five (XII.1-5) of the fifteen lines added in his final year mark a brief caesura "Betwixt the world destroyed and world restored." The Phoenix of *Samson Agonistes*, "then vigorous most / When most unactive deemed" (1704–5), is perhaps the last instance of Milton's choice trope for ambitious but unexpected achievement: bursting out into sudden blaze. After the great conflagration makes ashes of the first creation, the Phoenix-drama will again be played: "The world shall burn, and from her ashes spring / New heaven and earth" (III.334–35). Rising from the court of Chaos, Satan "With fresh alacrity and force renewed / Springs upward like a pyramid of fire" (II.1012–13)—the pyramid being, according to Plato, the precise shape of fire's atom.[15] Satan is literally in his element, forging character from rage, "the hot hell that always in him burns" (IX.467). It is an image of thrilling self-creation, of disciplined energy wrested from the elemental self-defeat (see II.890-910) of Chaos. Milton's large sympathy for those fireballs who surge upward from exile and despair can be measured in his tellingly excessive condemnation of Belial, the most sensible speaker at the demonic council, whose penetrating indictment of the folly of opposing omnipotence is greeted with the narrator's crusty "Thus Belial with words clothed in reason's garb / Counselled ignoble ease, and peaceful sloth, / Not peace" (II.226-28). However insightful Belial might have been seen, he had certainly not been *noble*. Resurgent energy, the proud refusal to rest, is not an infirmity of noble mind. It is rather nobility itself—what, for Milton, a mind must be in order to *have* infirmities.

The successful completion of *Paradise Lose* was Milton's private theodicy. To bargain with the Heavenly Muse, trading blindness for illumination, Milton had to dismantle the youthful crystallization of his poetic identity, and this in turn meant a repetition of, and realignment of, his Oedipus complex. One secret of his late creative revival was his ability, not just to retain, but to renew and fortify, through sacred symbols, his identity as a son.

In the first stage of his career, sensual sacrifice paid for inspiration. The key text in this regard is the Ludlow masque. Its author—a Cambridge graduate still living at home, deferring his worldly career and fending off what he called the "potent inclination" for wife and family—made of virginity a sage and serious doctrine.[16] Its exponent becomes worthy of heavenly confidences, and may well get put in the way of receiving them. For like all virtues, virginity has to be tried. But virginity, unlike other virtues, may be taken by force. So the moral coherence of the universe requires celestial guardians to protect virginity from unchosen loss—hence the theodicial force, in *Comus*, of Sabrina and the Attendant Spirit, who together extricate the Lady from the lair of her tempter. But as presented in *Comus*, this ideal suffers from its own internal inconsistency: it cherishes a grudge. Though wholly submissive to the "no" of a primitive superego, virginity as supreme value points inevitably to the guilt of parents. Within the context of this essay, one might say that Milton's psychic representative in the masque, the Lady, is a Miranda infinitely indebted to the largess of her father, but also an ambitious Miranda who would prove her brave new virtue superior to the fatherly bounty of marvellous Prospero by refusing to act her part in his marriage masque. She will have one of her own—a masque of virginity, paralysis, and veiled malice, not toward the young, as in Prospero's, but toward progenitors.

In the anti-masque of *Comus*, Milton presents an aggressive indictment of the community of parents, who, with their grave saws and reverend advice, burden children with a law of chastity they themselves nightly defile. Theodicy has ominous rudiments: in psychic development, at least, the source of good is also the source of evil. The hostility bound into the virtue of the masque surfaces in the transcendent destiny foretold by the Attendant Spirit's final speech. Here oedipal conflict is tuned to the triumph of "Youth and Joy." The momentary paralysis of the Lady gets transferred to the parental generation (Venus and her consort—the recuperating but still wounded Adonis), while "far above" Cupid and Psyche embrace before their nuptials at the decree of Jove. How to transform the superego into a consenting rather than denying power? How to lift the paralysis of Oedipal obedience, and detach poetic ambition from an over-whelming sense of indebtedness to a prosperous father? How to be ag-gressive and therefore guilty, as all mature men are guilty, while at the same time be found among the chosen? These were the difficult and deep-rooted problems that Milton solved during the second and triumphant phase of his artistic life.

For the late Milton, all the bounties of inspired creation—maternal protection, paternal potency, narcissistic entitlement, extended vision—are given through the structure of a superego reaffirmed as God the Father. This transformation opens a vast realm of psychic positions and resources otherwise unavailable to the sons and daughters of Renaissance Prospero: in fact, the immediate result, one that Protestantism both exploited and feared, is the escape of conscience from this world. But Milton did not need mere righteousness. He required a sanctioned imagination, able to believe that its own purchase on the drama of sacred history could do full justice to the human, the demonic, and the divine. In part he secured this warrant from an identification with Christ: obedient to a superego identi-fied with the Father, the ego becomes an analogon of the Son. Because the Son of his mature theology is not coeternal with the Father, but rather the first of the Father's creations, Milton is sometimes thought to have jealously withheld from Christ the degree of worship due him in an authentic Christianity. It is true enough that Milton's is not the Christ of ritual, nailed to the Cross and bleeding sacraments. Yet an identification with the Son of his heretical Godhead—who need only turn back, in a Protestant version of the neoplatonic epistrophe, to the will of his own creator, in order to gain what is uniquely his (merit) and the privilege such merit earns (inheritance of the Father's power in the execution and management of all subsequent creations and judgments)—gave Milton psychic title to a religious vision extraordinarily free of the usual obstructions. Once again, the justification of God has been called a hopeless and pridefully rational undertaking. But Milton's epic shows us that a religion centered about the question of God's justice will at least have done with some few soul-shrinking features—blind deference, the perpetuation of traditions be-cause they are traditional, the undramatic or melodramatic rendering of evil, the erection of mysteries wherever a human account of things seems to be running into trouble.

The orthodox Son reigns eternally in world without end. The Miltonic Son is indebted for the gift of life, like every other creature save Satan, who becomes evil by refusing to acknowledge his existence as a gift. But Milton was able through blindness to *reverse* this debt. Before seeing, he had been blinded. Before enjoying the privilege, he had suffered the feared punish-ment. "So much the rather thou, celestial light / Shine inward" (III.51): recompense is now his due. Blindness became, not a handicap overcome, but a strict precondition for artistic success. Accepting this death or premature entombment ("Myself, my sepulchre," his Samson laments, certain that the "moving grave" [S.A.102] of his blind body is worse than "decrepit age"), this castration (the narrator of the epic feels himself "from the cheerful ways of men / Cut off" [III.46–47]) as both his guilt and his punishment, the once militantly virginal Lady of Christ's got pregnant with light:

> Instruct me, for thou know'st; thou from the first
> Wast present, and with mighty wings outspread
> Dove-like sat'st brooding on the vast abyss
> And madest it pregnant: what in me is dark
> Illumine. . . .
>
>   [I.19–23]

Already in the first invocation becoming pregnant with God's bright seed is contiguous with illuminated blindness. In the days of Milton's late creation "ever-during dark" (III.45) was the vast abyss, the void and formless infinite, the apeiron, the receptacle, the womb. In Book III divine light is invited inside a feminine head: "the mind through all her powers / Irradiate, there plant eyes." (III.52–53). The ritual Christ of Christian tradition often possesses a maternal side. The Miltonic Son, too, before he could fill the vast womb with the Father's light, had first, womb-like, to absorb that light, that will. Milton also imitates this moon sun.

Elsewhere the Muse is feminine. In Book VII Milton solicits the full dream of an invulnerable mother from his deity, becoming Orpheus perfected. The paralysis of *Comus* derived from a fusion of the two great anxieties of man in psychoanalysis—separation from the mother and castration by the father. The "easy" and "unpremeditated verse" (IX.24) of *Paradise Lost* represents its own felicitous flow as the inverse of these dreaded ruptures—reunification with the mother and the receiving of a phallus from the father. The price, once again, was a demand on his blindness. Moving from private to public theodicy, Milton had to acknowledge what he resisted in all the explicit statements we have concerning his condition. Namely, he was guilty: blindness was both a punishment *and* just. The epic poet, elsewhere so vehement about his innocence, represents the deterioration of postlapsarian Adam as the primal case of *gutta serena*.[17]

This is a long story, and one I have told elsewhere, but perhaps I can convey the gist of it from a slightly new angle by noting how, once again, his own psychic arrangements resonate in his portrayal of deity. Thus Milton deftly remembers in his final invocation the sovereignty of anger in the motivational structure of classical epic—"the wrath / Of stern

Achilles," the "rage / Of Turnus for Lavinia disespoused," and the divine
ire of Neptune and Juno that made so intricate the journeys of Odysseus
and Aeneas (IX.14–19). The poet intends a strong contrast with the wrath
of the deity his poem celebrates:

> on the part of heaven
> Now alienated, distance and distaste,
> Anger and just rebuke, and judgment given,
> That brought into this world a world of woe,
> Sin and her shadow Death, and Misery
> Death's harbinger. . . .
>
> [IX.8–13]

This is no small anger. But it is the great argument of the poem that this
wrath has submitted, as an absolute limit, to justice. And in Christianity,
if divine wrath is overmastered by justice, divine justice is overmastered by
mercy. Inserting his poetic hopes into this Christian sequence, Milton (like
the good man in Plato, like Prospero) directed his wrath over his affliction
against itself by rendering Adam's blindness deserved, while simultaneously, illuminated by inspiration, he reaped forgiveness from a merciful God.

SOME FURTHER RENAISSANCE VARIATIONS
ON AUGUSTINE'S MODEL LIFE

One dominant life pattern in Milton's culture was the iamb of Augustine, wherein the "da" of youthful wantonness is followed by the
"DUM" of pious accomplishment. Variations were plentiful—in the son-
neteer's farewell to false love, in the neoplatonist's ascent from sensual
object to divine idea, in the movement of someone like Bunyan from the
coprolalia of his youth to the abounding grace of Scripture. England
produced a near-perfect replica of the Augustinian life pattern in the career
of John Donne, at first the priest of a libertine Apollo, at last the minister
of God. This model could readily be fused with the literary exemplum of
the Vergilian career, moving from the fires of frustrated love to the confessions offered St. Augustine in Petrarch's *Secretum*. But Milton did not
sport with Amaryllis in the shade. His was a stainless and studious youth,
he several times tells us, lived in "disdain of far less incontinences" than
those "of the bordello."[18] The later Milton had three wives, wrote in favor
of divorce, defended polygamy, came to detest the church, left out those
bizarre Augustinian notions of voluntary erection and elastic hymen from
his representation of Eden, gave angels an intriguing sex life, made Adam
argue with God in order to attain a mate, and pretty thoroughly scourged

the airy demons that held his attention during youth: "who bids abstain / But our destroyer, foe to God and man" (IV.748–49). The Miltonic iamb is in this sense a reversal of the Augustinian.

One remark to be made here is that creative achievement late in life may *not* be a matter, as the professionals now tell us that geriatric sex is, of preserving old habits, keeping on keeping on. I think it is often the result of felt deprivation, an attunement to the lost chances of an imperfect or frustrated youth. Assumptions current in literary criticism today would lead us to expect that late creativity must be deeply enmeshed with attitudes toward succession: is not someone writing for a world he must soon leave going to be grappling primarily, as Prospero doubtless was, with conflicts over the subsequent? But we often observe that the aged, precisely for this reason, become relatively disinterested in the future and relatively fascinated with the past—the world they *have* inhabited, have touched or continued or somehow made an impression on—and it seems to me that, in line with this observation, the abiding characteristic of good late poetry is its layered temporal depth, folded over, as it were, on the early work, wrinkled deep in time.[19]

When late poetry is very good, as it is in Donne's hymns, or in Milton and Yeats, this layered address to the early achievements may be suspicious and quarrelsome. Perhaps the secret lies less in staying youthful, renewing without dissatisfaction one's identification as son or daughter, than in correcting and redesigning youth. An aged writer's concern with succession might well get channeled into such a project, for the "da" of youth might be the imaginative heir to the "DUM" of age. All us human beings have at least one child: our own youth. This psychic offspring must be more than an effect of time, a fixed expanse of memories to be pored over and reinterpreted. It gets pored over because it really is a child, one that may be nourished and comforted, but also advised and rebuked, its deficiencies made up. The man is father to the child. (Since my thesis is turning Wordsworth inside-out in the name of a pre-Romantic life model, it may be fair to remark in passing that this trochaic poet, burdened by the idealization of his youth, led a long and uncreative old age.) As treatment, psychoanalysis recommends some such project—the renarration of youth, not as ideal, but as the place where something first went wrong in the story. The derivation of late creativity from deficient youth makes sense within the Augustinian life pattern as well as within the Miltonic reversal of it, for Augustinian youth is also deprived—not of sensuality, of course, but of truth. I suspect that just before his conversion Augustine welcomed the Plotinian idea of evil as non-being in part because to become a Christian meant feeling his own evil, or in effect, the emptiness of his youth. Conversion may be reversion, putting something into the past that was not originally there, prying loose the fixation points. Without prior insufficiency, no fulfillment. Montaigne fought against the Augustinian model in "Of Repentance," but in the end exemplified it in his gradual conquest of his youthful skepticism, finding in a rapturous regard of his habits, selfhood's sediment, the fixed center missing from his youth.

In fact, one of the most arresting Renaissance transformations of the Augustinian model makes explicit this early deprivation in truth. The occult, quasi-scientific, loosely Neoplatonic traditions of the Renaissance typically present us with a life rhythm marked by repeated disillusionment in youth, and after these encounters with the emptiness of received verities, conversion to a truth that must be sought for, worked out, pursued. In the lives of Giordano Bruno and René Descartes, among others, the forthcoming conversion was announced in powerful dreams.[20]

I will take Jean Baptiste Van Helmont as my example here. At seventeen he was studying philosophy at a French university. On the night before his examination for the degree of Master of Arts, a book lay open before him, but his attention was elsewhere. He was assessing his knowledge: what, really, had he gained from these studies? "I found myself," he would later write, "inflated with letters and, as it were, naked as after partaking of the illicit apple—except for a proficiency in artificial wrangling."[21] *Naked*, as Adam found himself in the shame of his alimentary crime, and *inflated*, as if bloated from an ill-nourishing meal: that night Van Helmont would fuse these ideas into a most remarkable examination dream.

He dreams that he is—not that he is in, but that he is—an enormous inflated bubble, empty and diffuse, stretching between heaven and earth. Above him is a tomb, below him a yawning darkness. This dream confirmed his waking assessment: viewed truly and nakedly, his mind was inflated, nebulous, nothing. He never took the examination. Withdrawing in disgust from the empty learning of the philosophy faculty, he went on to study other subjects, only to repeat the same experience. After enthusiastic assimilation would come that inner sense of falsehood and depletion. Finally he took up medicine. He read, he tells us, over six hundred treatises in Greek and Latin. He memorized Aristotle and Galen and Paracelsus. This, too, was wasted time: "I had learned, 'tis true, to dispute problematically concerning any disease, but I did not know how to cure even a toothache."[22] So he rejected everybody's central tenets—the four elements, the four humours, the Paracelsian triad of salt, mercury, and sulphur. His many subsequent treatises are invariably divided into two parts, the first a taunting diatribe against the "emptiness" of orthodox medical belief. "I ever found his reason stronger at demolishing the doctrines of ancient pillars of our art, than erecting a more substantial and durable structure of his own," his earliest English translator remarked.[23] But the bogus and the authentic are virtually inextricable in his work. He took a dose of wolfsbane, and in the hallucinations inspired by this illicit fruit, received a visionary revelation: something in his stomach, not in his head, was directing his thought and imagination. Turning to the study of that organ, he made a number of genuine advances, moving hermeticism toward true empiricism. He discovered that acid caused chylification, and understood the neutralizing alkalis in the small intestine. In another vision he saw his own soul: a tenuous substance, part air and part light. This prefigured his major discovery, the one for which he is primarily remembered. Van Helmont burned charcoal and realized that he had produced something different from air. Adapting a Greek word that Paracelsus had used to designate air, he called this substance *gas*. This, he theorized, was the vector of specificity in all matter; nature's germens were gaseous clouds imprinted by God with the plans for all things. The man who kept seeing his youth as an inflated bubble came back to that truth in his maturity: all things are, once you break through to the true shaping *quidditas* inside of them. The fulfillment of mature truth is a revision of the emptiness of youth. All is vanity, saith the preacher. But sometimes out of vain chaos comes . . . gas.

The idea that a good youth is an incomplete one, even a failed one—a youth that in any case leaves something left to do—belongs to the traditional wisdom of Western culture. Unlike the Romantic life model, which warns against losing touch with the glorious energies that are ours at first, the traditional wisdom is iambic, a plot for fulfillment in the end. In the belief that culture is not subject to old age, despite the vitality of the modern, I offer from the *De senectute* Cicero's advice about how to stay sexually active right to the end. Taken literally, it may be no more than average advice, but I have tried to show how as metaphor, folded over in a new wrinkle, this old chestnut flowers. "In any case," Cicero writes, "when failures of bodily vigour do occur they are to be blamed upon youthful dissipations more often than upon old age. A youth spent in immoderate debauchery transmits to later years a body that is already worn out."[24]

MY ITALICS

Two aspects of this study of late creativity in the Renaissance seem to me distinctive.

I have, first of all, given unusual stress to the vitality of the superego. The rhetoricians of antiquity debated the relative contributions of *ingenium* and *iudicium* to the creative process.[25] The rhyme and reason of their debate have been reborn in dualisms such as invention/imitation, genius/artifice, romantic/classic, primary process/secondary process, to forge in the smithy of my soul/the uncreated conscience of my race, the most durable and accurate revival being neoclassicism's *paragone* of Fancy (or Wit) and Judgment. Psychoanalytic accounts of artistic composition have mostly fallen on the side of Fancy. Often it is said that this emphasis should be civilized by improved attention to the just formalities of meter, genre, design, form in general. This can readily be done, though the familiar result is to place everything conventionally "literary" under the sign of defense: "Defense, in a literary work," Norman Holland says, almost indistinguishable from Harold Bloom in this instance, "takes one of two general modes: meaning or form."[26] But psychoanalysis should have something more interesting than this to say about Judgment, and especially about Judgment in the strongest sense—the moral weight of literature, and the role of moral judgment in its creation. The superego is often enabling as well as defensive. A more sensitive exploration of its function in the genesis of art would not remove psychoanalytic criticism from its native territory. For the id, after all, is only one sector of the unconscious, and Freud himself pointed to the radical collusion between id and superego. The deep and conflictual marriage of *ingenium* and *iudicium* generates the two artistic furors examined in this essay. There is something all at once libidinal, aggressive, and virtuous in the late tempests of Shakespeare and Milton—the moral narcissism of Prospero making a virtue of necessity, his testy display of enchanting but enforcing magic a choice example of what Jacob Burckhardt termed "that enigmatic mixture of conscience and egoism";[27] the epic narrator of *Paradise Lost* steadying anxious ambitions with a sense of earned trespass and stored forgiveness, sanctions derived in part from a long enraging youth when, making a necessity of virtue, the ego could seduce the id only because the superego had blocked off all other candidates.

Finally, there is my largely positive emphasis on the vitality of real fury. It is not to be found on the surface of our inherited wisdom. It makes for tragedy. Its dignity, hinted at in symbol and myth, rarely survives its open expression. Integrity, Erik Erikson maintains, is the virtue specific to the eighth and last of his ages of man:

> The ego's accrued assurance of its proclivity for order and meaning—an emotional integration faithful to the image-bearers of the past and ready to take, and eventually to renounce, leadership in the present. It is the acceptance of one's one and only life cycle and of the people who have become significant to it as something that had to be and that, by necessity, permitted of no substitutions.[28]

I do not dismiss these words lightly. As a last disposition, this seems to me both possible and desirable. The past, being outside the influence of will, is for everyone at every time a necessity. Psychoanalysis teaches that we bear this obvious truth, in sickness or in health, unwillingly, but one imagines that, as the past enlarges and the future lessens, this infuriating necessity, this terrible falling away of possibility, might at last make human sense. Perhaps in the end the relentless, angry, hot works of mourning and wishing might cool, and there might be in this new ability to let things be some rooted peace with the people in one's life—an end to wanting them otherwise. But, however much we feel this last disposition answerable to the promises of life, we must not imagine that they have failed, or been failed, who cannot go so gently. The ambition to remake the world, even as it confronts a progressively more final frustration, may never slacken. Certainly there are elements of tenderness, nurture, and integrity in Prospero's handing down of a wealthy world, Milton's continued attention to his mistaken youth, and Van Helmont's desire to empty and then fill the spirits of his readers. Yet these are, I believe, fierce tendernesses. Those of us who are not old, and may not be lucky enough to become old, would do well to realize that those people we have such trouble looking at, their bodies slow and breakable, are not always subdued or quiescent in spirit, but enraged, and some of them sublimely.

Notes

1. Marsilio Ficino, *Marsilio Ficino and the Phaedran Charioteer*, trans. Michael J. B. Allen (Berkeley: Univ. of California Press, 1981), p. 82. Ficino is commenting on *Phaedrus* 245a.

2. I quote Keats's famous letter in *English Romantic Writers*, ed. David Perkins (New York: Harcourt, 1967), pp. 1209–10.

3. *Phaedrus* 245a, in *The Collected Dialogues of Plato*, ed. Edith Hamilton and Huntington Cairns (New York: Pantheon Books, 1961), p. 492.

4. On *thymos*, see *Republic* IV.439e. Here I am much indebted to an advance reading of Gordon Braden's *The Senecan Tradition in the Renaissance: Anger's Privilege* (New Haven: Yale Univ. Press, 1985).

5. *Republic* IV.440b, in *Collected Dialogues*, p. 682. One of the things Plato disliked about poetry was its invitation to indulge passions such as anger and grief: in literature the breast-beating gives us pleasure rather than encouraging us to turn wrath inward against itself; the poet "waters and fosters these feelings when what we ought to do is to dry them up" (*Republic* X.606d).

6. Ficino, pp. 188, 230.

7. John Milton, "Animadversions," *Complete Prose Works of John Milton*, ed. Don Wolfe et al., I (New Haven: Yale Univ. Press, 1953), p. 664.

8. *Republic* IV.441b, in *Collected Dialogues*, p. 683.

9. *Republic* IV.440b, in *Collected Dialogues*, p. 682.

10. Arnold Modell, "The Origin of Certain Forms of Pre-Oedipal Guilt and the Implication for a Psychoanalytic Theory of Affect," *International Journal of Psychoanalysis*, 52 (1971), pp. 337–46. For the development of a complementary idea in

social anthropology, see George Foster, "Peasant Society and the Image of the Limited Good," *American Anthropologist*, 57 (1965), pp. 239–315, and "The Anatomy of Envy: A Study in Symbolic Behavior," *Current Anthropology*, 13 (1972), pp. 165–202.

11. Augustine, *Confessions*, trans. R. S. Pine-Coffin (Baltimore: Penguin, 1961), p. 28.

12. See Edward S. LeComte, *Milton's Unchanging Mind: Three Essays* (Port Washington, New York: Kennikat Press, 1973), pp. 5–69.

13. I allude to Milton's Sonnets VII and XIX.

14. On this theme see Victor Harris, *All Coherence Gone* (Chicago: Univ. of Chicago Press, 1949).

15. See Plato, *Timaeus* 50–56.

16. I quote from Milton's so-called "Letter to an Unknown Friend" in *Complete Prose*, I, p. 319.

17. An extended discussion may be found in my book *The Sacred Complex: On the Psychogenesis of Paradise Lost* (Cambridge, Mass.: Harvard Univ. Press, 1983), pp. 256–60.

18. Milton, *An Apology*, in *Complete Prose*, I, p. 892.

19. *Antony and Cleopatra* is itself "wrinkled deep in time," being a middle-aged rendition of *Romeo and Juliet*.

20. Those of Descartes have occasioned a minor literature arguing that they are indeed prophetic. See, for a sampling, Lewis Feuer, "The Dreams of Descartes," *American Imago*, 20 (1963), pp. 3–26, and Alice Browne, "Descartes's Dreams," *Journal of the Warburg and Courtauld Institutes*, 40 (1977), pp. 256–73.

21. Quoted in Walter Pagel, "The Reaction to Aristotle in Seventeenth-Century Biological Thought," in *Science, Medicine, and History: Essays on the Evolution of Scientific Thought and Medical Practice*, ed. E. Ashworth Underwood (London: Oxford Univ. Press, 1953), I, p. 491.

22. Quoted in Lynn Thorndike, *History of Magic and Experimental Science* (New York: Macmillan, 1923–1958), VII, p. 220.

23. Walter Charleton, "To the Reader," *Deliramenta Catarrhi*, by Jean Baptiste Van Helmont, trans. Walter Charleton (London, 1650).

24. Cicero, *Selected Works*, trans. Michael Grant (New York: Penguin, 1971), pp. 224–25.

25. See Ernst Robert Curtius, *European Literature and the Latin Middle Ages*, trans. Willard Trask (New York: Harper, 1953), pp. 293–301.

26. Norman Holland, *The Dynamics of Literary Response* (New York: Oxford Univ. Press, 1968), p. 189.

27. Jacob Burckhardt, *The Civilization of the Renaissance in Italy* (New York: Harper, 1958), II, p. 428.

28. Erik Erikson, *Insight and Responsibility* (New York: Norton, 1964), p. 139.

"THE CLAMOR OF EROS":
Freud, Aging, and *King Lear*
***
Carolyn Asp

> I am . . . inclined to adhere to the view that the fear of
> death should be regarded as analogous to the fear of
> castration and that the situation to which the ego is
> reacting is one of being abandoned by the protecting
> superego—the power of destiny—so that it no longer has
> any safeguard against all the dangers that surround it.
> —Freud[1]

WITHIN THE RICH COMPLEXITY OF *King Lear* is an eloquent, if fearsome,
representation of the pain of the aging male, the patriarch, who makes
himself dependent upon the tenuous bonds of the social construct called
the family.[2] With a ruthless, almost anti-humanist clarity, the play depicts
the implacable conflicts that exist between the generations: the narcissistic,
infantile, and latently incestuous demands made by the aging father on the
daughters and the aggressive rejection of these demands by the offspring.
In deciphering the latent antagonisms between parents and children,
Freud shows the extent to which the family is founded on a fearful debt.
Simply, the child owes his parents his life: but nothing is more dangerous
than obligation, especially one that is unsought, built into a structure over
which the child has no control, no choice. Obligation is the result of
submitting to the enormous burden of the other's generosity; it is created
by being threatened with a blessing. The concept of debt, an intensifica-
tion of the idea of obligation, describes a system of absolute equivalence; it
creates an economy ruled by price. And here lies the difficulty in structures putatively organized around love (the family), a word and concept
traditionally associated with the idea of freedom, divorced from the system
of equivalences. Commenting that it is difficult, almost impossible, to give
back what you cannot pin down, Hélène Cixous criticizes the debt-
creating structure of the patriarchal family that enforces "love."[3] Within
the parameters of this ambivalence, the parent, the father, no longer
young, comes to collect the debt he thinks his children owe him and calls it

grateful love. Once again it is a question of paternal choice to which the child can merely respond: one is selected to bear the burden of great inheritance so as to guarantee the oppression of obligation. If the child is female, and the parent an elderly male, the situation in our patriarchal culture is a particularly explosive one—tragically so, as *King Lear* emphasizes.

In his essay, "The Theme of the Three Caskets," Freud argues that *King Lear* is organized around the themes of the illusory nature of choice, the symbolization of death as love, and the originary myth of female power. Significantly, the fact that Shakespeare makes the man who must choose between three women an aging, dying king, brings us very near what Freud called the "ancient idea" of the "great Mother goddesses," who were perceived simultaneously as founts of being and destroyers. The fact that the three women are daughters locates the choice within the economy of the family. Finally, the nature of the choice lays bare the mechanism of the reversal of the wish.[4] As we know, the apparent contradiction of the situation in *King Lear* is that man's free choice among women falls on "death," which no man knowingly chooses. The natural tendency of desire, as Freud says elsewhere, is "to exclude death, to put death on one side."[5] Desire is convinced of its own immortality.

Man imagines that he exercises choice and that what he chooses is not death but youth and love; in reality, he obeys the compulsion of nature. The latent content (death) of the object he chooses is veiled from him at the moment of choice, thus allowing him to "forget" that he is a victim of destiny. How can this contradiction be explained? Freud appeals to certain forces in mental life called reaction-formations which tend to bring about replacement by the opposite. These formations create a defensive system which conceals the specificity of ideas and fantasies involved in the conflict, "keep[ing] the opposite feelings under suppression, and enabl[ing] us to postulate the operation of a process which we call repression."[6] In the face of disbelief in our own death, in the face of intense fear of death, how can one come to that acceptance of mortality which defines ultimate wisdom? Surely the subject recognizes the fact of death intellectually, but then in a process of (de-)negation (a function of repression), refuses to accept it affectively. Acceptance of the inevitable is not reducible to knowledge of necessity; acceptance is an affective task, a work of re-vision directed toward desire. How the repression of death is undone, how the acceptance, however partial, of death which defines wisdom is achieved— these are the questions posed by *King Lear.* Try as Lear will to escape, he must renounce love and choose death, familiarizing himself with the necessity of dying, lessons imposed upon him in great part by female power, by women, his daughters, who themselves renounce the bond of daughterly debt.

I

Freud enumerates the three inevitable relations a man has with a woman as "the mother herself, the beloved who is chosen after that pattern, and lastly, Mother Earth who receives him once more."[7] Far from encouraging the gratification of desire, the mother represents necessity and the laws of time, death, and difference; an improper object of desire, she imposes restraint, deferral of gratification. The son's fantasy of an original experience of total bliss at the mother's breast is a dream projected into the past, without a present or a future. As Sarah Kofman writes, what the mother teaches is to resign ourselves to death.[8] Freud wrote of his own experience:

> When I was six years old and was given my first lessons by my mother, I was expected to believe that we were all made of earth and must therefore return to earth. This did not suit me and I expressed doubts of the doctrine. My mother thereupon rubbed the palms of her hands together—just as she did in making dumplings, except that there was no dough between them—and showed me the blackish scales of epidermis produced by the friction as a proof that we were made of earth. My astonishment at this ocular demonstration knew no bounds and I acquiesced in a belief which I was later to hear expressed in the words: "*Du bist der natur einen Tod schuldig* ("Thou owest nature a death").[9]

The mother teaches that every life must be given back. The first lesson, the foundation of the pedagogic order, comes by way of maternal education. This first lesson, one we are all destined to learn, is also the last.

Lear's intent in the first scene of the play is to renounce in order to retain: to renounce the responsibilities and cares of an old king to retain the love of women, who, he hopes, will be mothers to him. In exchange for the inheritance, the daughters must voice words of love which privilege their aged father over all other objects of affection. As Lear crawls to death, he still demands: "which of you, shall we say, doth love us most?"[10] Preferring Cordelia to his other two daughters, Lear desires to occupy the position of her child, thus competing with her husband for attention, conferring on her the offices of the nursery ("I lov'd her best, and thought to have set my rest / upon her kind nursery" [I.ii.123–24], outwitting age and death by making her his mother during his second childhood. But Cordelia remains dumb (her silence is deathly), and the paradox of the play lies in the fact that Lear, in trying to expell the Goddess of Death represented by Cordelia, opens himself up to the real—not symbolic— threat of death. By banishing her, Lear forces the enactment of the very dynamic he sought to escape. The absence of the female exerts a power to which he can only submit.

What particularly strikes us about the daughters he was forced to choose by default, "these daughters" who actively "seek his death" (III.iv.163), is their self-sufficiency, their inaccessibility, their cold indifference. As the play progresses, as Lear grows desperate, images of women and female genitalia excite his disgust and rage, replacing desire (I will come back to this later) with loathing. As rejecting mothers, Goneril and Regan remind him of his need and dependence, but they will do nothing to alleviate it. As devouring mothers, they seek his doom: "She hath . . . look'd black upon me, strook me with her tongue, / most serpent-like, upon the very heart" (I.iv.160–61). This deprivation of nurture arouses in him an oral rage which expresses itself in curses directed specifically at the womb:

> Into her womb convey sterility,
> Dry up in her the organs of increase,
> And from her derogate body never spring
> A babe to honour her.
>
> [I.v.278–81]

In an exercise of verbal cannibalism Lear devours his own grandchildren.

In "On Narcissism: An Introduction," Freud discusses the self-sufficiency characteristic of female narcissism which poses such an enigma for the male who is always seeking the nurturing aspect of the woman: "Men come under the spell of their childhood, which is presented to them by their not impartial memory as a time of uninterrupted bliss."[11] The self-sufficiency of female narcissism compensates for the woman's loss of prerogative in the choice of a love-object and exerts great attraction over the male who transfers his original narcissism onto the sexual object, thus overvaluing it. What is attractive about this type of female is that she retains what the male has lost—that original narcissism for which he retains nostalgia. Always seeking the lost paradise of wholeness, the male is doomed to unhappiness. He envies the inaccessible position of this woman who has known how to keep her narcissism in reserve while he has impoverished himself; in seeking union with her, he seeks the lost part of his own narcissism. Anaclitic, or object-love, enables the female to play the role of nurturing mother to the male, a situation in which the male, then, assumes the role of the needy child: "Even a marriage is not made secure until the wife has succeeded in making her husband her child as well and in acting as a mother to him."[12] With regard to the male, then, the female position is either one of idealized maternal nurturance, as Lear wishes to find in Cordelia, or that of enigmatic indifference and self-sufficiency, as we see in Goneril and Regan ("Let them anatomize Regan; see what breeds about her heart" [III.vi.76]).

Goneril and Regan enact the destructive, non-nurturing aspects of the narcissistic female in her (non-)maternal role. In describing the power of these female types Freud compares their "unassailable libidinal position" to that of large beasts of prey, or to that of the great criminal as represented in literature. All have this in common: they are envied for having known how to protect their narcissism, their terrifying inaccessibility to the claims of others, their independence, their high self-esteem. They "compel our interest by the narcissistic consistency with which they manage to keep away from their ego anything that would diminish it."[13] Unmediated by the reaction-formation (love and beauty masking death so that the illusion of choice is left to man), Goneril and Regan cannot be accepted; but since they stand in the position of necessity, they cannot be expelled either.

In this confrontation between the demanding "child" Lear has become and the rejecting mothers they show themselves to be, insatiable (pre-Oedipal?) desire meets remorseless denial (castration?), and the spectacle moves us as few others have the power to do. A repetition of the Oedipal struggle in time, it represents our experience of subjective need and desire frustrated by the denying subjectivity of the other. The aging male, denied maternal solace, may be forced to re-suffer the terrors of the castration complex without, any longer, finding the rewards of an ego-ideal. (An aside: the fact that no male can destroy Goneril and Regan may point to the fact of the terrifying power of this particular female principle—at least as perceived by men.)

The relentlessness of all three daughters (even Cordelia is unmoving in her "truth") not only enrages him; it shames him by evoking from him specifically female reactions: hysteria, or "the mother," and "unmanly tears." As he begins to experience the victimization associated with the female position, he begins to react as a woman and begs his gods in desperation: "touch me with noble anger / and let not woman's weapons, water drops, stain my man's cheeks" (II.iv.276–77). These indifferent and fatal daughters force upon him the reality of his age and weakness, stripping him down to symbolic zero: "What need one?" (II.iv.263), asks Regan as she names her bid in the negative auction. Unable to accept his depotentiation, his "feminization" (the "mother" is even within him, rising up), Lear flees into madness: "this heart / shall break into a hundred, thousand flaws / or ere I'll weep. O Fool, I shall go mad!" (II.iv.284–86).

Lear's particular form of madness, analogous to hysteria, is, as Hélène Cixous puts it, "characterized by silence. . . . They [the great hysterics] are decapitated (or, castrated), their tongues are cut off and what talks isn't heard."[14] Lear is not literally aphonic—he seems to dominate the stage with his voice—but his speech is not "heard" by those around him. How many times he makes demands that are ineffectual, asks questions that remain unanswered! In the order of signification, Lear comes to occupy the place of the female (as do many of the aged in this culture). That place is the place "outside," marginal, cast out and powerless. Even if it is heard, language coming from that place is without power. Truly, Lear suffers from "the mother."

The hysteric is the unorganizable feminine construct that does not recognize him (her) self in the images the other may project. Lear, refusing to accept the image of powerlessness his daughters try to thrust upon him, and by refusing, alienating himself beyond the place where language has power (politics, society, the family), inhabits the place of silence, the improper. Fleeing beyond the boundaries—perhaps we could say, beyond the constraints of the symbolic order—Lear becomes a disturbance. Paradoxically, because he refuses to submit to the other's projections, he becomes heroic; indifferent within the space of his own subjectivity, he becomes an object of fascination, a center of power outside the center. Outside culture he speaks a savage language that goes beyond the bounds of censorship, beyond those relations of power and regeneration constituted by the family. His activity takes the form of wandering, of excess, unpredictability, and is therefore, intensely threatening. The daughters, in one way or another, try to put an end to the disturbance: Goneril and Regan seek his life; Cordelia seeks his restoration.

II

This play, which depicts the futile efforts of an aging patriarch to elude death, is structured, on one level, around the dynamics of repression and negation. Although Freud modified his definition of the term "repression" several times, he made his definitive statement in the 1915 essay: "the essence of repression lies simply in turning something away, and keeping it at a distance, from the conscious."[15] Negation is a type of repression which is a function of the intellectual judgment: "A negative judgment is the intellectual substitute for repression; its 'no' is the hall-mark of repression, a certificate of origin—."[16] The negation that Freud describes creates a split between intellectual function (consciousness of repressed material) and affective process (non-acceptance of such material); the subject brings the content of a repressed image or idea to consciousness and then negates it.[17] In negation then (or *denegation* as the French call it), "repression continues in its essence under the guise of non-acceptance."[18] In the play, both processes intertwine to form the basis of its tragic action.

What does Lear repress and negate? I believe he negates (or attempts to) not only the reality of his mortal condition, but also the passive position his own regressive scheme has created, that is, he is aware but refuses to accept. He represses (keeps unconscious) the incestuous desires for Cordelia that form the sub-structure of his scheme. In "The Theme of the Three Caskets" Freud points to the contradiction of combining an aging male with the structure of the bride-choice: "it is in vain that the old man yearns after the love of women as he once had it . . . : the third of the Fates alone, the silent Goddess of Death, will take him into her arms."[19] But Lear refuses to choose that third and by his refusal, attempts to negate his mortality. Like a young man, he wants to choose for Eros, but since sexual relationships are unlikely, the choice is displaced into the family, among the daughters; its sexual component is repressed and sublated into filial gratitude. Later, when he must suffer the consequences his own choices have created, he represses any evidence that would contradict his vision of himself as an "old, kind father, whose frank heart gave all" (III.iv.20), a man "more sinn'd against than sinning" (III.iii.60). What he refuses to acknowledge is that his attempt to enforce affection through the imposition of gift and debt is a response to the terror of loss.

The repetitive motion of the play is one of banishment or exile, a representation of the concept of negation. Freud sees both negation and affirmation as located within the field of the pleasure principle and dominated by what he calls "the judgment of attribution. . . . Affirmation—as a substitute for uniting belongs to Eros; negation—the successor to expulsion—belongs to the instinct of destruction."[20] Lear's ego thrives on repression and negation which establish clear and narrow boundaries— one of his favorite commands is "out of my sight!" It is Cordelia who catalyzes both activities. The manifest content of her behavior in Act One is a refusal to participate in the economy of gift and debt; the latent content points to entities far more threatening than defiance: death and incest. The form her resistance takes brings dangerously close to consciousness the latent content. Her silence bespeaks limit; her "nothing" utters the reality of her symbolic position and the man cannot choose her knowing what she represents: the Goddess of Death. Her words, which establish the daughterly limits of her love, echo the very demands of his repressed desire. Even as she discriminates between the duties of wife and daughter, she uses the language of the marriage vow: "Obey you, love you, most honor you" (I.i.98), thus bringing the two roles into proximity. Then she quantifies—not "all" but only half her love and duty go to him. In the very process of foiling she bring to light Lear's desire to keep her bound within the Oedipal triangle, that is, to be her father-lover, father-child. Insofar as Cordelia signifies all that he must repress, he has no choice but to banish her. But not only does he banish her, he "undaughters" her and disinherits her, the price she must pay for marriage.

After Lear banishes Cordelia, her signification is displaced onto the Fool. By undoing repression the Fool makes a space in which Lear can see his true situation: "thou mad'st thy daughters thy mothers . . . when thou gav'st them the rod, and put'st down thine own breeches" (I.iv.172–73). This jesting death's head, like Cordelia, says "nothing" yet is allowed to stay; his speech is figurative, not "plain," allowing Lear to both confront and yet not confront the distressing facts of his predicament. Lear's "boy," he neutralizes the tension of the relationship with the daughters, while at the same time providing the concern of a child for an aging parent. His function is to tell truth, but with a difference, in the form of jokes and riddles. As Freud explains, jokes are structured according to processes of the unconscious: condensation accompanied by the formation of substitutes; displacement; absurdity; indirect representation; and representation by the opposite. By special arrangements of these processes, thought, otherwise repressed, can be expressed as a joke.[21] The Fool's tendentious jokes are both hostile (toward the daughters) and obscene in that they expose Lear in his structural place vis-à-vis the daughters—as a child with its bottom exposed or a depotentiated old man. Even though he loves and suffers, the Fool falls within the blank-spot of Lear's eye; he can be ignored because Lear wants nothing of him.

The absence of Cordelia, the void at the center, also works to lift repression because it keeps her, and, concomitantly, Lear's desire, always before his mind's eye. As external reality presses upon him in ways he cannot deny, as repressed material forces its way into consciousness, Lear's subjectivity becomes increasingly fragmented until it collapses. His madness is threatening because it represents a failure of repression, an irruption that implies regression and a return to primary process thinking. Because it is activated by trauma-associated impulses (fear of the recurrence of the overwhelming helplessness of infancy caused by non-gratification of needs and separation anxiety), its impact is universal. In this state, Lear levels devastating critiques at the systems of the "sane" world, the world of sex and self sanctioned by reason. The imaginary unity of the ego shatters; sexual impulses bare themselves in all their polymorphous perversity. It is only within this reversed world of madness that Lear confronts and seems to accept his own mortality. A "bare, fork'd animal" he "smells of mortality" (IV.vi.133). Lust and guilt are everywhere. Lear's vision is of a world stripped of the protective parameters established by the super-ego; all must submit to nature and to nature's appointed end.

Looking at this spectacle we might ask ourselves: what is the point of so much suffering? The lifting of repression reveals a certain truth about the world and about himself to Lear, but it is problematic whether or not he can use that truth for any purpose of consciousness. As the Fool had warned him early in the play, "thou shoulds't not have been old till thou hadst been wise" (I.v.44). How beneficial is a process of lifting repression (psychoanalysis, for example) for those who are too old, too vulnerable for the truth? In "On Psychotherapy" Freud suggests that analysis with old people is unlikely to effect much change because there is not enough libido in them for a strong transference. This is certainly not the case with Lear who refuses to renounce libido—that is part of his problem—and remains obsessively attached to the object of his desire. Elsewhere Freud comments that "near or about the age of fifty the elasticity of the mental processes upon which treatment depends, is as a rule lacking—old people are no longer educable—and on the other hand, the mass of material to be dealt with would prolong the duration of treatment indefinitely."[22] These comments, on the other hand, rather accurately describe Lear: his rigidity must be shattered before he can learn, and this shattering is an intensely painful process. A lifetime of self-absorbed willfulness and self-deception cannot be changed in the short time left to him; he can feel "burning shame" and guilt for his behavior but he does not seem able to break out of the pattern. The brief moment of insight—"I am a foolish, fond old man"—is deflected before it can bear fruit, and it is deflected, paradoxically, by Cordelia.

When Cordelia returns to "rescue" her father, negation and repression return with her. The price of her ability to function as a merciful female presence is a denial of her father's unkindness and a displacement of blame and guilt onto her sisters. She engages in a species of reaction-formation in which she sees him only as a "poor *perdu*" and herself as the forgiving victim, powerful to save him. The reconciliation between father and daughter is based on a denial of the past, however moving and noble we think the action. In discussing the nature of Cordelia's response, S. L. Goldberg writes: "However necessary is the truth of Cordelia's 'no cause, no cause,' . . . this is still not the whole of the truth. . . . What has happened in the first scene and has happened since is also real. Lear has something to feel guilty about. . . ."[23]

Although Lear tries to expiate his sins and thus exorcise himself from guilt, Cordelia will neither let him off so easily nor will she play the role of revenger: "she has triumphantly refined the victim's role . . . and she has done this by denying . . . the cause."[24] This negation of the past brings it to awareness only to repress it, keeping it alive but unresolved. By regressing both father and daughter to a time prior to the abdication scene, by returning him to the world of the imaginary, I believe that this denial accounts for Lear's "uneducableness." Denial of their mutual complicity in creating the conditions of disaster, however, may be the only grounds on which reconciliation can occur.

III

Early in the play Cordelia tried to escape the fearful debt of obligation by rejecting the latent content (Goddess of Death) of Lear's choice, leaving that to her sisters. As Harry Berger comments: "Cordelia, for reasons of her own—not all of them available to her—accepted Lear's challenge, . . .

and by stonewalling helped him to bring on her plight. At the same time she helped Lear commit himself to her sisters' professed bosoms. . . ."[25] She can escape both the manifest and the latent content of the role her father expects her to play by insisting on her daughterly role, the role of divided loyalties: father and husband are kept separate, equal and in competition. Yet in the end, it is the father who wins. Lear's depotentiation de-fuses the threat of her righteousness: "fond and foolish," he appeals to her pity, trying to regain mastery through weakness, attempting to re-establish the mother-beloved/child structure she originally had rejected. By stressing his suffering and her exaltation—"you are a soul in bliss, but I am bound / upon a wheel of fire" (IV.vii.45)—he ensnares her.

Strong as she is, Cordelia cannot escape the lure of the devouring father, the narcissistic parent who destroys his children. As C. L. Barber comments: "How fully Shakespeare understood the destructive side of the bonds whose value he so movingly expresses is manifest in his having changed the happy ending of all his sources."[26] But she knows what she does. She reminds him that his cause has ruined her: "For thee, oppressed king, I am cast down" (V.iii.5). Once again Lear is the cause of her banishment, this time to prison and death. Oblivious of the danger, he once again imposes his regressive fantasy upon her; the prison cell will be the "kind nursery," epitome of male bliss. Here I agree with Stanley Cavell's reading: finally succeeding in displacing her husband, "he has found at the end a way to have what he has wanted from the beginning. . . . 'Hidden together we can love.' "[27]

Because Lear refuses to admit the nature of his love for Cordelia, that "it is too far from plain love of father for daughter,"[28] he is caught in a pattern of repetition. While he retained power, Lear could never love Cordelia as his darker purpose dictated; he could not even acknowledge the intensity of his desire: "what Lear is ashamed of is not his need for love . . . but the nature of his love for Cordelia."[29] The scheme of his abdication with its domestic arrangements is a ploy to secure a place with her both legitimate and wish-fulfilling. The prison cell replicates and intensifies the marginalizing tendencies of such a scheme. As is the case in so many circuits of desire, what the subject strives to obtain, what he thinks is the true object of desire, is withdrawn and a substitution made. Ostensibly what he does not desire is provided. Such is the case at the beginning of the play; such is the case at the end.

Unaware of the oppression of his ecstasy, Lear presumes that Cordelia is willing to forego ambition and mock its loss, finding in him enough. We never know, except through hints, how she feels about having been caught by both her father and her enemies; her feelings are overpowered by Lear's fantasies. Her tears indicate that she realizes the deadly nature of his love, and Edmund's alibi, that she fordid herself through "her own despair," though not literally true, may have guessed at her state of mind. If, at the end, she had desired revenge, her death would have been the perfect means: to kill this father through excess of loss and call it perfect love.

Cordelia dead in Lear's arms—this is death not decreed by inevitability but by chance; a few minutes would have saved her. This death—not decreed by Atropos, "the inevitable," but by Lachesis, "chance within the laws that govern fate"[30]—cannot be chosen; it eludes mastery, wisdom, sublation. One comes to wisdom by learning to submit to the common fate of mankind, but the element of chance makes death absurd. For the child to die before the father defies the law of natural progression: as Lear comes onstage carrying Cordelia in his arms—the gesture of a bridegroom—we are confronted with the intolerable tableau of inversion. The aging male carries the youthful female, dominating the omnipotence of death by a symbolic supplement of patriarchal power, a futile assertion in visual terms of escape from the originary domination of the woman and death. He cannot survive this fictive mastery which precipitates his death and nullifies his knowledge.[31] The mother/beloved is completely beyond the demands of his desire; the loss (castration) has no compensation in the realm of culture.

In the opening of the action, Cordelia refuses to reverberate Lear's desires back to him; she will not enact his fantasies and allow regression. Confronted with her silence, her difference, he inflicts a symbolic death on her, wishing her dead rather than defiant; he resists the traumatic moment in which he could recognize and accept his own death, insisting on regressive fantasy as a basis of love tainted by incestuous and infantile desire. It is this very love that is so oppressive to Cordelia, leaving her no choice but confrontation and estrangement. Lear's terrible dilemma results from the fact that his love is incompatible with any opportunity for living it out; the loss or sacrifice of that love, on the other hand, is intolerable. Unlike Prospero, whose project detaches him from Miranda, the cherished daughter, Lear comes to the end of his life clinging more tenaciously than ever to the love of women. Prospero is "so wise a father" whose wisdom defines itself in a submission to Ananke—a daring to face and accept the harshness of life which culminates in death. He accepts the difficult paternal vocation of giving to his daughter only to give her up, to separate. Lear is a "fond and foolish old man" whose foolishness consists in attempts to escape and deny that harshness in a desire for childhood consolations. He gives only to receive; his goal is fusion, not separation. By acting on the desire to arrest temporality and thus avoid death, Lear only succeeds in becoming enmeshed in a pattern of repetition that he defines as the future.

The terror of the play lies in the spectacle of so little wisdom garnered at the price of such immense suffering. Even at the end, Lear's desire seems not to have been re-educated to accept either his death, a release rather than a culmination, or Cordelia's. He has not seen how his desire precipitated the deadly conflicts within the family that destroyed her, nor does he understand that the inevitable fate of the devouring parent is rejection. Perhaps Freud is right: we cannot wait until the end of our lives to seek out wisdom because age makes the re-education of desire immensely painful. Lear's "education," such as it is, is thrust upon him in such a way that he resists most of it; what he cannot resist comes too late for him to use.

But what of us, readers or spectators? We are greatly troubled by this play because it stages to our eyes, desires and necessities we would prefer to repress. The old man seeking a mother is a return to pre-Oedipal desire (which involves unacknowledged incestuous demands) that we thought successfully sublimated. Both fear of loss and the inevitability of loss dominate the action, thus reactivating the terrors of the castration complex. Like most of us, Lear has no tragic destiny but to suffer and die. How will we come to grips with this destiny? Will we be rejected, abandoned in old age through the workings of our own narcissism? If we are young, do we not secretly wish for the power and wealth jealously guarded by the elderly? Is it not folly for the elderly to give up their only sure hold on the young: the inheritance? The lack, or loss of a nurturing maternal principle within the world of the play is the terrifying absence at its heart which bars recovery. The spectacle returns us to the unmoored helplessness of the child deprived of protective mediation, for what other position is there for us, young or old, in the face of death, our solitary destiny?

Notes

1. Sigmund Freud, *The Standard Edition of the Complete Psychological Works*, trans. James Strachey (London: The Hogarth Press, 1953), XX, p. 130.

2. Unlike maternity, which is self-evident, paternity must be "proved." It can be subject to question; it is a purely social relation, "a hypothesis, based on an inference and a premise" (Freud, *SE*, XXIII, p. 114).

3. Hélène Cixous, "The Laugh of the Medusa," *Signs*, 1, No. 4 (Summer 1976), p. 890.

4. Sigmund Freud, "The Theme of the Three Caskets," in his *On Creativity and the Unconscious* (New York: Harper and Row, 1958), p. 63.

5. Freud, *SE*, XIV, p. 296.

6. Freud, *SE*, XX, p. 106.

7. Freud, "The Theme of the Three Caskets," p. 75.

8. Sarah Kofman, "Ex: The Woman's Enigma," *Enclitic*, 7 (Fall 1980), p. 22.

9. Freud, *SE*, IV, p. 238.

10. William Shakespeare, *King Lear* (I.i.51), in *The Riverside Shakespeare* (Boston: Houghton Mifflin, 1974).

11. Freud, *SE*, XXIII, p. 71.

12. Freud, *SE*, XXII, p. 133–34.

13. Freud, *SE*, XIV, p. 89.

14. Hélène Cixous, "Castration or Decapitation," *Signs*, 7 (Autumn 1981), p. 47.

15. Freud, *SE*, XIV, p. 147.

16. Freud, *SE*, XIX, p. 236.

17. According to J. Laplanche and J. B. Pontalis, *The Language of Psychoanalysis* (New York: Norton, 1973), the German word *Verneinung* is far more complex than its English translation as "negation." It "denotes negation in the logical and grammatical sense . . . but it also means denial in the psychological sense of rejection of a statement which I have made. . . . In this second sense *verneinen* comes close to *verleugnen*, to disown, deny, disavow" (p. 262).

18. Jean Hippolyte, "Commentaire Parle sur la *Verneinung* de Freud," *La Psychanalyse*, 1 (1953–55), p. 32. This lecture, with the accompanying "Réponse" by Jacques Lacan, form a philosophical discussion of the Freudian concept of negation/denial.

19. Freud, "The Theme of the Three Caskets," p. 75. An old man such as Lear cannot choose between three women except as daughters; the erotic, incest theme becomes latent but no less powerful as a result of this structure.

20. Freud, *SE*, XIX, p. 239.

21. Sigmund Freud, *Jokes and Their Relation to the Unconscious* (New York: Norton, 1963), pp. 29–44.

22. Freud, *SE*, VII, p. 264. At the time he made these remarks, Freud was forty-nine.

23. S. L. Goldberg, *An Essay on "King Lear"* (London: Cambridge Univ. Press, 1974), pp. 32–33,

24. Harry Berger, Jr., *"King Lear:* The Lear Family Romance," *The Centennial Review*, 4 (1979), p. 355.

25. Berger, p. 371.

26. C. L. Barber, "On Christianity and the Family: Tragedy of the Sacred," in *Twentieth Century Interpretations of "King Lear,"* ed. Janet Adelman (Englewood Cliffs: Prentice Hall, 1978), p. 118.

27. Stanley Cavell, "The Avoidance of Love," in *Twentieth Century Interpretations of "King Lear,"* p. 84.

28. Cavell, p. 85.

29. Cavell, p. 85.

30. Freud, "The Theme of the Three Caskets," p. 75.

31. Kofman, p. 23.

THE INTERMEDIATE AREA
BETWEEN LIFE AND DEATH:
On Samuel Beckett's *The Unnamable*

***

Gabriele Schwab

> "Strange task which consists in speaking of oneself.
> Strange hope, turned towards silence and peace"
> —Samuel Beckett[1]

IF WE ARE INTERESTED in literary images of aging, Samuel Beckett's texts are a scandal. Many of their characters are aging or even dying men and—more rarely—women who indulge in observing their decrepitude and corporeal decay. The grotesque disintegrations of their bodies and minds as well as the deformations of their relations to others and to the surrounding environment give rise to a black comedy of old age staged in exuberant speech performances.[2] And yet these texts display the most ingenious strategies to resist our attempts at reading them as literal presentations of old age. *The Unnamable* is perhaps the most extreme in this respect. Nevertheless, I want to read this last part of Beckett's trilogy as a speech voiced by an old narrator who fantasizes about questions of life and death. I should mention that this reading has not grown "organically" out of my years of reading Beckett, but rather out of the "exterior" motivation to write about aging, literature, and psychoanalysis. Surprisingly enough, this reading has uncovered a dimension that remained latent in my former readings, which had carefully avoided focusing on the obvious, namely, that most of Beckett's texts are framed as visions of old age, unfolding ever more artistic variations on the theme of death yet endlessly displacing death in never-ending endgames. This "repression" certainly has some of its roots in my having started to work on Beckett while I was taking care of my dying sister. In the very face of death I obviously needed to displace it as much as Beckett's characters do. Thus I never asked directly what meaning these texts could assume if they were seen as voicing a process of dying. In part, of course, I was justified by their very forms, which never are simply "about" death, which refuse to be seen as "representations" and defy allegorical readings. Instead, they even display strategies which invite us to project upon them our preconceived notions and philosophies of life and death in order to undermine those very projections through a complex process of transference between text and reader/audience.[3]

If I now deliberately read *The Unnamable* as the speech of an old man facing death, I am aware that I am engaging myself in the very paradoxes inherent in the Unnamable's speech. "Where I am there is no one but me who am not" is not only the expression of a paradoxical subjectivity beyond the notion of a self, it is also the expression of a voice that is conscious of the paradoxes of its own performance.[4] These paradoxes will affect any reading, regardless of its focus, destroying our ease with such basic categories as life, death, time, language, self, and other.

It was this very paradox of a voice trying to grasp a mode of being beyond categories that separate living and dying, I and Not-I, self and other, that suggested the theoretical frame of my reading—D. W. Winnicott's concept of the "intermediate area."[5] According to Winnicott, the infant creates an intermediate area of experience in order to cope with the pain of separation. Helping to effect the necessary separation from the mother and the differentiation between self and world are "transitional objects," which are perceived as I and Not-I at the same time, and which function to permit a transition into "reality." Paradoxical experiences and a flexible handling of the fluid boundaries of the self are characteristic of this mode of being, which should not be judged by norms derived from the requirements of the reality principle. Winnicott assumes that this intermediate area, with its paradoxical forms of experience and its transitional modes of being, remains valid throughout life in our experience of cultural objects. One of the primary functions of cultural objects is to provide for an area that, free from the constraints of the reality principle, allows for a continuous restructuring of the boundaries of the self.

In the intermediate area primary and secondary processes or modes of experience coexist with varying dominance. If we conceive of poetic language as an intermediate area of speech, then one of its functions would be to take part in the structuring of self-boundaries. This is valid for the receptive process as well as for the creative process.[6] The Unnamable's speech performance would, then, not only create the boundaries of his own subjectivity, it would also work upon the boundaries of the reader's subjectivity. I have, in another context, interpreted the Unnamable as an "intermediate character" created by an "intermediate area of speech" that challenges our notions of subjectivity and language.[7] Now, reading this speech as voiced by an old man concerned with his own dying, I am interested in how this mode of being in the intermediate area might relate to a specific experience of old age.

Winnicott insists that our fear of death is indissolubly linked to our earliest experiences of loneliness and separation. It is surely significant that the intermediate area of infancy is created to cope with separation anxieties and to master the transition into reality, and that in old age we have to prepare, instead, for the transition out of reality and to cope with the anxieties of an ultimate separation from the world. Thus it seems natural that reactivating the modes of being of the intermediate area might help with the transition from life to death, easing our way *out* of reality as they once eased our way *into* reality. In old age, the "intermediate area" might again absorb more and more of our everyday life, providing a sanctuary where we can learn to let go, to dissolve the boundaries of our self, and to cope with the menacing dissolution of the body.

Seen in this way, the speech of the Unnamable can be understood as a symbolic object in the psychoanalytic sense which the Unnamable has created to wean himself from reality, from his body, from others, and from his self. We all need psychological crutches to face the facts of aging and dying, the fear of solitude, decrepitude, and death. Psychoanalytic theory, having rooted the original function of symbolic objects in our need to cope with presence, absence, and separation,[8] thus helps us understand the function of symbols in old age that serve to wean us from reality.

In an essay on Samuel Beckett's *Malone Dies*, Kathleen Woodward makes a striking transference of Winnicott's concept of the transitional objects of infancy to the objects and symbols Malone creates to face the pain and suffering of dying.[9] Malone gradually withdraws meaning from the last remains in his environment until he finally concentrates on the last possession, his exercise-book, which he uses as a transitional object: "The exercise-book is the place of both the I and the Not-I. And as Malone is increasingly alienated from his disintegrating body . . . the I comes to exist in the book itself."[10] Yet, this displacement of the I into language or, more precisely, into a speech that is used as a transitional object, does not leave the I unchanged. The I renounces the fiction of being clearly delimited, continuous, and differentiated from the outside world and from others, and transmutes itself instead into the paradoxical I of the intermediate area that is always Not-I or vice versa, it can play the game of presence and absence (Fort-Da) with the first person pronoun, thus abstracting the I into a linguistic dimension or an epistemological problem. This is the very point at which *Malone Dies* ends and *The Unnamable* begins. "I, say I. Unbelieving," (p. 3), or "I seem to speak, it is not I, about me, it is not about me." (p. 3). Is this I still connected with (the fiction of!) a "living" voice? Nothing seems less sure with a narrator decidedly denying it. Instead, one of his most obsessive fantasies is the impossibility of defining his self between the boundaries of life and death. This notion of death as inherently linked to birth gives rise to prenatal and postmortal fantasms, evoking the paradoxical image of a very old decaying being whose foremost task is to be born. Thus the categories of life and death, freed from their ontological foundation, tend to function as pure elements in a language game that playfully investigates their linguistic possibilities. And yet, contrary to the Unnamable's declared intentions, these categories life and death never cease to assume psychological connotations because even in their abstract artistic form, they resemble familiar fantasms and metaphors of the self. As such, they interfere with the Unnamable's transitiónal speech performance which depends upon refusing *any* representation of the self.

As for Malone—and for the Unnamable too, this game is achieved with only intermittent success. The intermediate area of old age is a refuge threatened by the intrusion of the real. In the case of Malone, the real takes the form of his disintegrating body reasserting its claims, but even Malone is disturbed by the irreducible autobiographical implications of his writing because they threaten to refer his words back to himself.[11] For the Unnamable, the threat is even more abstract: it is the principle of representation itself that brings too much of the real into his transitional speech. Behind this, of course, hovers the notion of "presence with no illusion."[12] For the Unnamable, however, this "presence" is not desired but rather an impossible task requested by anonymous others who want to "snap him up among the living" (p. 81). The Unnamable seems less obsessed with a presence without illusion than with the illusion of absence. As long as you can hide in the intermediate area of speech, death cannot get you, because it is always out there in the realm of the real where you are not. And yet death haunts the Unnamable's transitional speech in the fantasms that displace him until the illusion of absence is fused with the notion of death: "a sperm dying, of cold, in the sheets" (p. 129), a being longing "to suck his mother white" (p. 69), a non-being craving for death, a fake human whose paradoxical death is expected by anonymous others—all these (self) images circle around the fantasm of a being that can neither live nor die. Two alternatives—coming into the world unborn or being buried before one's time—finally materialize in the form of creatures like Worm,[13] thus delimiting linguistically a non-being that conceives of himself as limitless: "he the famished one, and who, having nothing human, has nothing else, has nothing, is nothing. Come into the world unborn, abiding there unliving, with no hope of death, epicentre of joys, of griefs, of calm. . . . The one outside of life we always were in the end . . ." (p. 82).

The physical shapes, invented to displace his self, recall Lacan's "phantasms of the fragmented body," the ambiguous "other" of our notion of the unity of a self.[14] In order to prevent such body fantasms from becoming the material base of an identity, the Unnamable produces imaginary bodies in endless variation. Highly artificial constructions, they are kept in the realm of artistic inventions. Even establishing the position of the body becomes a matter of logical speculation. At first, the Unnamable seems still to hold on to the notion of a humanlike shape. "I have always been sitting here, at this selfsame spot, my hands on my knees, gazing before me like a great horn-owl in an aviary" (p. 6). He even feels tears on his face, but in his distrust of any expression of emotion and his deliberate reduction of himself to reflective functions, he declares, ironically, these tears to be "liquefied brain." This suspiciousness extends to his sense organs—or whatever seems to remain of them. Only half-convinced that he can still hear, his eyesight reduced to the perception of the near surroundings, he tries to logically deduce his corporeality from its remaining functions, assuming, for example, that he has hands because he writes. Paradoxically however, he is convinced that he cannot lift his hands from his knees. The more he uses his capacity for reflection to establish an idea of his body, the more his body images are transformed into pure abstract fantasms:

> But what makes me say I gaze straight before me, as I have said? I feel my back straight, my neck stiff and free of twist and up on the top of its head, like the ball of the cup-and-ball in its cup at the end of the stick. These comparisons are uncalled for. [p. 22]
>
> no, no beard, no hair either, it is a great smooth ball I carry on my shoulders, featureless, but for the eyes of which only the sockets remain. And were it not for the distant testimony of my palms, my soles, which I have not yet been able to quash, I would gladly give myself the shape, if not the consistency, of an egg, with two holes no matter where to prevent it from bursting, for the consistency is more like that of mucilage. [p. 23]

The principle of forming and shaping becomes independent from the constraints of self-observation. This process seems to be full of secret delights for the Unnamable, who uses his transformations of the image of the coherent body into geometrical forms to violate the boundaries and taboos we normally associate with our body images: "Why should I have a sex, who have no longer a nose? All those things have fallen, all the things that stick out, with my eyes, my hair, without leaving a trace. . . ." (p. 23). Sometimes he fantasizes that others impose bodily shapes on him, which he, in turn, of course rejects: "The poor bastards. They could clap an artificial anus in the hollow of my hands and still I wouldn't be there alive with their life. . . ." (p. 38). Increasingly, he favors pure abstract forms, like that of a ball or a foil: "I am a big talking ball" (p. 24), or, "perhaps that's what I am, the thing that divides the world in two, on the one side the outside, on the other the inside, that can be as thin as foil, I'm neither one side nor the other, I'm in the middle, I'm the partition, I've two surfaces and no thickness. . ."(p. 134).

We know that such geometrical body fantasms may result from an effort of the I to resist tendencies of dissolution from within.[15] The use of simple forms with a simple order can help us cope with a complexity that threatens to become chaotic by reducing that complexity to primary structures.[16] Thus they are creations complementary to the fantasms of the fragmented body that underlie them. The image of the "I as surface," for example, can help neutralize anxieties, for without an "interior," the I, as a "*projection* of a surface," can overcome a threatening symbolic depth.[17] Reducing himself to the two-dimensionality of a sign-being, a being without symbolic depth, is for the Unnamable, who likes to invert such psychological implications, just another strategy to avoid being trapped among the living. If, however, we interpret these body fantasms as fantasies of an aging and dying man, we cannot avoid relating them to the ominous actual dissolution of the body. But the Unnamable's fantasies are not mere fantasms of the fragmented body. At the most, they are deliberate stylizations of such fantasms that make use of their ambiguous appeal, evoking their threats as well as their pleasures and keeping a delicate balance between the two. The secret pleasure we might derive from them—including uncanny pleasures—is not reduced to the fantasies as such, but is intensified by the creative act that forms and redissolves them at will. It is this constructive act that distinguishes them from mere fantasms of the fragmented body and lends them the qualities of transitional fantasies. In the realm of these transitional fantasies, the Unnamable reacquires an imaginary mastery over his body that allows him to confront its decay.

As readers, we are faced with a double shocking awareness: we witness an image of old age that, instead of repressing or lamenting bodily decay, centers on it, exposes it, and indulges in artistic modulations and explorations of its possible and impossible forms. But coping with physical decay and decrepitude is not the only function of the fantasies. From early childhood on, fantasms of the fragmented body symbolize the boundaries of the self as well as those of the body. Thus they can also be related to the dissolution of the self in old age. With respect to both the body and the self, their function is ambiguous and polyvalent: they may be used as defenses, reactions, therapeutic devices, and artistic creations at the same time. And yet, the Unnamable's constructive use of them seems to involve a paradox that comes to pervade his whole discourse: he sets out to voice various forms of self-dissolution or self-lessness, but in voicing them, he is unable to prevent himself from creating and shaping a kind of secondary, linguistic self on a different level. We might expect this to be a stabilizing device if one were concerned to counteract the threat of self-dissolution in old age. The Unnamable, however, clearly presents it as an artistic paradox—the impossibility of speaking from beyond the self without simultaneously creating a self. Each new and deliberate attempt to keep the notion of self out of speech seems doomed to defeat. The Unnamable faces the paradox that there is neither a self-less speech nor any identity with the selves that emerge out of his speech. But can one then still speak of an "I"? Like Malone, the Unnamable resolves "never to say I again," but like Malone he will necessarily fail.

As a counterpart to this impossible speech, the Unnamable evokes the notion of "silence," which he cherishes like a private myth and uses as the teleological orientation of all talk and noise. We, from our perspective as readers, can hardly prevent ourselves from seeing this silence as a linguistic substitute for death. But for the Unnamable, who does not want to be trapped among the living, it is impossible to conceive of his own death. To do so, he would have to admit the idea of having a self. Thus paradoxically, the extrusion of the self from one's speech produces the extrusion of death as well. That is why, though the Unnamable's transitional speech verges on the theme of death, it eternally defers the notion of death. Is this not, perhaps, a sophisticated postmodern version of the age-old theme of "writing in order not to die"? For the Unnamable, silence is peace of mind and absence of speech, a positive utopia, an impossible project. But as with the body fantasms, silence is highly ambiguous, too. The Unnamable can revel in his mind being at peace, that is to say, empty" (p. 31), but he can also abhor the silence imposed on him by others. "They think I can't bear silence, that some day, somehow, my horror of silence will force me to break it" (p. 85). The "horror vacui" seems to lurk from within as much as from without, and to oppose it, there is only the never-ending speech with its dream of a peaceful silence at its core. Paradoxically, not only the notion of death, but the very notion of self is transferred to this silence. Speaking, the Unnamable can only invent himself without ever becoming himself. One could say, with Kierkegaard, that he is "desperately not aware of having a self."[18] Kierkegaard has named this mode of being "sickness unto death." Its paradoxical result is a "diffusion of the self into eternity" *(Verfluechtigung ins Unendliche)*. It is this, precisely, that is one of the results of a speech situated in an intermediate area between life and death, between I and Not-I. The self voices itself in an imaginary realm of abstract endlessness ("abstrakte Verunendlichung") or in abstract isolation, lacking itself and growing further away from itself.[19] Such a self simply cannot die. If this were a fantasy of old age, would it be a consoling or a devastating one? And can we say that such fantasies create a myth of silence and self-lessness or a defense against death? We will find no answers for such questions in Beckett's texts. On the contrary, they urge us not to ask them.

Instead, they draw us into their actuality and materiality. We are supposed to give up looking for what they might represent in order to experience the effect they have on us. The further we follow the endless spirals of the Unnamable's speech, the more we are drawn toward its materiality, toward changing rhythms, sounds, repetitions, and echoes. This again is a reactivation of the possibilities created by the infant in the intermediate area. For the infant too can use language as a transitional object long before it learns to use it as a means of communication. It can produce sounds that it perceives as I and Not-I at the same time. Astonishingly enough, the first use of language is to produce difference and differentiation at a time when language is not yet even separated from the self. Again, the Unnamable seems to invert the process. Towards the end of his discourse, he uses language more and more as if it had been decomposed into the transitional objects of sounds and rhythms. His speech increasingly loses its conventional qualities, shifting its emphasis from meaning to sound. It seems as if it now helps to dedifferentiate the self as much as it once helped to differentiate it. The dissolution of syntax and semantics appears to be equivalent to a diffusion of the self into language by dissolving the mutual boundaries between language and the self. The ordering of the speech into passages and sentences is relinquished in favor of a flow of speech that becomes intensely rhythmical and sonorous. Formal qualities are emancipated from constraints of meaning, and the qualities of the primary process begin to dominate. According to Freud, such a use of language increases the energies with which language is invested. This results in a loss of distance towards language that might seem strangely opposed to the utmost reflective control over language that the Unnamable prefers at the beginning of the text. His hypersensitive reflexivity gives way to nonsense-play that resembles certain forms of glossolalia: "I'll laugh, that's how it will end, in a chuckle, chuck, chuck, ow, ha, pa, I'll practice, nyum, hoo, plop, pss, nothing but emotion, bing bang, that's blows, ugh, pooh, what else, oooh, aaah, that's love, enough, it's tiring, hee, hee . . ." (p. 170). It seems as if the Unnamable is seeking to empty his speech from the burden of meaning that he has accumulated throughout life. His techniques might remind us of children playing with language by repeating words until their meaning dissolves behind the sounds, or of the mantras in Eastern meditation techniques that aim at emptying our mind from its semantic fixations.

According to Freud, such increasingly asemantic conglomerations of language are usually a sign of the dominance of the pleasure principle over language. And yet, the original cathartic function that we find in early childhood productions of transitional sounds, glossolalias, or nonsense words seems to be absent from the Unnamable's speech. The reason is that he does not produce them spontaneously but has to invent them; they are "inarticulate murmurs, to be invented" (p. 170). As a result of his deliberate reflective act of subverting the referential qualities of language, these transitional sounds ultimately fail to provide the freedom from the constraints of the symbolic order of language that the Unnamable seeks. This suggests that it may not be so easy after all to reactivate the pleasures of the intermediate area deliberately, even if the partial and temporary freedom from the semantic constraints of language can be seen as a kind of weaning process. While the Unnamable dissolves more and more into the rhythm of his speech, he never achieves that peace of mind he longs for. His ever-wary alertness toward the snares of meaning turns into a negative fixation. Instead of moving towards peace and silence, his speech moves away from them. Its rhythm does not become more harmonious, but more hectic and fragmented. The more he fastens his mind on silence, the more it evades him: "I want it to go silent, it wants to go silent, it can't, it goes for a second, then it starts again, that's not the real silence, it says that's not the real silence, what can be said of the real silence. . . ." (pp. 170–171).

The text ends with this open contradiction. It does not provide us with an unambivalent image of old age. The Unnamable is neither helplessly exposed to the destructive forces of old age, nor does he peacefully master the unavoidable. We face a character's struggle to voice his own dissolution, using his own voice to wean himself from his body, his self, and his language. He is provisionally able to do this by taking shelter in the intermediate area of speech, by manipulating language as a transitional object and thus transforming himself into a kind of transitional character who hovers between life and death. But the intermediate area of old age is nothing less than the regression to an imaginary paradise of lost childhood. It remains constantly threatened by the intrusion of the real.

If we as readers witness this process, we are drawn ourselves into that intermediate area of experience where our commonplace notions of life, death, time, and self lose their validity. We are forced to follow the Unnamable in giving up the boundaries we have drawn in our relation to ourselves and the outside world. We will be tempted to imagine the Unnamable as an old dying man, but his voice will dissolve any conventional notion we might connect with such an image.

It is important to stress that it is our preconceived images of old age that are undermined and not so much the experience itself. We might, for example, be tempted to project existentialist notions onto the text, interpreting the Unnamable's speech either as an expression of the solipsistic enclosure in old age that speaks to the human condition in general, or even as an expression of the desperate resistance of the individual will against this enclosure. Or we might project romantic notions, seeing the Unnamable as the solitary aging artist and outcast who transcends his grim fate through his artistic creations. The text itself partly invites such interpretations because it is full of existentialist or romantic "echoes." And yet, at the same time, it undermines the very projections it invites by inducing an irreducible "otherness" in the various familiar frames which are chosen. This "otherness" prevents the text from being completely identified with or absorbed by any philosophy, be it of old age or of the human condition in general.

On the other hand, that the text evokes these familiar interpretive frames, inviting us to project our preconceptions onto it, is an important strategic device that guides our response. It makes the text assume qualities of a "mirroring other." Each time we see one of our preconceptions undermined by those abundant details, tones, or styles that do not fit or even counteract them, we find our preconceptions mirrored back to us through the text. We now can discover them ourselves as what they are: projections to reduce otherness. This is, briefly, what I meant when I referred earlier to a complex transference between text and reader/audience.

Thus, in *The Unnamable*, instead of being presented with any fixed image of old age, we are provided with a singular experience of old age, transformed into a speech that intentionally explores the paradoxes of a speaking voice that wants to create its own mode of being between life and death. Most readers have struggled with the fundamental "otherness" of this mode of being, but at the same time, it is this very otherness that has caused *The Unnamable* to be one of the most influential and provocative modern texts, resisting any reduction to a stereotype. By gradually familiarizing ourselves with this otherness, we allow it to work upon and infiltrate the boundaries of our own subjectivity.

One paradoxical effect of the Unnamable's speech derives from the fact that it is a literary speech. The image of the Unnamable as a dying old man fades behind that of a narrator who, with the skilled perfection and artfulness of a pedant, refuses to allow any self to materialize in his speech. With a pedant's delight, he rejoices in the processes of differentiation and dedifferentiation needed for this task, and this delight is only barely veiled by the manifest complaints that provide the negative emotional energies for his speech. As readers, we participate in the ambiguity of the situation: what seems the most sophisticated version of a postmodern subjectivity can also be seen as one of the grimmest, but nevertheless most playful and hilarious practices in the art of dying. Or the other way round: what we could read—if we focus our attention on the situation of a dying narrator (which remains dubious in itself)—as a practice in the art of dying, can be seen as an expression of postmodern subjectivity. This indissoluble ambiguity and the fact that the text undermines any reduction to *one* exclusive meaning, while at the same time inviting the most different provisional constructions of meaning, is perhaps one of its greatest achievements.

A voice situated in the intermediate area becomes so overdetermined that it can transgress the boundaries between youth and old age. The dying voice can take on qualities of transitional voices in general and convey something about the potential of intermediate areas of speech. By following the Unnamable's voice, we experience a subjectivity that transgresses the boundaries between I and Not-I. The secondary undifferentiatedness that the Unnamable achieves through his voice is at the same time a hyperreflective form of individuation. In the intermediate area of his speech, individuation and undifferentiation are not exclusive, just as neither primary nor secondary processes belong exclusively to the domain of intermediate experience. This is important for our understanding of the intermediate area of old age. The Unnamable can dissolve secondary-process orders and recuperate primary-process functions without giving up the function of judgment or the reflectivity of the secondary process.

Seen in this way, the intermediate area of old age undermines the reductive stereotype of aging as a second childhood. Our cultural heritage, based on the exclusion of primary processes from the symbolic order, may tempt us to see all forms of undifferentiation or dedifferentiation as regression or deviation. This, in turn, is reflected in the exclusion of the elderly from many social functions. We do not like to, or even know how to, acknowledge the potentials and the otherness of old age, which we instead relegate to the domain of cultural waste. This practice has a decisive influence on the very forms of old age that our society can produce: it has a debilitating function. The elderly we find in "nursing homes" or psychiatric hospitals provide us with a distorted image of what old age could be. For a culture socializes its elderly as much as its children. In "The Negated Institution," an analysis of mental hospitals, the Italian psychiatrist Franco Basaglia argues that we cannot know what mental illness is, because what we see is only mental illness *plus* the effects of isolation, discrimination, and hospitalization.[20] The same is true for the elderly. This unavoidable internalization of the gaze of the other that carries the norms of socialization up to our old age, might account for the powerful role of persecution played by the anonymous others in Beckett's text. They are the trans-individual instances of a paranoid cathexis of the real. But the Unnamable's paranoia remains a "creative paranoia" throughout.[21] He gives way neither to the notion of total absorption by the gaze of the other, nor to that of a possible freedom from it. His very intermediarity denounces the two to be false alternatives. Throughout his whole speech he continues to demonstrate, if only ex negativo, the insistence of the subject in an alien speech.

Thus Beckett also frees the subject from our petrifying stereotypes of old age. The Unnamable's voice testifies to a mental alertness beyond those categories and realms where we usually look for them. At the same time, he uses his unconventional voices of old age to undermine our conventional notions of subjectivity in general. He does this by showing, among other things, that they are based on those very exclusions that tend to ignore early childhood *and* old age in the conceptualization of subjectivity. The Unnamable's intermediate speech demonstrates the reductiveness of any such conceptualization based on secondary-process categories alone. His intentional, reflective attempt to move into the borderline area between I and Not-I, the real and the imaginary, life and death or not-life, body and bodilessness, time and timelessness, or speech and silence becomes more, then, than simply a weaning process. It expresses those imaginary parts of our subjectivity that extend to all its manifestations but that we tend to confine to or imprison in the intermediate areas of play and art. It also reveals a potential in and of old age itself that we usually do not see and might never experience. This involves the creation of subjectivity through language, and to voice or experience it, one has to face the paradoxes of the intermediate area and find a voice that transcends the I. Finding such a voice in old age might, on the other hand, be a task that helps us in our transition towards death or even reveals some aspects of the "old heart's wisdom."[22]

Notes

1. Samuel Beckett, *The Unnamable* (New York: Grove, 1958), p. 31.

2. I have chosen the term "speech performance" because I think it is more adequate to express the performative qualities of Beckett's prose than the terms "language game" (Wittgenstein) or "speech act" (Austin/Searle). I even think that a detailed analysis of these performative qualities might provide an interesting contribution to the contemporary debate in analytical language philosophy. For the importance of the performative dimension in post-modern literature and theory (and for the postmodern sensitivity to performance), see also Herbert Blau, *Blooded Thought: Occasions of Theatre* (New York: Performing Arts Journal, 1982).

3. This is an argument I have developed at length in my book *Samuel Beckett's Endspiel mit der Subjektivitaet: Entwurf einer Psychoaesthetik des modernen Theaters* (Stuttgart: Metzler, 1981). A summary of the book in English appears in *English and American Studies in German: Summaries of Theses and Monographs* (Tübingen: Max Niemeyer, 1981), pp. 106–08. See also my "The Dialectic of Opening and Closure in Samuel Beckett's *Endgame*," *Yale French Studies, Concepts of Closure*, ed. David F. Hult, No. 67 (1984), pp. 191–202.

4. Beckett, p. 94.

5. D. W. Winnicott, *Playing and Reality* (London: Tavistock, 1971). See also his *The Maturational Processes and the Facilitating Environment: Studies in the Theory of Emotional Development* (New York: International Universities Press, 1965).

6. For an elaboration of this, see my "Genesis of the Subject, Imaginary Functions, and Poetic Language," *New Literary History*, 15, No. 3 (Spring 1984), pp. 453–93.

7. I am referring to a chapter on Beckett's *The Unnamable* in my forthcoming

book on modern fiction tentatively titled *Subjects without Selves: Subjectivity and Aesthetics of Reponse in Modern Fiction*.

8. See especially Freud's analysis of "Fort-Da" in his *Beyond the Pleasure Principle*, trans. and ed. James Strachey (New York: W. W. Norton, 1961).

9. See Kathleen Woodward, "Transitional Objects and the Isolate: Samuel Beckett's *Malone Dies*," unpublished manuscript.

10. Woodward, p. 8.

11. Woodward, p. 8.

12. See Blau, *Blooded Thought*, where he analyzes "presence with no illusion" (p. 154) as one of the most prominent latent desires in postmodern thought.

13. See Margaret Mahler, Fred Pine, and Annie Bergman, *The Psychological Birth of the Human Infant* (New York: Basic Books, 1975). Mahler analyzes the necessary conditions for a psychological birth (a psychological birth requires much more than a biological birth), and the psychological problems of living without being born. There is a striking similarity in the metaphors Beckett uses in *The Unnamable*.

14. Jacques Lacan, "The mirror stage as formative of the function of the I as revealed in psychoanalytic experience," in *Ecrits: A Selection*, trans. Alan Sheridan (New York: W. W. Norton, 1977), pp. 1–7.

15. Leo Navratil, *Schizophrenie und Kunst* (Munich: Deutscher Taschenbuch Verlag, 1965), pp. 69–80.

16. See Gilles Deleuze, *Logique du Sens* (Paris: Editions de Minuit, 1969), pp. 11–20.

17. See Sigmund Freud's definition of the "I" as the "projection of a surface" in *The Ego and the Id* (1923), trans. Joan Riviere, rev. and ed. James Strachey (New York: W. W. Norton, 1962), p. 16.

18. See Søren Kierkegaard, *Die Krankheit zum Tode* (Duesseldorf/Koeln: Eugen Diederichs, 1971), p. 396 (my translation).

19. See Kierkegaard's notion of the diffusion of the self into eternity in *Die Krankheit zum Tode*, pp. 414–16.

20. Franco Basaglia, *L'Istituzione Negata* (Torino: G. Einaudi, 1968).

21. I have borrowed the term "creative paranoia" from Thomas Pynchon's *Gravity's Rainbow* (New York: Viking Press, 1973).

22. See James Joyce's poem "Bahnhofstrasse" (1918), in *The Norton Anthology of Modern Poetry*, ed. Richard Ellmann and Robert O'Clair (New York: Norton, 1973), p. 275.

Contributors

CAROLYN ASP has recently completed a translation (with Robert Con Davis) of Jacques Lacan's "La Famille," and is working on two books—a collection of her essays on Lacanian theory and Shakespeare, and a postmodernist critique of Jacobean drama. The author of a number of essays on Renaissance literature, she is Associate Professor of English at Marquette University.

HERBERT BLAU, until recently artistic director of the theater group KRAKEN, was co-founder (with Jules Irving) of the Actor's Workshop of San Francisco and co-director of the Repertory Theater of Lincoln Center in New York. He is Distinguished Professor of English at the University of Wisconsin-Milwaukee and is the author of *The Impossible Theatre, Blooded Thought: Occasions of Theater*, and *Take Up the Bodies: Theater at the Vanishing Point*. He is currently at work on a book tentatively titled *The Audience*.

LESLIE A. FIEDLER holds the Samuel Clemens Chair of American Literature at the State University of New York at Buffalo. He is the author of many seminal works of literary criticism, cultural history, and fiction, including *An End to Innocence, Love and Death in the American Novel, Freaks*, and *What Was Literature? Class Culture and Mass Society*.

DIANA HUME GEORGE is the author of *Blake and Freud*, nominated for a Pulitzer Prize, and *Epitaph and Icon* (with M. A. Nelson). George, an Associate Professor of English at Pennsylvania State University, Behrend College, has just completed a book on the poetry of Anne Sexton entitled *The Zeal of Her House*.

NORMAN HOLLAND is Milbauer Professor of English and director of the Institute for the Psychological Study of the Arts at the University of Florida at Gainesville. He is the author of *Psychoanalysis and Shakespeare, The Dynamics of Literary Response, Laughing: A Psychology of Humor*, and most recently, *The I*.

WILLIAM KERRIGAN, Professor of English at the University of Maryland, is the author of *The Prophetic Milton* and *The Sacred Complex: On the Psychogenesis of Paradise Lost*. He has edited (with Joseph Smith) *Interpreting Lacan* and *Taking Chances: Derrida, Psychoanalysis and Literature*. Kerrigan is working on a book on the love poetry of John Donne.

MARY LYDON is an Assistant Professor in the Department of French at the University of Wisconsin at Madison. She is the author of *Perpetuum Mobile: A Study of the Novels and Aesthetics of Michel Butor*, and her essays have appeared in *SubStance, Contemporary Literature*, and *Diacritics*. She is currently working on a book on contemporary French philosophy and feminist theory.

JOHN P. MULLER is a clinical psychologist and senior researcher at the Austen Riggs Center in Stockbridge, Massachusetts. He is co-author (with William J. Richardson) of *Lacan and Language: A Reader's Guide to the Ecrits* and co-editor (with Richardson) of the forthcoming *The Purloined Letter Reader*.

ELLIE RAGLAND-SULLIVAN, Associate Professor of French at the University of Illinois at Chicago, is the author of *Rabelais and Panurge* and *Jacques Lacan and the Philosophy of Psychoanalysis*. Her articles have appeared in *SubStance, The Modern Language Journal*, and *The Literary Review*.

GABRIELE M. SCHWAB, Associate Professor of English at the University of Wisconsin-Milwaukee, is the author of *Samuel Beckett's Endgame with Subjectivity* and essays in *New Literary History, Yale French Studies*, and *Diogenes*. Presently she is working on a book to be titled *Subjects Without Selves: On Subjectivity and the Aesthetics of Response in Modern Fiction*. She has taught at the University of California-Irvine, and the University of Constance, West Germany.

MURRAY M. SCHWARTZ is Dean of the Faculty of Humanities and Fine Arts at the University of Massachusetts at Amherst. He has taught in both the Department of English and the Department of Psychiatry at the State University of New York, Buffalo. The author of numerous essays and reviews, he is co-editor (with Coppelia Khan) of *Representing Shakespeare* and is currently working on a book to be titled *Toward a Shakespearian Identity*.

KATHLEEN WOODWARD is director of the Center for Twentieth Century Studies and Associate Professor of English at the University of Wisconsin-Milwaukee. She is the author of *At Last the Real Distinguished Thing: The Late Poems of Eliot, Pound, Stevens, and Williams* and editor of *The Myths of Information: Technology and Postindustrial Culture*. She co-edited (with Stuart Spicker and David Van Tassel) *Aging and the Elderly: Humanistic Perspectives in Gerontology*.